WALL: OUR NORTHUMBRIAN V

CW01190162

WALL: OUR NORTHUMBRI

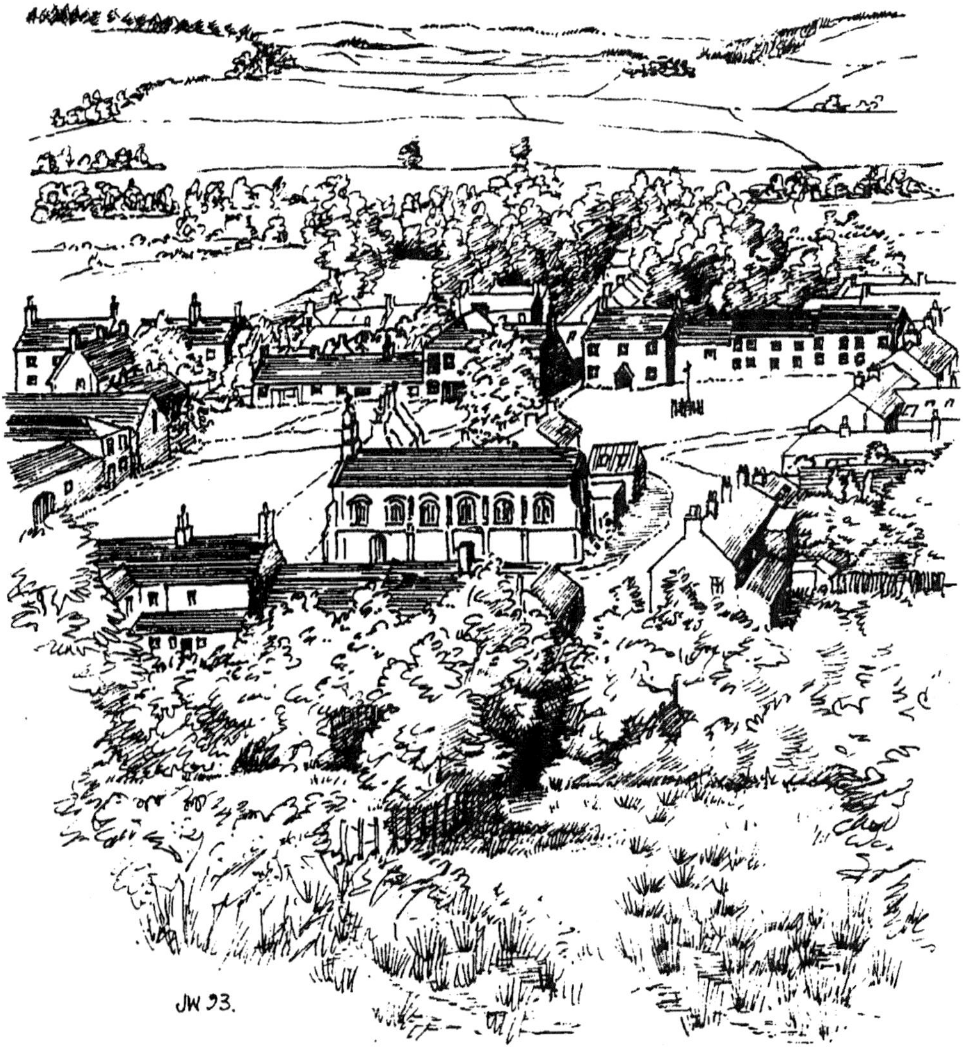

Wall village seen from Wall Fell

ACKNOWLEDGEMENTS
From The Members of the Book Group

Without the financial support of the following people it would not have been possible to produce this book in the way you see it here. As each donation and grant came it was a positive boost and the Book Group's spirits rose, as we began to realise we could actually do this and produce a community work that could be printed.

We take pleasure in thanking all the people who have attended fund raising events in the village for this book, without you it would not have 'got off the ground'. Your generosity was the start of what followed. We are most grateful for the faith you have shown in this project and in our village of Wall. Our hope is that you will feel it has been justified as you read and discover the life and history of Wall, Our Northumbrian Village.

Community Foundation Tyne & Wear and Northumberland who accepted our application for a grant for the printing costs, and selected the following trust fund which they felt would be interested.

I'Anson Family Fund who responded so generously and quickly, giving us the amount we requested to add to the amount raised in the village in order to cover the printing costs.

Wall Parish Council and Wall Village Hall Committee whose generous donations both exceeded our expectations

Northumbria and Cumbria Estates who over many years have bought and sold properties for clients in Wall. With their donation towards this book, they have continued their link.

Pattinson Photography, Hexham whose work on restoring many of the photographs and committing them to disc ready for the printer, freely given, is greatly appreciated.

Leonard Evetts Trust who graciously gave us permission to sell his books, and to keep 50% of each sale for our book.

Several individuals voluntarily offered financial sponsorship of this book and we are pleased to acknowledge their contribution here, and thank them for their support.

P G & C F Bull, Mr W R Herdman, Prof N & Mrs M M Laws, Miss D Mitchell, Ms N Reasbeck, Mr & Mrs A & S Slater, WSW & D Soulsby.

All rights reserved. No part of this book may be reproduced, reprinted, photocopied or utilitised in any form without prior permission from the author and publisher.

Typeset, Printed & Published by Robson Print Ltd.,
Hexham, Northumberland NE46 3PU
Telephone: 01434 602975
robsonprint.co.uk

October 2013

ISBN: 9780956428738

TABLE OF CONTENTS

Title page – Wall - Jemima Westle
Acknowledgements - Sponsors and Grants ii
Foreword – Steve Cram MBE iv
Preface – Ella Hill v
Introduction – Mary Herdman vi
Chapter One – OUR HISTORY 1
Chapter Two – OUR ENVIRONMENT 21
Chapter Three – OUR COMMUNITY 39
Chapter Four - OUR NATURAL HISTORY 65
Chapter Five – OUR INDUSTRIES, TRADES, SHOPS AND SERVICES 85
Chapter Six – OUR CHURCH, CHAPEL AND SCHOOL 115
Chapter Seven – OUR CLUBS AND SOCIETIES 127
Chapter Eight – OUR RANDOM MEMORIES 139
Chapter Nine – ISABELLE'S WARTIME STORY 145
Chapter Ten – OUR CELEBRATIONS 157
AND FINALLY 169
List of Contributors 171
Bibliography 172
Wall Civil Parish Map .... Inside Back Cover

FOREWORD
Wall: Our Northumbrian Village

As a fairly recent arrival to the beautiful village of Wall it might have taken hundreds of visits to its cosy and welcoming village pub to glean even a fraction of the local knowledge contained within this lovely book. Both my liver and I are therefore very grateful for the time and dedication given by all those involved in its production. The authors have carefully combined meticulous historical and ecological research with captivating personal memories and perspectives. It catalogues wonderfully the development of Wall and its surroundings, reflecting warmly on bygone days but in so doing offering an understanding and application of the village and its residents today.

All too often our fast moving modern lives give little time for the social interaction and environmental engagement which was once so integral to everyday village life. Happily this superbly detailed book serves as a timely reminder that the decisions we make in our local communities today have an impact on those who will become part of the parish in the future. Wall is a fabulous village with friendly and loyal residents, both of which, I now feel I know a lot better.

STEVE CRAM MBE

PREFACE

I have been asked to write a preface because I am one of the oldest residents in the area. I grew up here in a farming family and my grandchildren are now the fifth generation living in the Parish of Wall. After I married in 1954 I then lived in Essex for thirty two years but always returned to Wall several times a year and kept in touch with family and friends. When my husband retired in 1987 we hastened back to Wall to live in the house in which my parents had spent their retirement. Wall had been my home when I was young and it still felt like home. It had changed very little then and I slid back into life in Wall as if I had never been away. There have been quite a lot of changes since 1987 and there are many younger people in the village now but the feeling of community is still strong and this book bears witness to that.

When the Millennium Wall Hanging was made it was decided that a book to accompany it would be put together so that the background to the enterprise would be explained. We now have the Wall Hanging Book in its own box underneath the hanging in the village hall so that it is available for all to read.

Later a more comprehensive view of Wall Village and the surrounding area was suggested for a new book. Joan Proudlock and Mary Herdman took on the daunting task of collecting memories and stories from anyone who had something interesting to tell about the people or places in the area. They encouraged us all to write down what we could remember and hand in our snippets for sorting and editing into a book for publication. It has been an interesting exercise and has brought many memories to the surface reminding us of things forgotten over the years. Most of the contributions in the book are from people who are living now but some items are about people who are dead and we all have reason to regret that there is no-one left to answer our questions or verify the facts. This book, therefore, will be a useful reference for those in years to come who would like to find out a bit about the history of the village and its development.

ELLA HILL

*****

LUCY GRACE DUGGAN

In the week that this book went to the printers our village learnt of the tragic fatal accident of Lucy at eighteen years of age. Lucy was the daughter of Barbara and Ralph Duggan and sister to Jack, the grand-daughter of Ella Hill who has written the preface, the great grand-daughter of Jack Wardle of Planetrees and the great, great grand-daughter of John Wardle of Fallowfield and Bibury.

Lucy enjoyed helping at village events such as the fête and the soup lunches, which she attended, first as a baby. In later years she baby-sat many of the village children.

Lucy's roots were in Wall, she grew up amongst us, outgoing and happy.

This book is dedicated to her memory.

Lucy at St Oswald's with Mollie and Dash

INTRODUCTION

This book is a community project celebrating our village of Wall and its Parish.
Wall is like Christopher Robin's favourite stair, "It's not at the bottom, and it's not at the top." It is stands halfway between the fell top and the North Tyne. Our village enjoys an environment full of history, and is surrounded by beauty. The oldest houses form the nucleus. They cluster around the village green with the old water pump, the pant, at the centre. These houses are built of stone and many are hundreds of years old. Away from the green there have been more recent, mainly harmonious, additions. The War Memorial stands on the green too, as testimony to local men who gave their lives for their country.

To understand our environment, as it is today, we have explored both our human and our natural history, and the ways that they have shaped our village. And we have a lot of history! We have the remains of an Iron Age settlement on the fell above us. Hadrian's Wall bisects our parish and gives us our name. Through St Oswald's church at Heavenfield and the fabled battle of that name, we are associated with the royal saint. Five hundred years ago the region was a troubled place, subject to cross-border raids and warring families. These were the days of the reivers when bastles, defensive houses, were built. Wall has an ample share of these. Later, after the Jacobite rising, the military road was laid near, and partly on top of, the line of Hadrian's Wall. In the nineteenth century a notable preacher of his day preached his first sermon on our green. This was depicted by Ralph Hedley, a famous northern artist.

Over the centuries religion has played an important part. Our churches all have an interesting history and a big role in the present day. Our clubs and societies show our leisure time interests and enthusiasms. Everyday life is shaped by our schooling and our businesses, trades and industries, both past and present. As we are a rural community, farming is, as it always was, very important. Quarries and mines have also played a part. The tourist industry has become important today.

In days gone by most people were employed locally. Families would remain and work in the parish for generations. Now, with better transport, a larger percentage of our population can commute. Many of our youngsters have moved away seeking employment. People from other areas have been attracted to live in this lovely village and have also retired here to enjoy the tranquillity. The older families are now in the minority. Many who have joined us are active and add their skills and enthusiasms to ours.

We are interested in our past, present and our future. We hope that our efforts will be of interest and help to generations yet to come.

MARY HERDMAN

CHAPTER ONE
OUR HISTORY

THE PARISH - Mary Herdman

For the purposes of this book we are looking at the civil parish rather than the more extensive ecclesiastical one which includes Bingfield and Hallington.

Wall Village is four miles north of Hexham, on the A6079 which crosses the B6318 and continues to Colwell Five Lane Ends and the A68. At Brunton Crossroads from the A6079 take a left turn and either follow the B6318 west on the line of Hadrian's Wall or circle Chollerford roundabout to travel the route up the North Tyne to Wark and Bellingham. The A6079 is situated near the western border of Wall Parish which is formed by the river North Tyne. The eastern boundary is just beyond the A68 which follows the route of Dere Street, the ancient Roman road. East to west it is bisected by the B6318, which is known as the Military Road. To see the extent of our parish, refer to our parish map. We have a population of about 500. This is a rural parish, fairly hilly. The land rises up from the North Tyne, levels out somewhat, especially where the village stands, and then rises more sharply. There is quite a steep hill, known as Brunton Bank, leading up the B6318 to Heavenfield. On the lower areas can be seen mixed farming whilst more of sheep on the higher land. Small mixed woodlands are scattered throughout the area.

The parish has numerous disused mines and quarries. There are on-going attempts to reopen one of the quarries. This idea is raising stiff local opposition. The tourist trade is thriving as we have part of the popular Hadrian's Wall and Trail within our boundaries.

We no longer have a school, or shops. Our local medical centre, shop and Church of England Primary School are two miles away in Humshaugh parish. Apart from farming, the old industries, with their employment opportunities, are gone. We are within commuting distance of Newcastle and Hexham is a good shopping centre.

This is a good area to bring up families, and a good place for retirement. We are lucky to live in such a beautiful and historic part of Northumberland.

THE EARLY DAYS

Bronze Age burials have been found in the parish, one at Grottington and another, at Chollerford, which was discovered when the Border Counties Railway was built.

On the fell above the village is the site of an Iron Age defended settlement which would have consisted of six or more round houses inside an oval enclosure. It would have been a good defensive position with a marvellous view. It was at this very same spot that a group of villagers gathered on Millennium night to light a bonfire. On a clear, frosty midnight, they too had a wonderful view, of fireworks and bonfires all along the North Tyne. Two thousand years of history were linked.

Another settlement straddles two fields, the Long Slip and the field leading to Fallowfield. Here it is possible to see the outlines of walls and ditches.

Roman times brought Hadrian's Wall. This World Heritage site runs right across the parish and has given us our name. In the Roman period small farmsteads were built near Grottington Farm and at Redhouse Crags. These were more rectangular in layout, with no more than three round houses.

In early medieval times the battle of Heavenfield was fought somewhere in the area. The actual site of the battle is hotly debated, but the church of St Oswald and the roadside cross commemorate the rallying point. Medieval times saw a number of small villages and hamlets at Keepwick, Beukley, Great Grottington and East Errington. These were vulnerable to attacks by the Scots in the 14th and 15th centuries. Eventually they were deserted.

Reiving became widespread throughout the borders in the 16th and 17th centuries, with territorial feuds and opportunistic raiding. Defensive pele towers and bastles were erected. Pele towers reflected the need of the gentry. They had more storeys than bastles, but served the same purpose. There is a good example of a pele tower at Cocklaw. Bastles were vernacular buildings, defensible farmhouses. In times of trouble animals and supplies would be secured on the ground floor, the living area on the upper floor would be reached by a ladder which was then pulled up. Wall is a village with bastles.

When border warfare came to an end industry took on a greater role in the economy. Farming had always been a part of rural life. Coal mines were opened. From early man, stone had been quarried to build shelter and protection. Quarrying was important again. Limestone was burned commercially in kilns at Cocklaw, linked to the railway. There were now many more employment opportunities.

In the 20th century the two world wars left their mark on Wall. The worldwide effects were devastating. We will see how they affected our parish and its people, some of whom have given us their first hand memories.

The village we now know has expanded to meet today's needs. Old occupations, priorities and mode of life have changed to fit the patterns of modern society. They will continue to do so as we move on to the future.

OUR ROMAN LEGACY - Jenny Harrington

The village of Wall is about half a mile from Hadrian's Wall. The name is not a coincidence and several of the old houses have Roman stones in their masonry. After the conquest in 43AD the Romans gradually pushed north – indeed tried to conquer Scotland but decided it wasn't worth the effort. Finally Hadrian became emperor in 117AD and the boundary, Hadrian's Wall, was fixed along the line running from present day Wallsend to the Solway Firth.

Was there ever Roman occupation of Wall? There has been conjecture that there might have been a temporary marching camp and, looking at sections of the map of the village, it has been claimed the typical playing card shape of a Roman fort can be made out. Certainly there were quarries nearby such as Written Crag

Brunton Turret

where there was an inscription PETRA FLAVI CARATINA, perhaps that of a quarryman or a legionary commander. The inscription is now in Chesters museum.

Over the centuries builders plundered the Wall for good well dressed stone. Far worse for the wall was the building of the Military Road. After the Jacobite rebellion of 1745 General Wade was given the task of surveying and building a network of military roads, including a new route from Newcastle to Carlisle. Much of this road was actually built on top of the line of the Roman Wall. Our present day idea of conservation and respect for archaeology is comparatively new, and fortunately Hadrian's Wall is now a Unesco World Heritage Site, so it and all the monuments are under the protection of English Heritage.

Roman Pillar

The idea of a National Trail following the line of the Wall was mooted in the early 1990s. After many problems and setbacks, including the foot and mouth outbreak in 2001, the Hadrian's Wall Trail was officially opened in 2003. It means that it is now possible to view at close hand much more of the line of the Wall than before.

Hadrian's Wall Trail enters Wall parish a little west of Stanley Plantation, crossing the Military Road at an access road to Errington Hill Head. Walking westward there are some magnificent lengths of the northern ditch with its V- shaped section. The trail re-crosses the road at Planetrees. Here one can see a substantial section of the Wall. This is thanks to

William Hutton, a 78 year old Birmingham shopkeeper who, in 1802, decided to walk the length of the Wall and back again. When he reached Planetrees, he found a workman about to demolish the masonry on the orders of a local landowner. Hutton prevented this from happening. It is a good section of the Wall to examine, because visible are both the broad foundation and the narrow foundation after the Roman builders changed their minds about the width of the Wall. Crossing the next stile and walking steeply downhill to Brunton Copse there are both the northern ditch and the vallum, the huge earthwork built to the south of the Wall. In the copse there has been evidence of a much more recent military episode, when a wartime weapons dump was discovered. The trail had to be diverted for a few days while the army disposed of the dump.

The trail now follows the New Lane into Wall. Originally, the plan was to take the trail through fields to Brunton Turret and then across the A6079 to Chesters, but this proved impossible. On the other hand, the change in route has been very good for the Hadrian Hotel as walkers often stay there. They can also camp on the back green for one night free of charge, and it is a common sight to see tents on the green. After the village the route follows the A6097 to Brunton crossroads. It is a must to stop off and enter a field to look at Brunton Turret. There are six complete courses of masonry still in place and the turret rises to a maximum of eleven courses. A massive stone doorstep on the south side is still in place. On the north side it is possible to see how the north ditch breaks off to allow the turret to jut out. From the turret it is possible to see how the Wall ran in a straight line to Chesters. Before crossing Chollerford Bridge there is a footpath on the left which leads to the banks of the North Tyne. Here on the east bank, still in Wall parish, can be seen a section of the Wall joining on to the Roman bridge abutments. There were actually two bridges here. The first was a foot bridge and it is thought that it was swept away in a flood. The second one was a much grander affair and was built to carry a road over the Tyne. The stones of the abutments are huge. Each one weighed 600kg. Lewis holes can be seen in some – this is where lifting gear would be used to raise the stones into place. It is also possible to identify the base of a pier from the first bridge. It is a lovely spot on the banks of the river. On the other side, in Humshaugh parish, can be seen the Wall and the famous bathhouse.

Right from the start of the trail archaeologists have been worried about the damage so many feet can do to remains just under the surface. This is particularly true in the winter and, with this in mind, circular walks have been devised to take walkers away from the Wall. Our local route goes from Wall village green to Fallowfield, to Written Crag to Crag House and down the Old Lane back into Wall. This is just one of many lovely local walks. Wall is a good area for walkers!

Dennis and Jenny Harrington became volunteer wardens on the trail in 2003. Their section runs from Brunton Turret to Heavenfield. They have to walk their section at least once a month, pick up any litter (very little), cut back vegetation round stiles, report on any problems with signage, keep an eye on the archaeology and, most important of all, talk to any trail walkers they meet. The walkers come from all over the world and by and large are most enthusiastic about the trail.

HEAVENFIELD

In 731 St Bede completed his Ecclesiastical History of the English People which chronicled Oswald's raising of the cross before the battle, through to the site becoming a place of pilgrimage. Many miracles thereafter were attributed to the saint, with pieces of the original cross being taken as relics by pilgrims in the hope of cures.

The place is called in English Hefenfelth, meaning Heaven's Field, a name given it in ancient times in evident anticipation of what was to come.... It lies to the north near the Wall... The brothers of the nearby church of Hagustaldesea (Hexham) long ago established the custom of gathering each year on the anniversary of King Oswald's death....

To this day there is an annual pilgrimage from Hexham Abbey to St Oswald's Church at Heavenfield, taking place in early August as the saint's feast day is 9th August.

Not much is known about the battle of Heavenfield. St Bede tells us that it was between the tyrannical Cadwalla of Gwynedd, king of the Britons, who was occupying the Northumbrian Kingdoms and Oswald, 'a man beloved of God'. Oswald had a small army 'protected by their faith in Christ'. On the eve of the battle they erected a cross and prayed for divine assistance. The following day saw Cadwalla's superior forces scattered and Cadwalla himself killed at Rowley Burn, three miles south of Hexham, but this is open to conjecture!

Should it be Cadwalla or Cadwallon? Both names appear in the many scholarly works on this subject.

A BASTLE VILLAGE - Julia Grint

The following is an extract from Bastles: An Introduction to the Bastle Houses of Northumberland by Julia Grint.

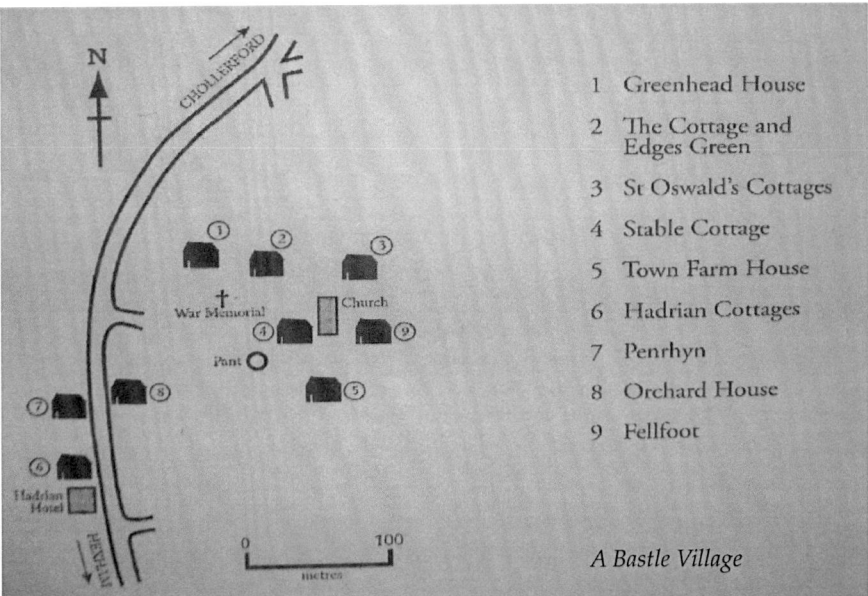

A Bastle Village

Wall is well known for being a 'bastle village', although it is peaceful and tamed nowadays, with relatively little evidence of its reiver past. Nonetheless there are houses that have kept some basic characteristics and the layout of the older dwellings is roughly as it was – a defensive circuit around the village green. As you wander round the village you may note that the houses include masonry taken from Hadrian's Wall, which of course lies only a stone's throw away.

Park in the centre of Wall; the buildings are best viewed by strolling around. Greenhead House (number 1) stands at the north west corner of the village green, overlooking the war memorial. These days it has rather a grand air about it, but close inspection shows that although much altered it was a bastle in its youth. Seen at a glance are its thick walls made of large stones. The remains of the original, gently arched byre doorway can be seen very clearly to the left of the 'new' porch; note that in this case entry to the byre was in a long wall rather than a gable end, probably because Greenhead was part of a terrace. Certainly traces of another, perhaps older building can be seen in the left (west) wall. Above the porch are traces of the doorway to the living quarters, which would be reached by a ladder. Also to be seen are blocked up windows to the left and right of the porch, although these would surely be added later, perhaps in 1631 when times were somewhat safer; a stone with that date has been re-situated in the (much later) porch. The stone also bears the words, FEARE GOD IN HART, as does a very similar stone over the doorway of the end St Oswald's Cottage, (number 3). The earliest Greenhead bastle would almost certainly have had only slit vents to the ground floor byre. No doubt any traces of the original upstairs windows were destroyed when much larger and later windows were installed.

Walking from Greenhead House towards the church you will see The Cottage (number 2), once a bastle, which although much altered is easily recognizable by its masonry and its blocked side slit vent. This is now one with Edges Green, which has a new front wall; apparently the original wall fell down during the removal of an ancient fireplace. Both have enormously thick walls and were undoubtedly bastles.

Further along again in a more or less straight line, passing St George's church on your right, you will find St Oswald's Cottages (number 3). An early photograph of Wall, taken by the well-known Hexham photographer and polymath J P Gibson in about 1865, clearly shows that the east gable end of St Oswald's Cottages retained an external stone staircase to the upper floor. As mentioned above, this cottage also has an inscribed stone over its doorway, similar to that of Greenhead House although with the slightly later date of 1642: FEARE GOD 16BKTK42 IN HART*, and again this date must relate to the reconstruction work that went on in the mid 17th Century. The gable ends of both cottages have original slit vents. Although it is thought that these terraced bastles would all have had doors facing inwards, there are traces of an old door at the west end of the terrace as well as a glimpse of the original plinth.

Returning to the village, the next obvious bastle is just around the corner from the church. Stable Cottage (number 4) has a blocked up door to the first floor and has a steeper roof than other houses around it. The huge and rough masonry can easily be seen.

Across the green with your back to Stable Cottage you will see the back view of Town Farm house (number 5), which now faces away from the rest of the village but which presumably in its earliest form would have faced inwards as part of the defensive circuit. There is little to see, but the walls of the original house, which has been much altered, are immensely thick, and are undoubtedly very old. Just across the green, further west and in between Stable Cottage and the back of Town Farm is the 'pant' or village water pump and trough built in 1858.

Our next bastle (number 6) is on the opposite side of the 'main road' through Wall, immediately up the road from the Hadrian Hotel (a good place to have a break). It could be that this entire line of buildings formed the western side of the green, before the buildings in between became the 'new' western boundary. Either way these two cottages were once a bastle, and what was once the doorway to the upper floor is now a false window, seen above the new doors.

Further along again, at right angles to the main road is Penrhyn (number 7), the exterior of which is very much of the early 19th Century. This house shows no discernable trace of its ever having been a bastle, but the interior walls are very thick, and there is what appears to be a blocked slit vent in the kitchen wall inside the house. Even less bastle-like these days is Orchard House (number 8), on the opposite side of the road from Penrhyn, and like Town Farm facing the 'wrong way' if it were indeed once a bastle. The much changed exterior may be seen on Keys to the Past website, which suggests that it was "probably originally a bastle", but there are no details to support the statement. It seems very likely to me that other houses in Wall Village, old but not as old as bastles, were built where bastles once stood, completing more fully the defensive circuit. Fellfoot and Fellfoot Cottage (number 9) fall into this category. As one who lives in the village, looking over the green, I am heartily glad that these days neither Roman nor Reiver is likely to disturb our peace.

*Perhaps the letter K in "FEARE GOD 16BKTK IN HART might refer to the surname Kell, at that time a well-known name in the area.

COTTAGE No 2 - Michael Bruce

On taking the Jacobean floorboards up in the bedroom I found money dating from 1775-1948 covering four reigns, George III, Queen Victoria, George V, and George VI. I also found under the floor, handmade child's shoes, a tooth with a big black hole in it, a mummified cat, straw thatch bundles (for roofing) and a poacher's gaff.

Whilst excavating the fireplace which involved removing the 1950s tiled one, then two others, I ended up with a large open fireplace with a beehive oven set in the back. Someone thought perhaps it might have originally been the village bakery! The lintel over the front door had a sunburst carved in it. The outer wall of the house was one metre thick and at one time had been the village outer defence wall. The stair well I filled in with matching oak beams brought from the House of Correction in Hexham, (they were being burnt on a bonfire). When I removed the wood panelling on the living room wall I found a message left on a cutting of wood which read,

"John Vincent Cattermould of Chollerton Cottages 1914 of April 20th. The house occupied by Mr Smith, wife and sons and daughter." On the other side it read "I am an apprentice joiner for the Benson Estates and today we are panelling this wall".

*A William Cattermould joined the Navy during the First World War, then emigrated to Australia and joined the police there. He ended up as Superintendent in one of the state provinces.

The house next door to the cottage, the home of Helen Clark, had a priest hole in the flue. When the house was altered it is believed it was removed and was taken to the Moot Hall in Hexham.

This record came from a previous owner of The Cottage, (No 2 on the plan) Mike Bruce, who now lives in Gibraltar. He and Liz, his wife, and children, Nicky, Clare and Calum lived there for several years. Mike was a builder and very interested in doing renovation work to fit the style of the house, and that is what he did in The Cottage.

THE MILITARY ROAD

The B6318 is a road with a history. Part of it runs east to west through our parish. It is widely known as the Military Road. It was built after the Jacobite rebellion of 1745. Bonnie Prince Charlie had advanced down the western side of the country, taking Carlisle. General Wade, with his troops, was billeted in Newcastle. He should have been able to cross the country to intercept the Scots but this was not possible. Because of the lack of good roads and communication he only succeeded in reaching Hexham.

This fiasco brought the condition of the highway to public attention. In 1749 the local gentry petitioned the House of Commons, claiming that the country between Newcastle and Carlisle was often impassable, and that the lack of communication had endangered the kingdom during the '45 rebellion. They requested national assistance. A surveyor was appointed and the construction of the road was ordered by Act of Parliament in May 1751. In our parish, as elsewhere, this construction was very destructive of archaeology. Workers would clear and level Hadrian's Wall to lay the road. From Portgate to St Oswald's it was built upon its line. After this point the road runs alongside it to cross the North Tyne at Chollerford, which is upstream from the Roman bridge abutment.

The B6318 is well used by visitors from all over the world who flock to see what is left of the famous Hadrian's Wall. Not so many know about the history of the road on which they are driving.

THE CHESTERS SALE - Mary Herdman

Nathaniel Clayton came to the north east in the 18th century as a Minister in the Church. He was a descendant of John Clayton of Clayton Hall, High Hoyland, Yorkshire. Robert Clayton, his eldest son, became Sheriff and later Mayor of Newcastle and Nathaniel, his second son, served for 37 years as Newcastle's town clerk. In 1796 this Nathaniel bought the Chesters Estate, where he died in 1832. His son John succeeded him as town clerk in 1822. He had received a classical education and became involved with the rebuilding of Newcastle in the neo-classical style. John expanded the Chesters Estate, buying any land bearing a portion of the Roman Wall as soon as it came onto the market, with a view to excavating and recording it. John remained a bachelor. On his death in 1890, he was succeeded by his nephew Nathaniel George Clayton who was the son of his younger brother Richard Clayton.

Nathaniel married Isabel Ogle in December 1860. They had three sons. Chesters Estate was inherited by the second son Edward Francis Clayton, born in 1864, who married Jeanne de Fougeres at Dinard in Brittany in 1900. They had a son and a daughter. This son was John Maurice Clayton who was born in 1902. His grandmother, Mrs Isabel Clayton died on 6th May 1929. By the time of her death, her grandson, John Maurice, had run up considerable gambling debts. In his interests, and those of the family, it was necessary to sell off part of the estate.

By the time of the sale the Chesters Estate had become one of the best known and most extensive domains in the County of Northumberland. In total it ran from Heddon-on-the-Wall through to Greenhead in the west. The main estate was along the line of the Military Road, about 22 miles from Newcastle and inclued Vindolanda, Brocolitia and Borcovicium. The Clayton family owned many stock raising farms in the valley of the North Tyne, described as having some of the richest land in the county, including hill farms, numerous small holdings and a sporting estate on the River Irthing. They owned practically the whole of Wall Village and our parish.

In the Old Assembly Rooms, Newcastle upon Tyne, on Wednesday and Thursday, 19th and 20th June1929, auctioneers Hampton & Sons of London in conjunction with Messrs Turner, Lord and Dowler also of London, offered 112 lots for sale. These were described as extensive and valuable portions of the Chesters Estate, Humshaugh.

Throughout the estate the buildings were advertised as being in an unusually good state of repair, and the farms as equipped with very good homesteads and labourers' cottages. The auctioneers drew attention to the fact that farming in this locality was a prosperous and thriving industry, to a very great extent unaffected by the current depression. They predicted increasing prosperity in stock farming.

Of the 112 lots, 64 concerned Wall. The sales catalogue gave a detailed listing of all the properties, naming the tenants. Brunton House, the Cocklaw and Brunton Limestone Quarries and the Smith's Arms (now the Hadrian Hotel) came in for special mention in their catalogue. Each property was numbered and their location shown on colour coded maps. The properties were described in great detail. In properties other than small cottages the number and purposes of the rooms and outbuildings were listed. Not only was acreage of the land given, but also the uses to which fields were put. Annual rents were quoted. The Farmhouse lots included the farm cottages. The village school included the master's house.

The general memoranda covered a variety of subjects such as mineral rights, water supplies, shooting and fishing. Any disputes concerning fencing were to be referred to the vendor's estate agent, A M Allgood Esq. The vendor reserved the right to alter the mode of lotting, to amalgamate any two or more lots, or withdraw any lot or lots either before or at the time of the sale.

The following is a description of one of the Lots.

Lot 15: Fallowfield Farm.* This was described as a highly attractive agricultural and sporting property, lying most compact and embracing almost the whole township of Fallowfield. It comprised of a finely placed superior farm residence, extensive farm buildings, four good cottages, with some 161 acres of sound arable and 402 acres of grassland. Included also are about 60 acres of woodland and the Fallowfield Mines of 26 acres, making a total area of about 664 acres.

The Farmhouse itself was detailed as occupying a commanding position facing south in the centre of the farm and containing: two good sitting rooms, kitchen, back kitchen, cellar, five bedrooms, two attics, bath room and wc. It also enjoyed a garage and a two-stall nag stable with loose box.

The farm buildings consisted of: Byre for 4, large loft, byre for 8, straw barn and threshing house, stable for 7, loose box, hen house, piggeries, yard with two loose boxes, implement shed, seven bay cart shed, two fine ranges of feeding boxes for 18 with turnip house and hay house, fine byre for 36 with feeding passages, turnip house and hay house, rick yard with seven bay Dutch barn, yard with byre for 16, hay house, etc.

The water supply was from a spring pumped by a windmill to storage tanks supplying house and buildings.

The schedule of land is minutely detailed under the title: Parish of Fallowfield. It consisted of 577,247 acres of arable land and pasture (this included the house, buildings and gardens), 60,470 acres of woodland and 26,635 acres of scrubland: a total of 664,352 acres. Let to Mr J S Wardle, the rental was £586 per annum.

This lot was sold privately.

*Mr Wardle, having lost Fallowfield House and farm, had land in the village on which he built the house known as Bibury. He had farming connections in that part of the Cotswolds, and the lovely sandstone cottages of Bibury perhaps reminded him of the Northumbrian sandstone with which Bibury is built. He duly attended the Chesters sale, buying several of the cottages in Wall Village, Town Farm and Low Barns Farm in order to keep the tenants in place.

In 1840 the major part of the village and parish was in the ownership of the Tulip family of Brunton. John Clayton owned only 16 plots in Wall. In 1876, John bought Brunton from Brunton House was described at length, and in very great detail, but again was one of the lots withdrawn from the sale.

The list of the lots is a good source of information about the people of Wall in 1929 and they have been included at the end of this chapter. It will be seen that Lots 13 and 14 are missing from this list as they were in Acomb parish.

There are several Chester sale books retained by the descendants of 1929 village residents.It was certainly a sale which must have raised great interest but it is good to note Wall survived pretty much as it was, whereas now developers might have moved in and transformed some the cottages and houses beyond recognition.

From the buildings of Wall and out-bye we now move on to some of the people who lived and worked in and around the village as it was. Before the 1929 Chesters sale came the 1914-1918 Great War and this is where we start by remembering those young men who served their country and did not return.

THE WORLD WARS AND WALL

We are grateful to Alan Grint for permission to use the following article taken from his book with the title- Silent Fortitude - A Tribute to the Men of the North Tyne Valley who died in the Great War

Lieutenant William Lee aged 26 - Royal Air Force
5th (Service) Battalion Royal Irish Fusiliers Died 19 August 1918

William was the only son of Thomas and Mary Lee of Low Brunton, Wall. Before joining the Colours he was employed as a draughtsman by the North Eastern Railways in their Divisional Goods Manager's Department at Forth Banks, Newcastle. In early 1915, William enlisted in the Officers' Training Corps at Armstrong College. After receiving his commission in the Royal Irish Fusiliers he was sent to Salonika. In September 1917 the Irish Rifles returned to Egypt and were part of the force destined to capture Jerusalem. William later joined the RAF and was acting as an instructor in Egypt when he met his death in a flying accident.

William is buried in Suez War Memorial Cemetery.

****

Gunner George Gray aged 28
168th Brigade, Royal Field Artillery Died 1 September 1918

George was the youngest son of William and Margaret Jane Gray of Wall. He was educated at Wall School. Before joining the army he was employed by Messrs William Weir and Co at Hexham Saw Mill. In May 1917 he enlisted in the Royal Scots Greys (a cavalry regiment) and was subsequently transferred to the Royal Field Artillery. He had served in France from April 1918.

George is buried in Daours Communal Cemetery Extension.

****

Guardsman William Cuthbert Robson aged 20
3rd Battalion Grenadier Guards Died 27 November 1917

William was born in Wall and was the youngest son of William Cuthbert and Mary Robson of Front Street, Wall. He was one of six brothers serving with the forces. Before he enlisted he had been employed for over five years as a butcher by Mr. R. Hedley of Humshaugh. William was posted to the guards in October 1916.

William is commemorated on the Cambrai Memorial to the missing.

****

Lance Corporal John Thomas Bell aged 21
1/4th Battalion Northumberland Fusiliers Died 18 September 1916

John was born in Wall and was the fourth son of John and Elizabeth Bell. The Wall Parish Roll of Honour records that he was an old boy of Wall School. The 1911 census shows that at the age of fifteen John was working as a domestic servant. He was wounded in action on 15 September and died in hospital in Abbeville.

John is buried in Abbeville Community Cemetery Extension.

****

Private Robert Maddison aged 22
1/4th Battalion Northumberland Fusiliers Died 20 September 1916

Robert was the son of Robert and Isabella Maddison of Wall. In 1911 at the age of 16 he was working as a coachman and was living with his widowed father in Wall. He married Hannah (née Robson) in 1914 and was the father of a girl called Frances, who was born in early 1915; a daughter who would never really know her father. He was wounded in action on 15 September and died of his wounds at one of the hospitals near Etaples.

Robert is buried at Etaples Military Cemetery.

****

Lance Corporal William Stephen Hepburn aged 23
2nd Battalion Yorkshire Regiment Died 8 July 1916

William was born in Monkton, Durham, the son of William and Fiona Hepburn. Although no details of his connection to Wall are known, he is mentioned in the Wall, Bingfield and Hallington 'Roll of Honour' published in the Parish Magazine for

January 1915. He arrived in France in early October 1915.
William is commemorated on the Thiepval Memorial to the missing.

****

Private Robert Thomas Curry aged 18
51st Graduating Battalion Durham Light Infantry Died 1 March 1918

Robert was the only son of Robert and Isabella Curry of Brunton Banks, Wall. He had been in the army for only a few months when he died. He was educated at Wall School. While stationed at Durham he contracted pleurisy and was transferred to a military hospital in Newcastle; he developed pneumonia and died. The funeral, conducted by Reverend W W London, was attended by a large gathering, including the teachers and pupils of Wall School.

Robert is buried in St Oswald's (Heavenfield) Churchyard, Wall.

****

Private Albert Walton aged 21
1st Battalion Durham Light Infantry Died 10 September 1917

Albert was born in South Shields, but from an early age he was brought up by his mother's sister, Margaret Fisher of Wall. He was employed as a woodman and he initially enlisted into the Northumberland Fusiliers. He was later transferred to the 1st Battalion Durham Light Infantry. Albert died of Enteric fever at Cherat, India.

Albert is commemorated on the Delhi Memorial.

****

Private William Baird aged 40 Military Medal
'C' Company 7th Battalion Seaforth Highlanders Died 1 October 1918

William was born in Dumfries, Scotland. He was the son of Robert and Catherine Baird of Kirton, Dumfries. He was married in early 1914 to Jeanie(née Best) who lived in the Hexham registration area and left a son, William, born in late 1914. The Wall Parish Magazine for April 1915 in its Roll of Honour reported that William Baird of Hallington had been accepted into the 9th Reserve Cavalry Battalion. The Battalion War Diary for October 1918 lists the name of William Baird as a recipient of the Military Medal, presumably posthumously.

William is buried in Dadizeele, New British Cemetery.

****

WAR EFFORTS 1914-1918

The minutes of the reading room give some information on support efforts during the First World War.

In 1914 Mr Wm Graham donated his prize money of 18/6, won in the billiard and the domino handicaps, to the War Relief Fund. The committee also voted to give £5.5s.0d. to the Lord Lieutenant's Fund. The Reading Room was made free to all local soldiers.

In 1915 £20.0s.0d was invested in the war loan.

1916 saw Mrs Waddilove organizing the Ladies' Working Party. She was allowed to use the premises on Thursday afternoons for her sewing meeting which made garments for wounded soldiers.

THE SECOND WORLD WAR

In every city, town and village throughout the land brave men and women answered the call of their country, many never to return. Each would have his individual story to tell.

There have been many characters who for many reasons have found their place in the life of Wall, but in the Second World War Wall had its own hero. The following is part of Norman Craig's story. He said he was the lucky one, he came home.

Norman Craig
"No Legs - but he drives his own car."
First ministry gift is presented to Wall Man

During the next two weeks Mr Norman Craig of Front Street, Wall will take his wife and two children for a ride in their new family car. Six years ago Norman thought that would never be possible and so did his family. For on Anzio beachhead in Italy, where he was serving with the Yorkshire Dragoons a German shell crashed into a dugout which he occupied with two comrades and so shattered both his legs that they had to be amputated. (Both his comrades died). In spite of his handicap, Norman has been a young man of hopes and ambitions ever since he came out of hospital. He found employment as chief office clerk at Fewsters sand and gravel works at Howford and it was here on Friday that he and his work colleagues welcomed a representative from the Ministry of Pensions who delivered Norman's neat little 8hp Morris Minor Saloon. Special extensions to the steering column enable the driver to control his acceleration and clutch with his right hand, while a joy stick at the side of the seat operates the foot brake. Otherwise the car is the same in design and construction as those which are going in such numbers for export these days. Norman told a "Courant" reporter who attended the handing over ceremony that he was grateful to the Ministry whose gift would enable him to get more easily to work and to give his family a few outings.

*The above article was taken from the Hexham Courant and detailed an event which changed the lives of Norman and his family.

During all the years Norman never regarded his artificial legs as a handicap to his getting on with life. As reported he worked for Fewsters at Howford Quarry and then when it closed he moved to Mootlaw, working on the weighbridge there. He became the secretary of the Wall and Humshaugh Leek Club and is remembered for that post which he held for many years. When he retired he enjoyed driving to Grassholme and Kielder to enjoy fishing, whilst still carrying on the trade which he knew so well, plastering. There are many folk in Wall whose walls or ceilings were plastered by Norman. One bride to be found him standing on a table plastering her kitchen ceiling, as a wedding present, she being completely ignorant of his leg situation.

Another story which indicates the strength of Norman was when returning from a fishing trip to Kielder, a car driven by a Scandinavian doctor drove into his car. The

Roll of Honour

emergency services, including the air ambulance helicopter were called as Norman was trapped. The police arrived, and one of them who knew Norman was able to lift him out of the car, leaving his artificial legs behind. Imagine the consternation of the paramedics in the helicopter when they arrived and saw Norman lying on the ground with his retrieved legs lying beside him! Norman's reaction to the accident was excitement at having a helicopter ride to hospital and, as he said "It's not everyone who can lose their legs twice!" His sense of humour carried him through.

Norman was a familiar sight walking with his sticks in the village. He and Mona, a Wall girl, were married for seventy years contributing much to the richness of village life. Today wounded servicemen return with a raft of support facilities and the benefit of modern surgery and technology. There was none of that available for Norman. He counted himself lucky because he did come home. Like many he did not speak about his war, he just got on living. He would never have considered himself a hero but in the history and life of Wall village he was and is most definitely Wall's Hero.

Norman Craig

THE MILITARY

The military appeared very soon after the beginning of the war. This was a marvellous area for the distribution of ammunition dumps which were hidden in the woods around the New Lane. They were manned by Military Police. Civilians had to have passes to go up and down the New Lane. The manual work of moving the huge boxes was done by the Pioneer Corps. Accommodation was in six large Nissen huts on the back green below the school. There were Nissen huts at Brunton crossroads too. The verges above the cricket field were often busy with the loading or unloading ammunition into or from lorries. By the riverside near Dunkirk, soldiers practised putting pontoon bridges across the North Tyne. On at least one occasion they used hand grenades to break the ice. Some of the older members of our community today remember an aeroplane crashing very close to St Oswald's Farm. The crew were Polish and there were no survivors.

THE HOME GUARD

Every village had its 'Dad's Army'. Wall was no exception. Most of the local lads took part in the Local Defence Volunteers, which became the Home Guard, before being called up.

The Local Defence Volunteers legally came into being on 17th May 1940. Its primary function was to observe German troop movements in the event of an invasion. In late July 1940 it became the Home Guard. Few villages had a purpose built armoury but they were encouraged to improvise and use whatever means they could in defence of their area. The captain was Charlie Watson. His lieutenant was Cecil Herdman. The Home Guard had access to rifles and ammunition. Working in close collaboration with the military, they had meetings in the Hall, went on exercises and, occasionally, weekend manoeuvres. Sunday morning exercises on the back green finished up with lunchtime discussions in the Hadrian Hotel.

Some members of the Home Guard who showed a special aptitude were recruited to a secret guerilla army, the Auxiliary Unit. They were highly trained to cause maximum disruption to the invaders. They were all hand-picked volunteers who laid down supplies of both arms and food, ready to go into hiding the day the invasion started. Their job was to slow the invasion by blowing up arms and fuel dumps, bridges and railway lines: to cause confusion to the enemy. They knew that they could be on a suicide mission. An intimate local knowledge and skill of concealment was essential, plus the willingness to kill those who might be tempted to collaborate – perhaps their neighbours! Specially constructed bunkers were excavated, their locations remaining secret. Were any of our local men members of this elite corps? If they were, they never revealed it.

In charge locally was the 'Intelligence Officer for Northumberland', Anthony Quayle, (who was to become the famous actor). This is Joan Proudlock's story of how she met him in Wall.

In June 1988, when Sir Anthony Quayle's Compass Theatre Company was performing at the Newcastle Theatre Royal, he stayed at the Hadrian Hotel in Wall. At the start of the week his car developed a problem and he took it to my husband John's garage, to be repaired. This presented him with a problem as he needed to shop for food for his dog Tiger, so I was pressed into service with my car. We had two dogs then and, after a little discussion, he happily came home with me to collect some tins of dog food. I offered to take him to a place where he could walk Tiger before going to the theatre. He chose Fallowfield Fell, a place he seemed to know, and as he walked he told me of his connection with Northumberland during the early war years and how he had served in the Auxiliary Unit setting up operational posts. He had chosen the Hadrian Hotel to stay, because he could look across the river to Warden Hill where he had set up one of these observation posts with an escape tunnel. I was amazed – and even more so when he told me what was required of the men he recruited. Having seen both Ice Station Zebra and The Guns of Navarone and knowing his acting history, you can imagine the privilege it was for me to share such memories he had of his real-life wartime career in a county, of which he told me, he was very fond. He was a charming and humorous man who sadly died the following year. I am left with the memory of a June summer morning standing on Fallowfield Fell, looking across the valley to Warden Hill, listening as Sir Anthony Quayle told me of his time in the Wall area.

At the beginning of the war, when there was fear of an invasion, every name on every road sign was obliterated. Post Offices had their names removed. There was traffic going through Wall at all hours of the day and night, the night traffic using dimmed headlamps. This all led to navigation difficulties.

WALL'S WARTIME CHILDREN

Some children today are rich in material possessions but during the Second World War things were very different. Everything was in short supply, rationing applied to so many things. The eldest child had new clothes, if there was not an older cousin or friend to obtain them from. Younger siblings usually wore hand-me-downs too. Little girls wore frocks made from the best bits of mother's old dresses. Toys were very hard to obtain. The creative skills of parents were put to good use, using whatever they could put their hands on, be they wooden ships or rag dolls. Santa Claus did much of his shopping in Colman's Second-Hand Saleroom, in St Mary's Chare, Hexham.

Children too were inventive. Old dried egg boxes were just the right size for dinky car garages. Milk bottle tops were precious. They were made of waxed card and made great miniature frisbees. Those with the holes in the middle that were poked out for inserting drinking straws were just right for making pompoms from any left over wool. Old cardboard boxes were valuable. Sat in, they could be tanks, ships, cars or aeroplanes. They could be used upside-down as tables for dollies' tea parties. Flattened, they made summer sledges. Their use was only limited by a child's imagination. Paper was in very short supply to the extent that slates and slate pencils came back into use in some schools. Blank backs of any redundant documents or letters were often used for drawing.

The Christmas stocking contained far less than it does today. They were filled with whatever was available at the time. They contained fruit, apples, oranges, nuts, small toys such as balls, yoyos or marbles, sugar mice and whatever sweets could be obtained. The stockings were the child's own rather than a pair of large rugby stockings borrowed from daddy.

There were difficult times for several years following the war, but the children of Wall were happy, blackout curtains taken down, the threat of invasion gone and families reunited. The outdoors beckoned, and as we shall find later amongst the memories, Wall gave children a secure place to grow.

WALL VILLAGE ARCHIVES - Mary Herdman

At the first committee meeting of Wall Local History Society various aspects of our history were discussed. I asked "What about today?" On being asked what I meant, I replied, "Today is tomorrow's history!" I was promptly told that that would be my job. The *archives were born.

It was quite a job setting them up. I scanned the newspapers and ran around the village photographing anything and everything. At the beginning I intended to concentrate on the here and now, post 1980, but as many people gave (and still give) me contributions of older photographs and documents, the archives soon expanded.

Once I had been watching four men with shovels spending idle hours round a hole in the road. I thought it a good subject to come under services, as road repairs. Finally two of them started digging. I rushed out and photographed them. They were alarmed. They thought I was a council spy! I reassured them. I refrained from suggesting that if I had been, I would have had plenty of time to take them leaning on their shovels. The incident taught me to ask and explain before taking photographs.

On behalf of the Village Society, the archives went on display in the Methodist Chapel schoolroom every year on the day of the Three Churches Fête. At first, when I had only five files we had to think of an added attraction but soon they filled the room! The files cover a variety of subjects ranging through our community; people, local photographs, shops, services, amenities, changes, events, aspects of history, art and artists, press cuttings and the Village Newsletters.

Initially the Society offered to pay my expenses, but I soon realised that I would be taking all their funds. The archives remain my personal property, for the use of the village. Often they go out on loan to local people. I impose rules. They must be returned to me, not passed on to others. Food, drink, or anything which can be spilt, must be kept away from them. I keep a careful register.

Only once has a book been damaged. A lady had to answer her door. On coming back she found that her young Labrador dog had pulled it from the table and was just settling down to eat it. The lady was very distressed about it, but the damage was minimal.

* Due to the vigilance of Mary in collecting and collating anything and everything that is newsworthy connected with Wall over more than twenty years, there has been a ready source of material to draw on for several sections of this book. Sadly now the Chapel has closed, so a new way of annually presenting Mary's collection is being negotiated.

Thirteen ways of looking at Wall - Patricia Gillespie

i) Wall Green, November, 1am.
   Mole dark,
   a leaf falls, and then another
   and that is all.
   Somewhere among beech twigs
   water beads succumb to gravity.
   Just three notes.
   Roots of grasses, buttercup,
   rowan, silver birch
   touch toes.

ii) Dawn races on crimson clouds.
    Flamingos line-dance at Lake Bogoria.

iii) Postman's van scatters
     nonchalant chickens.

iv) We harvest Sunset, Jonagold, Falstaff -
    lesser planets in a copper world.

v) Over Warden Hill
   skies of apricot, slate,
   turquoise and green.
   Wood-smoke.

vi) Owls in conversation
    on a late night jaunt.

vii) Village in the crook
     of a sandstone swell.
     Hebridean sheep inhabit the gradient.

viii) We climb 69 steps
      as, centuries ago, miners
      bound for Fallowfield.

ix) With buzzards' eyes,
    Iron Age settlement,
    landscape panorama.
    North Tyne Valley -
    its warp and weft.
    Far horizons of Deadwater Fell.

x) Below sycamore and wood sage,
   a secret crag inscribed,
   'To err is human
   To forgive divine'.

xi) A deer crouches in a far field,
    but it is dry thistle,
    long necks of willow herb.

xii) Farmer, John Lamb, aptly named,
     his tractor, cotton-reel hay aloft.
     On the Roman frontier,
     one white bull.

xiii) Heavenfield at twilight,
      candle time,
      looking north.

Chesters Sale catalogue

Lot	Holding	Tenant	Buyer	Price
12	Acomb High Barns Farm	M. R. Ridley	Sold privately	
15	Fallowfield Farm	J. S. Wardle	Sold privately	
16	Town Farm	T. Davidson	Mr. J. S. Wardle	£4.000.
17	Wall West Farm	W. T. & M. Lamb	Sold privately	
18	Wall North Farm	Mrs. J. Davidson & Son.	Sold privately	
19	Brunton House	G. H. Waddilove, Esq.	Withdrawn	
20	Low Brunton Farm	T. Lee	Sold privately	
21	High Brunton Farm	T. W. & M. Lamb	Mr. J. S. Wardle	£1,000
22	Cottage and Garden	Miss Fisher	Miss Fisher	£250
23	Cottage and Garden	G. H. Waddilove, Esq.	Withdrawn	
24	Two Cottages and Gardens	Miss Scott & Michael Scott	Mr J. S. Wardle	£250
25	Three Cottages, etc.	Various	Mr. J. S. Wardle	£370
26	Three Cottages and Gardens	Various	Mrs Knell	£250
27	Post Office and Cottage	Mrs. Laing	Mrs. Laing	£390
28	Two Cottages and Garden	J. Little & J. Bell	Mr. Scott	£240
29	Smith's Arms Inn	Miss Purvis	Mr E. Watson	
30	Buildings and Yard	Miss Purvis	Mr E Watson	
31	Tennis Ground	C. E. Watson	Mr C. E. Watson	£50
32	Cottage and Garden	Miss Herdman	Mr J. Herdman	£300
33	Wall Engineering Works	E. Herdman	Messrs J. Herdman	£400
34	Shop, Cottage, etc.	Mrs M. Muse	Mrs Muse	£580
35	Three Cottages, Stable, etc.	Various	Mr Coats	£340
36	Accommodation Land	R. Stewart	Mr Macdonald	£55
37	Wall Village School, etc.	Northumberland C. C.		
38	Accommodation Land	R. Stewart	Mr J. S. Wardle	£110
39	Cottage and Garden	T. J. Scott	Mr Cuthill	£170
40	Two Cottages and Gardens	W. Jackson & H. Rochester	Mr Cuthill	£240
41	Two Cottages and Gardens	H. Millar & T. Mason	Miss Thompson	£140
42	Stable, Slaughter House, etc.	T. J. Lamb	Mr. J. S. Wardle	£90

43	Cottage and Garden	J. G. Scott	Mr Bird	£230
44	Accommodation Land	T. J. Lamb	Mr. Bird	£65
45	Village Reading Room	In Hand		
46	Cottage and Garden	C. E. Watson	Mr C. E. Watson	£360
47	Cottage and Garden	G. H. Waddilove, Esq.	Mr Wood	£190
48	Cottage and Garden	Vicar of Wall	Mr J. Mitchell	£120
49	Ground Rent	Wesleyan Chapel Trustees	Mrs S. Wardle	£10
50	Accommodation Land	Miss Purvis		£15
51	Accommodation Land	Miss Purvis		£240
52	Wall Mill and Land	W. B. Ripley	Mr R. Stewart	£800
53	Plantation	In Hand	Mr Macdonald	£165
54	Keepwick Farm	J. L. Henderson	Mr Walton, Rawfoot	£9,000
55	East Cocklaw Farm	Wm. Tully	Messrs Dodds	£5,100
56	West Cocklaw Farm	C. Rutter & Sons	Withdrawn	
57	Cocklaw Quarries	Hexham R. D. C.		£3,500
58	St. Oswald's Hill Head Farm	W. Dickinson	Mr John Nichol	£2,900
59	Codlaw Hill Farm	Major Hornby	Sold privately	
60	Wall Fell Farm	J. & J. Johnson	Sold privately	
61	Planetrees Farm	A. Johnson	Sold privately	
62	Two Cottages and Gardens	Mrs Muse & A. Johnson	Mr Urwin	£210
63	Cottage and Garden	Miss Mews	Mr Purvis	£75
64	Small Holding	T. Stubbs	Mr Purvis	£565
65	Small Holding	Mrs R. Curry	Mr J. S. Wardle	£380
66	Cottage and Garden	J. F Rowell	Mr Caisley	£360
67	Cottage and Garden	R. Davidson		£80
68	Cottage and Garden	Service Tenancy	Mr J. S. Wardle	£140
69	Brunton Quarries	Geo. Armstrong	Mr G. Armstrong	£2,000
70	Cottage and Garden	Mrs Littlefair	Mr G. Armstrong	£165
71	East Dunkirk	A. Burns	Withdrawn	
72	West Dunkirk Farmhouse	T. Hill	Hexham R.D.C.	£290
73	Small Holding	P. Saint	Mr Caisly	£820
74	Small Holding	Messrs. Lamb	Mr G Johnstone	£320
75	Accommodation Land	J. M. Robson	Mr Dodds	£60

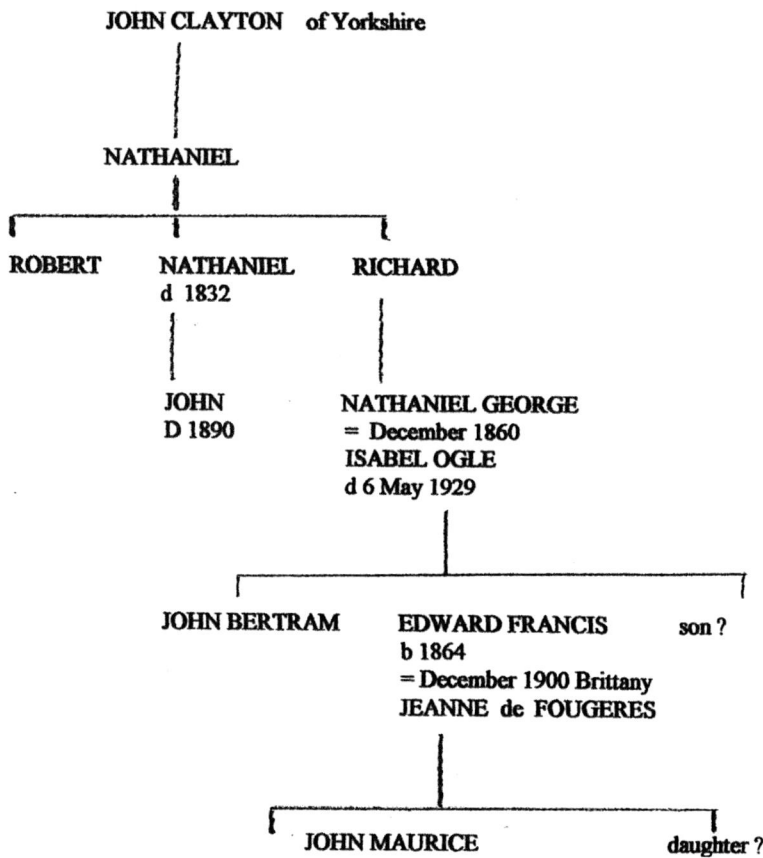

The Clayton Family Tree

CHAPTER TWO
OUR ENVIRONMENT

In this chapter we are looking at some of the features which make up our environment, giving us such a splendid place to live.

In April 1991 Tynedale Council designated our lovely village a conservation area, an area of special architectural or historic interest, the character or appearance of which it is desirable to preserve or enhance'.

Changes within the area, which contains listed buildings, are under the control of the planning department based in Hexham, which is eager to preserve and enhance our environment. They concern themselves with developments, alterations, demolition and protecting the setting of the area, which is indeed worth protecting. The older buildings, many of 17th and 18th century origin, are of stone construction with slate roofs. At one time heather thatch was often used but there are no longer any examples of this.

In October 2007 Tynedale Council imposed a ban on house building in communities which they deemed 'unsustainable' in not having sufficient amenities, such as a school or shop selling food. Wall was included on their list. Regarding extensions, the planners are very strict. In the central area and on Front Street they must be in stone, in keeping with surrounding buildings. (The houses to the south of The Chare do not come within the conservation area.) We cannot do as our ancestors often did and take the stone from Hadrian's Wall, but local barn demolitions can come in very handy!

Those of our attractive buildings which have been listed are:

The milestone built into the roadside wall on Front Street

Milestone Cottage on Front Street

Penrhyn and the adjacent outbuilding on Front Street, also Penrhyn's forecourt, walls and gate piers

The pair of cottages to the north of the Hadrian Hotel

Greenhead House and St Oswald's cottages at the north side of The Green

The Methodist Chapel with its attached wall, rails and gates

Town Farm house, on the south side of the green

The Dutch barn forty metres west of the farm house which was once part of Town farm buildings and is now converted into dwellings

St George's Church, plus the forecourt wall, gates and railings on the east side

Stable Cottage at the centre of The Green

The Pant

We start by describing the work of the Parish Council which looks after our affairs.

WALL PARISH COUNCIL - David Westle

Wall Parish Council is an elected body of six councillors who, along with hundreds, if not thousands of fellow parish councils throughout the country, represent the so called 'base of the pyramid' in the system of government. To qualify to be a councillor one has to be over eighteen and domiciled in the parish of Wall.

Although the council represents the 420 residents (according to the 2007 census) who live within the parish boundary, the majority of our deliberations and actions are concerned with matters pertaining to the main centre of population – the village of Wall itself.

It was the acquisition by lease of the village greens within Wall from Wentworth Canning Blackett Beaumont, Lord of the Manor, during the last years of the 19th century, and the subsequent compiling of the byelaws relating to the greens that represents some of the earliest records of the Parish Council. On 1 May 1900 a lease was drawn up whereby Wall Parish Council agreed to pay the princely sum of one shilling (5p) per year. One hundred and twelve years later we still lease the greens from the Allendale Estates, at the much inflated total of £5 per year!

One of the expressed terms of the byelaws is to ensure that the greens are protected and maintained for the recreation of the parishioners and, as such, the Parish Council, with the express permission of the Allendale Estates, has recently extended the existing facilities on the back green. Football posts and nets, a new set of toddlers' swings and a small adventure playground have been erected. Such projects are funded by the Parish Council from the precept which is set yearly by the council from the County's Council Tax. For several years now the Parish Council has striven, successfully, to maintain the precept at a constant £4,000. From this sum the council pays for much of the general maintenance around the village, such as extra grass cutting, occasional tree surgery, insurances and looking after the bus shelters. These are situated in the village and at Brunton crossroads and belong to the Parish Council. The council also provides the Christmas gifts for our pensioners, the village Christmas tree and makes donations to several local charities.

By far the most difficult and contentious concerns to be dealt with by the council are planning issues. In the past many recommendations made by the Parish Council regarding planning matters have been disregarded by the planning authorities. It is only since Wall has been classified by Tynedale Council, under their local plan, as a non-sustainable village (ie without a shop or school) that we have been spared the threat of any major development. Of course, now that Wall parish is part of the unitary authority of Northumberland County Council, Tynedale Council has been abolished, and with the changes to planning law as proposed by the Coalition government, we must wait to see the effect on future planning applications. We hope that our voice will be heard.

There are many other issues which the Parish Council discusses, as can be seen from our agenda which is posted in the village notice board prior to our meetings. These are held usually on the first Wednesday of every other month. Members of the public are invited to attend these meetings, although they are not officially allowed to contribute to discussions until after the meeting is over.

Our current members of the Parish Council are John Lamb, David Mason, Kathy Rogstadt, Roly Taylor, and our chairman, David Westle. Together with Joyce Lundy, who fulfils her duties as the current parish clerk, it is hoped that Wall Parish Council serves the parishioners of Wall fairly and satisfactorily, as have parish councils in the past and, hopefully, those in the future.

WALL READING ROOM

The first meeting of Wall Reading and Recreation room, and Library was held on 5 October 1903. 'Convened at the instance of Mrs N G Clayton of The Chesters to explain matters in connection with the Institute and to elect officers and committee for the ensuing year'. Mrs Clayton attended the meeting herself. She had prepared and furnished the rooms, bought a large number of books for the library and was paying the wages of a caretaker. She charged no rent for the rooms but retained the property. A billiard table was donated by G H Waddilove JP of Brunton Hall. 24 members were enrolled. By November 1904, this number had risen to 81.

Papers were ordered. The dailies were Newcastle Daily Journal, Newcastle Daily Chronicle, North Mail, Evening Chronicle and Evening Mail. Weekly papers were Hexham Herald, Hexham Courant, Athletic News and Illustrated London News. The Strand was added to the list shortly afterwards. Over the years this list was to vary and the number of books and games available was to increase.

The rooms were opened to members on 10 October 1903. Thereafter the committee seems to have been active in organising not only Billiard Handicaps, but also picnics at the Chollerford cricket ground with sporting programmes, suppers, dances and concerts in the schoolroom. In 1914 they proposed a sweet pea show but this was abandoned on account of the war.

1914, and 11 members had enlisted in the army. As members were 'called to the colours' membership fell to 30. The secretary's reports listed casualties, and on a happier note, the award of the Military Medal to Private Ridley Robson. Membership rose again when ex-soldiers returned.

Funds were invested in the War Loan. Mrs Waddilove was allowed the use of the Reading Room for her Ladies' Working Party on Thursday afternoons. Here garments were made for wounded soldiers. Mrs Clayton continued to take a personal interest for many years. Her name appears often in the minutes throughout the First World War and afterwards until her death on the 6 May 1929. 1923 saw the creation of the 'Roll of Honour' which still hangs in the Village Hall.

A big date in the story of the Reading Room was the sale of The Chesters Estate on 29 June 1929, when the property was bought for £75, by the committee as trustees, on behalf of Wall.

The minutes between 1931 and 1948 are missing; consequently we have no information concerning the Second World War however the minutes thereafter reported activities similar to those earlier. By this time boys over twelve could be admitted on Saturday nights from 6-8 o'clock, but only under supervision. The library had become a lending library. As the villagers were now the owners, repairs and maintenance were high on the agenda so money-making functions were important, particularly weekly whist drives.

By January 1958 there was discussion about the future of the Reading Room. Rowdyism had been taking place, with a lot of damage to fittings and furniture. The secretary was instructed to see the parents of the offenders and ask for their cooperation.

In 1963 trouble arose again in the form of damage to the table tennis table, pin-up photographs, lounging on the billiard table, entry through the window and horseplay. Where culprits could be caught, they were to be suspended. Bad behaviour was again being reported in 1966. With rising costs, especially of electricity, the financial situation was difficult. By 1968 problems with behaviour and finance were easing. Although members' subscriptions were one of the lowest sources of income, and many members gave no support at all, rentals from The Leek Club, the *Catholic Church and the Parish Council were useful. 1971 saw troubles recurring, involving vandalism and gambling. As great social changes had taken place, there were now two options: to remain open or to close.

1972 saw local interest waning. TV and the pub were blamed. The future was again discussed. A leaflet was distributed stressing that the committee were looking into the possibility of closing the Reading Room. Many further attempts to drum up interest and income were made. Vigorous efforts were made to save it, but there were many problems, both with finance and continuing untidiness and vandalism, which got progressively worse. After the increasing difficulties in running it the reading room was sold in 1980. The money was used to help with improvements to the Village Hall.

The Reading Room is now a private house with an upper storey and garage.

* As few local people had cars the Reading room was used by local Catholics for their services.

THE VILLAGE HALL

Mona Craig, an elderly Wall resident, wrote her memories of the hall's early days. "About 1924 the old vicar left after twenty-odd years. He travelled by pony and trap, so the present hall was a stable, coach house etc for the vicarage. In due course it was converted into the church hall, heated by portable oils heaters and a coal fire with a little 'set pot' for washing up and a kettle for the tea. The kitchen was behind the stage. They were now able to hold dances."

Major changes to the village hall came in 1987, instigated with great foresight by Dr Rachel Lowther, Chairman of the Village Hall Committee. Money had become available, through the sale of the Reading Room in 1980. The changes Rachel put forward were to enable the community to have a much enhanced hall. An extension was built on, divided up to house a purpose built kitchen with good storage space, and an area coming from it, to spread into when necessary. This was fitted with benches that hinged for use. When not in use they flapped down, and space was created for tables or chairs for small meeting groups. A stable door at the end of the kitchen could be used as a serving hatch. The rest of the extension became part of the hall, again creating extra space. Rachel also brought about a change in the tables and chairs. Previously there were rather unwieldy chairs which had come from Hexham hospital, but the stacking plastic variety were much easier to use and took up less space. Sixty were bought at first, the number has rising to eighty. The tables too are now easily stored in the little room behind the stage. Elva Mason made the curtains. The result of all this work was we had a village hall that was cosy yet spacious, attractively painted (there was much discussion over the colour) and earning praise from all the visitors who came to events. A plaque in the hall commemorates the extension.

Rachel also gave a great amount of her time to the transfer of ownership of the hall, from the Church Commissioners to Wall Parish Council, who now hold the deeds. It was a somewhat difficult transaction, with costly legal fees incurred by 'the other side' which we were required to pay, but finally it became the village hall.

The praise that the hall now earned did not just stop with the visitors. In 1993 we entered a British Gas competition and followed that up with another in 1995. The plaques commemorating our wins are in the hall for all to see, again a tribute to the work of Rachel and the community.

It is important to make note here, for all who read this book, that it was Rachel Lowther, who with her great belief in the power of community life brought the village hall from an occasionally used facility, to one that is in use every week and is the centre of community life in Wall. Rachel believed in people getting together. She was chairman from 1985 to 1997, when she retired due to ill health. She died in August 1997. She had worked selflessly and with wisdom, to the end. A plaque in her memory was unveiled in the hall on 29 April 2000.

In 1998, a local architect drew up plans for further development at the hall in order to enlarge it. There were grants available through the National Lottery Board specifically for village halls, and it was thought we could qualify. The idea was to extend beyond the stage into land that had supposedly been given for this purpose. This would have given a small supper and meeting room, so lessening the heating costs of using the main hall for meetings. The then chairman Mr Jim Jones, submitted the bid, but it was turned down. Instead more practical adjustments took place, using other available grants. The ladies' toilet facilities were extended to make a unisex toilet for the disabled and also a baby toileting area. The kitchen had a new cupboard installed, as we were all finding that bending down to put the crockery away was a little too difficult. A new, more manageable layout was introduced into the washing-up end, making more room for movement. The stage was shortened to allow more room for the bowls club and the piano was moved on to the stage, allowing the chairs to be stacked at the back of the hall. This point had to be reconsidered when computers took over that space in 2004.

Since its initial transition, the hall has played a leading role as a social hub for the village in providing a meeting place for the community. It is available for hire and is in great demand for many social gatherings and charity fund-raising events. It played a major role in both millennium and jubilee celebrations.

A very generous bequest by the late Gwynneth Wood, who had lived both at Middle Brunton and in the village for many years, enabled an updating of the kitchen again in 2007. This completely new and practical kitchen incorporates a modern electric cooker, commercial dishwasher and fitted kitchen units. The transformation was undertaken by our unsung 'Bob the Builders' kitchen fitters and decorators, alias

Nick Swan and Tony Cattermole. A number of attempts have been made to purchase, from the Church Commissioners, a small package of land from the vicarage garden so that the hall could be extended to accommodate today's user requirements, for example a meeting room. Regrettably, so far our requests have been declined.

In 2012 the Village Hall Committee instigated a change, in that the computer area of the hall became a secure storage space, followed by the most welcome arrival of comfortable padded chairs. Maintenance happens when required by members of the committee, and when a deep clean is needed it is all hands on deck, with all the hall user groups involved.

Within the hall are notice boards advertising and informing. The main focus on walking into the hall is the Millennium Wall Hanging at the back of the stage. In front is the purpose-made wooden box which contains the art book giving an explanation of every item in the hanging. On the right of the stage is the Millennium Photo-Montage containing as many images of Wall residents past and present as it was possible to assemble.

It is worth noting that the hall is a completely self-funded charity managed by a volunteer group of villagers comprising three trustees (Chairman, Treasurer and Secretary), a representative from each of the organisations which use the hall and, at present, two honorary members. The continued support of our village community and surrounding out-bye areas is vital in maintaining the fabric and structure of our village hall for future generations.

GROUPS WHICH HAVE USED THE VILLAGE HALL

TABLE TENNIS

During the 1960s a table tennis group came into being. A table was made by Ray Craig, John Proudlock, David Mason and John Elliott. Games took place every Friday night in the hall and soon a team was entered into the Hexham and District League. In the 1962/63 season they were second in the league, and then in the following four years, were top. Players included Ray Craig, John Elliott, David Mason, John Proudlock, and from out of the village, David Hedley, Colin Hogarth and Alan Burgon.

WHIST

In the early 1950s whist became very popular in the village and there were regular whist drives held in the village hall. In the late 1980s, this turned into a smaller group meeting in a private house.

WALLABIES

In 1988/89 it appeared there might be need for a place for young teenagers to 'hang out'. A group of parents at that time with teenager families got together, and The Wallabies was born. The parents were Neil Scholes, Clive Price, Chris Allcock and the Proudlocks, along with any other parents, who were available on a Friday night, to lend a hand. The hall was set up with various activities such as table tennis, soft drinks were available and for a while it all worked. Young teenagers however grow. Soon they were learning to drive or finding their leisure elsewhere, so the Wallabies quite naturally outgrew itself and ended.

RELAXERCISE

Relaxercise, or exercise without stressing joints and muscles, started in the 1990s and ran every other week for about three years. It was started as a result of Doris Herdman, then in her eighties, having a conversation with Joan Proudlock about how she loved to dance and move to music. Joan promised her she would find someone who could make this a reality.

This person was Joy McCollum who started a class of gentle movement to music, suitable for everyone, every other Thursday morning. Due to her nursing experience, Joy was able to make sure all the exercises brought benefits. As news went round the hall soon filled, and when it came to laying out the coffee cups they numbered over twenty. The social half hour after each session was enjoyed by all, and was as beneficial as the exercise!

ALEXANDER TECHNIQUE

This was run by Sharon Higginson, and had a good attendance but only lasted for the duration of the course. Sharon has gone on to work with great success with the young people of Humshaugh, Wall and the surrounding area in the field of amateur dramatics.

PILATES

This is an on-going class at this time, held each Thursday morning. It is run by Pat Waters and began with about six people, but now has risen, on average, to twelve, with some coming from Dilston, Chipchase and Wark. Following the class another social time and get together with coffee is enjoyed.

RAQS SHARQI - DANCE OF THE EAST

There are two sessions held in the village hall each week for Raqs Sharqi. On Monday evening the Bela Divas group meet for practising, as they give performances for WI groups, and also go into Care Homes as afternoon entertainment for the residents. On Thursday evenings it is a more social time where anyone who is interested can drop in and join the group. There is music, sometimes drumming and dancing.

LIFE DRAWING CLASS

One activity in the village hall which flourished for a few years was a life drawing class. About a dozen artists took part in raising money to hire models and occasionally a tutor. Our village hall can be very cold, so it was necessary to supply extra heaters for the brave models. A memorable occasion saw one of the painters' cars roll down the green from where it was parked and crash into the wall of the hall. A concerned resident on the green, not realising the class that was taking place came rushing in to the hall, only to beat a very hasty retreat!

WRITING ON THE WALL

For a time these were very successful evening and afternoon events staged by Julia and Alan Grint, who at that time lived in the village and ran Cogito bookshop in Hexham. They brought many writers to Wall to give talks on their books, and with a buffet supper or an afternoon tea included, there was great demand for tickets and it was much enjoyed by those who came.

OLD YEAR'S NIGHT

Rob and Alison Say and friends have organised this for several years and it is always a big success. It is a way of ending the year with folk music, stories, dancing, food and drink and is a great way for the community and friends to get together with entertainment thrown in.

NORTHUMBERLAND THEATRE COMPANY

Wall has presented many NTC productions which have somehow managed to be staged in our relatively small village hall. In October 1990 John and Joan Proudlock met and got talking to Stewart Howson, who was with a caravan advertising NTC at Alwinton Show! Ever eager to introduce something new for the community, Joan took on the role of bringing NTC to Wall. The first three productions, over three years, starting Friday 4 October 1991 were 'These Things Do Happen', 'Staying Here', and 'The Bondagers'. Colin Braithwaite then took on the role of organising with, 'On Yer Bike' another play written by Stewart Howson and now Susie Swan has successfully run this venture for several productions, which always attract a full house. NTC have an amazing way of bringing large sets and dedicated actors, who not only unpack the van, construct the set and lighting before the show, change costumes, play two or three characters, then take down the set and lighting and pack their van after the show, before next day, in a different venue, doing it all over again. Wall so appreciates their productions. At this time their future is in the balance due to financial cut backs in arts support. We can only hope they can somehow continue to bring this entertainment to so many villages and out-bye areas.

Groups, clubs and societies mirror a community's interests which can change with the passing years, and that is clearly shown in the variety that have come, stayed and gone in Wall.

THE VILLAGE GREENS

In Wall we are fortunate to enjoy two village greens. One is in the centre of the village surrounded mainly by the oldest of our houses. Three farms are grouped round it. Although the farmhouses are still here, their yards have all become housing estates. A group of buildings form an 'island within the green. This includes the Church and the old Reading Room. The village hall also opens on to the green.

To the north east is the back green. Here there are public toilets, swings, a climbing frame, a concrete cricket strip and goalposts. The back green is much enjoyed by dog walkers and children. Above it is a small enclosed wood and the house converted from the old school and master's house.

In 1900 a booklet of Byelaws was published by the 'Parish Council of the Parish of Wall'. These concerned 'the Village Green and open spaces held by the Council by virtue of an Agreement dated the twenty-eighth day of September, 1899, and made between Wentworth Canning Blackett Beaumont, Esquire, M.P., and the said council.' It was signed on behalf of the council by the chairman: George Waddilove, and two members: Joseph Bell and James Herdman. This was 'Allowed by the Local Government Board this fourth day of January, 1901'. In this booklet there are rules covering the erection of posts, rails, fences, tents, booths, stands, buildings or other structures. Do not do it without Parish Council permission! Further rules cover the playing of games: 'football, quoits, bowls, hockey, cricket or any other games'. These rules are not about banning games. They are more about the protection of the enjoyment of the participants against interruption.

Byelaw no 4 states 'No person shall improperly interfere with or interrupt any religious, political, or other meeting or procession on the Village Green or open spaces'.

Be warned - The penalty for any infringement of the byelaws is forty shillings!

THE PANT

In 1858 Lt Col Butler of Brunton House erected the pant for the village giving the villagers their first piped water supply. Previously they had to go to a spring up Spouty Lonnen: the lane up to the fell beyond the vicarage. The pant stands centrally on the village green. It was fed from a reservoir on the fell. The water flowed until 1996, although in later years it was declared unfit for humans though it was often used for watering horses and for washing cars. Unfortunately, when a housing development was built on the line of the feed pipe, the water was cut off. For some years the Parish Council tried to have it functioning again, but finally gave up, filled it with soil and planted flowers in it.

THE CORONATION TREE AND THE CIRCULAR SEAT

The original tree, planted to celebrate the Coronation, did not survive. Its replacement was the beech tree which stands in the centre of the green. In the 1980s a circular seat was built around it. This was damaged when it was hit by a car in 1990. It was replaced by Andrew Mullins who lived in Stable Cottage and was training to be a craftsman joiner. Eventually the roots of the tree made the seat uneven. It fell into disrepair. In 2005 it was replaced by another. This was presented to the village by Catherine and Tim Collier in tribute to Catherine's brother Steve Morris, who was killed, aged just 31, in the 2001 terrorist attack on the World Trade Centre in New York.

BRUNTON HOUSE

The first mention of Brunton House gives the name of Dawson on the muster roll of 1538, and also Dawson is a name in lists of tenants in Wall at that time. A Watch was ordered in 1552 from the mouth of the Erring Burn to Chollerford Bridge to be watched nightly by four men and Dawson was one of them.

At St John Lee, Acomb is the grave of William Dawson of Brunton House. Whether he built the house is not known, but old deeds dating back to 1672 show that this Mr Dawson became copyholder of land lying between 'Wall Close Gate' and the 'King's Street'. It is difficult to assess the extent of this land, as old names have gone out of use. His son, Robert, acquired more land in 1728, before dying in 1729. His estate included Brunton House, 'Hall-Poole Farm' (Town Farm?) and three houses in Wall.

A descendant John Dawson, who died in 1807, sold Brunton House to brothers Matthew and George Culley, of Wark, but retained it under a lease. John married Frances Smith of Haughton Castle, and after her death in 1806 The Gentleman's Magazine for May published the following extract:

'...She (Frances Dawson) introduced the Jennerian* vaccination into her neighbourhood and once a week had many cartloads of applicants for that improved mode of inoculation'. *Edward Jenner was the pioneer of smallpox vaccination and the father of immunology.

After the deaths of John and Frances the Dawson name disappears from the history of Wall.

Brunton house and its lands became part of the Chesters Estate. At the time of the sale in 1929 the tenant was G H Waddilove. It was described as a highly attractive residence 'situate in a fine position on high ground overlooking the North Tyne Valley yet nicely secluded, being protected by luxuriant growth of shrubs and trees... It is approached by a winding carriage drive, and is a pleasing low structure of stone with slated roof'. The sale catalogue goes on to describe in some detail the extensive interior: principal rooms, twelve family and guest bedrooms, bathrooms, domestic offices and servants' quarters. Listed also were numerous outbuildings: coach house, garages, stabling etc. The gardens and grounds were depicted as 'very attractive and beautifully timbered'. There were 'long herbaceous walks, lawns, a walled kitchen garden and a fruit garden with ranges of capital greenhouses'. In the event Brunton House was withdrawn from the sale.

In 1939 the Roman turret in the grounds was accepted by the Office of Works. It was restored by them after the war, in 1948. During the war years Brunton House was owned by Col and Mrs Wood whose son Drew, when he came home from his war posting in America, turned the stables and some of the out buildings into a home for his wife, Gwynneth and his children. It became Middle Brunton and Brunton House was eventually sold to Major and Mrs Bell followed by Mr and Mrs English and now Mr and Mrs Benson.

During the Second World War Brunton House had another use. The patients and staff from two units of The Newcastle Eye Hospital in the centre of Newcastle were evacuated to it. We are fortunate to have the memories recorded here, of a young nurse then, who actually worked there. Long since retired, after a full nursing career, she now lives in Humshaugh. Together with Joan Proudlock, at the kind invitation of Mr and Mrs Benson, the present residents, they spent an afternoon reliving her time there, turning rooms into wards and an operating theatre!

Like many of the writings in this book there is a story attached as to how they came to be here. Joan was coming out of the Chapel Schoolroom where Mary Herdman's Village Archives were on display at the summer fête in Wall when she met Margaret Gilhespy and they started talking. Margaret told Joan about her connection with Brunton House. Well, we couldn't miss out on those memories, especially as Joan discovered later, hardly anyone knew that Brunton House had

DID WALL HAVE A HOSPITAL?
Memories of a Student Nurse Margaret Gilhespy

Older people living in Tynedale will remember that some villages received hospital units from Newcastle hospitals during the Second World War. There was a widespread belief that industrial cities would be heavily bombed, and of course many were. Some of the more vulnerable patients were evacuated to country areas. There were two TB sanatoria near Hexham, and there were others units, for children at Ponteland and Ovingham. Newcastle Eye Hospital sent children and elderly who were due to have surgery to Brunton House. NEH was one of the many voluntary hospitals which depended on financial support mostly from wealthy people.

The NHS began in 1948, 4 years after the end of the Second World War. Prior to that time there were hospitals and clinics under a vast variety of management arrangements. However, as more factories, mines and shipyards opened during the Industrial Revolution it became increasingly common for working class men to make small, regular contributions to support the hospitals which they mostly used. In the 19th Century, Health and Safety were not a management priority and there were some dreadful injuries. During the war, beds in NEH were mostly occupied by such patients and servicemen, the latter often injured during training. In the population as a whole, there were, of course, many other ophthalmic conditions in the mid 20th Century and there were no antibiotics then, so infections often ensued. The NEH was housed in a lovely building in St Mary's Place and was opened about 1820. It was one of the Regency buildings vandalised in the 1960s to make way for the Civic Centre. The Eye Unit then moved to Walkergate Hospital for many years and is now permanently established at the Royal Victoria Infirmary.

My own home lay right on the coast between Seaton Sluice and Blyth. We were on the borderline between children being evacuated — or not. 3 September 1939, when war was declared was just at the end of the school holidays and it was decided that we would not be evacuated. The Government decreed that children in such areas were not to return to school until air raid shelters were built. Shelters were given priority to large cities so there was a great shortage of bricks, and it was months before we could return to school. We had weekly appointments with our form teachers to be given work in all subjects — and to return the previous week's work. We found that most of the younger teachers had left for the Services and we all thought that those who had come out of retirement were as old as Methusalah! Perhaps more importantly, their teaching methods were very different. Despite all the upheaval, most of us achieved the School Leaving Certificate, similar to O Levels, but much more demanding.

I was one of the many who persuaded their parents to allow them to leave school without taking Matriculation (A levels). My vision was to be received with open arms, to train as a State Registered Nurse at one of the great London hospitals! Well, I hadn't done my homework and soon discovered that one had to have passed one's 18th birthday to begin a statutory training anywhere. Not only that, the prestigious

London hospitals required their students to have matriculated, and my parents were adamant that I was going no further than Newcastle! It was made very clear that I was was not going to stay at home doing nothing, though there was always plenty of work on a farm in wartime.

My father noticed an advertisment in a local newspaper for student nurses of 17 and over, at Newcastle Eye Hospital. I wrote to the Matron and received a prompt reply giving a date and time for interview and to present myself - together with my mother! This seems hilarious today but was then usual. Matron was charming but addressed most of her remarks to my mother and hardly spoke to me. She explained that the Ophthalmic Nursing Diploma was a nationally recognised qualification and together with SRN was accepted all over the world. Because of the war, NEH had a country 'Branch' where some of the student's time would be spent. A complex description of the situation of Brunton House, Wall followed, but when she stopped to draw breath, my mother said "Thank you, but I know the area". I don't think Matron had ever met anyone who had said this. My mother's family had been farming in the South Tyne Valley for several generations, so I had been taken there all my life. The family had friends in the North Tyne area, so I remember coming in a pony and trap.

I began my training in February 1942 and in September I was told that I was going to Brunton House and I would be on night duty - alone! I had had no experience of this upside down world and was rather scared! The patients were the old and the young, which meant mostly cataracts and squints (at that time severe squints were treated by surgery). The cases "don't forget your text books", and trudged to the Haymarket for a bus to Hexham.

I don't remember anything about the rest of the journey but we were met at Brunton crossroads by a man with a horse and cart. He took our cases and the huge baskets of fresh laundry which had been taken to the bus in Newcastle by the porters, but I don't know about the transfer in Hexham. Of course we walked to our new home. Sister told us on the bus that as soon as our rooms were allocated we were to change into uniform, go downstairs to be introduced to the patients and help with their lunch. Many had to be fed, all toiletted and hands washed. This was easy, as there were eight of us on this one occasion. The two Sisters and eight students then had lunch together exchanging experiences before the Team whom we were relieving left to return to base. Some were sad to go as they found that they loved country life, while others looked forward to Newcastle. I can't think why, because it was as dull, dark and dreary as most other cities, London being a possible exception - and it was bombed more than anywhere else.

The residents of Brunton House were Col & Mrs Wood. At that time members of their family came and went as their Service duties permitted. I don't remember how many domestic staff there were but they were all friendly, motherly women, except the cook who was considered very strange, and some claimed that she was affected by the moon! I do know that on at least three occasions I found the back door open in the middle of the night, the light streaming out to be seen for quite a distance. No ARP Wardens here! Anyway, she was a wonderful cook and did marvels with strict rationing and the lovely local produce.

On that first day I was taken to the kitchen and introduced to her. She showed me how the stove worked and how much precious tea to put in the huge teapot (no teabags), also where my meal would be left and what I might take from the fridge. Sister then told me to go and unpack properly and then go to bed. I was called at 7.30pm in time for a bath and 'breakfast' before 'On Duty, Sister' at 8.30pm. She then sent the others off duty and I accompanied her while she gave out drugs and supervised me putting the correct drops in the appropriate eyes. Then she departed and I was alone with about thirty sleeping men, women and children.

There was no central heating, but a coal fire in each of the three wards. All had been lovely reception rooms still with smart light fittings and decorative plaster ceilings. The main hall had a small Courtier Stove which, I suppose, was better than nothing. I had to keep all these going which was no problem except in the women's ward. The men and children slept through my wielding the coal shovel, but the smallest sound would wake a woman who would want a bedpan, and before I knew it I was doing a full BP round! I soon learnt to lift one piece of coal at a time and place it gently on the fire. The blackouts were left until daylight and during the night, apart from a fox barking or the hoot of an owl there was utter quiet. I sometimes had great difficulty in keeping awake.

Every hour I did a round, shining my torch on my apron, rather than in patients' faces. Not that they would be disturbed as after they had surgery they had both eyes covered even though they had surgery to only one eye. The children had surgical repairs of squints and went home after a week. Nearly all the adults had cataract extractions and the adults stayed for three weeks – they were nursed with one pillow and strict bed rest for the first and second weeks. All came and left on Mondays – by bus. They were taken home via NEH so that they were examined before being discharged home.

As I recall, all the consultants were of Service age and all had departed. Most of the medical staff were immigrants from Nazi-occupied countries and much of their English was very difficult to understand. Because their qualifications were only given temporary recognition they could not become consultants, even though they were doing the complex work, which, no doubt they would have done in their own countries. Two of the retired consultants therefore came back to work.

Mr McRae, gracious, and at over 70, still a fine surgeon came to Brunton House every Tuesday morning in a laden car. He brought the following week's theatre equipment –instruments, dressings, theatre linen and any medications which Sister had ordered. Before lunch he did a round, speaking reasurringly to all who were to have surgery and telling all the other patients that they were 'doing fine'. He had lunch with the staff and then went to 'Theatre' to begin his list. This was the bathroom at the turn of the big staircase. A board was secured over the bath and covered with a thin mattress and a sheet. Sister then set out the trays of instruments, drugs and dressings helped by a local nurse who came in every Tuesday. I regret that I can't recall her name but she was the wife of the local policeman and lived in the house at Brunton crossroads. The patients were escorted on foot across the hall and up the stairs and brought down again by stretcher and carefully positioned in their beds. I suppose local men came to act as carriers, but I was supposed to be asleep so heard but didn't see what was going on.

On Tuesday mornings, weather permitting, I walked as far as I could go. My idea was to get so tired that I would sleep through the comings and goings. My bedroom however, was just at the top of the stairs so my plan rarely worked. I should explain that I couldn't go to bed until after the staff lunch, thus ensuring that I had a main meal every day - no microwave cookers then to warm a meal during the night. Our dining room was the main part of the large hall. The outer door was always open and there was (is) a large clear pane in the inner door. Sister sat facing the door and I, being the most junior, had my back to it. Col Wood had been severely incapacitated by a stroke but he was able to go for a walk most mornings. He almost invariably returned during our meal and Sister would say "Nurse, the Colonel" so I opened the door, removed his cap, large scarf and heavy overcoat, then ensured that he was safely into his room. I often wondered why, if all this was necessary, he was able to get around on his own out of doors, especially as I had to finish a meal, by then quite cold!

Having all these free mornings I got to know the area quite well and was delighted with Wall village. There were no modernised or modern houses and two or three homes still had thatched roofs. Of course, TV aerials and dishes were not invented and the area round The Green had probably looked the same for generations. Only rarely was a car to be seen and the one tarmac road ran diagonally from the church. The other paths were wide enough for horses and carts; the lovely local word 'clarts' was very appropriate! When I wandered around Humshaugh I never imagined that I would spend my retirement here. There were, I know now, seven shops but none were of interest, well, one was, but as I'd always used up my sweet ration coupons there wasn't any point in going into the sweetie shop.

I know now what I didn't know then - that it was a very responsible job. Elderly people, kept so long without moving were at risk of developing venous clots, often resulting in strokes or heart attacks. However, no-one had recognised these dangers at that time. Sister had said, on my first evening, that I was to call her if I was worried about any of the patients. The most senior of the day students warned me that I'd better not call if it was a false alarm; my head would be on the block in the morning! On only one occasion did I disturb Sister. A lady complained of chest pain so I gave her a drink and altered her position as much as I dared, she was still at the 'no pillow' stage. She couldn't settle and said the pain was worse. Fearfully, I crept upstairs and knocked on Sister's door and a sleepy voice bade me enter. I told my story and she muttered "Probably indigestion, give her a dose of Aqua Menth Pip. and come back if she hasn't settled in half an hour". This was the standard initial treatment – no Rennies or Gaviscon in those days. It was a few drops of concentrated peppermint oil and a few grains of sugar stirred into hot water making a sort of cordial. For the next few minutes I watched the patient like a hawk. She then gave a ladylike burp, sighed and went to sleep. Panic over!

Every morning, after a toilet round I gave the patients a cup of tea. This took ages because I had to hold the feeding cup for some of them. Tea, like almost everything else was rationed so I couldn't throw it out and make fresh. It was leaf tea of course as the ubiquitous tea bag had not yet been invented. The big metal teapot was kept warm on the stove so the second ward got well stewed tea. The men didn't seem to mind but there were always a few grumbles from the women. I tried to be fair and give first made tea on alternate days. The children were then roused and taken to the bathroom, boys and girls separately. I checked that they cleaned their teeth and combed their hair; the girls were usually quite biddable, but if not watched the boys would often get up to mischief. One can't blame them, they must have been bored stiff; no radio, TV, mobile phones, computers and not even allowed to read. I wonder how the children of today would behave in those conditions.

Now that I am old myself I can imagine just a little, of three weeks in bed not even able to feed oneself. What a long, weary time of loneliness that must have been, especially as they would have few, if any, visitors. They could, of course, chat to each other.

The following year I was sent to Wall, again on night duty, and this time I was the senior student. This didn't please Sister (a different one) as she wanted to be able to go into Hexham on Market Day in order to buy something – anything! She couldn't go off duty as there was no-one else sufficiently senior to be left in charge. My second tour was much like the first and in the autumn of 1943 rationing was even tighter. Now I felt somewhat more confident and didn't always feel that I must be watching the patients. The final exams were drawing near, so I could spend a little time with the text books. I always looked forward to the cold collation left for my meal by cook. I think the presentation almost gave as much delight as the food; the tray was always set with fine china on a lace cloth. It was so different from the white pots from which we and the patients normally ate. I washed the dishes with the greatest care as replacement would have been quite impossible.

When I look back now after all those years I realise how utterly peaceful it was at Brunton House at the height of that terrible war. In many rural areas people never locked their doors and in this area, even when hundreds of young soldiers arrived, they saw no reason to do so. Nor was there any suggestion that it was unsafe for a young girl to be rambling round the fields and lanes, on her own. I usually met some of these lads and was often 'chatted up' but I soon learnt to give as I got.

We got very little outside news and didn't have access to a radio, so I think the only war news was brought on Tuesdays by Mr McRae. Letters from our families were mostly about bombing and rationing. There wasn't much truthful news and we didn't know how heavily censored were the BBC and newspapers. Bad news was toned down and good news was exaggerated. Our blissful ignorance contributed to a sense of contentment but the 'vibes' of Brunton House were happy ones too. After so long I've probably forgotten the 'bad bits' and my abiding memory of my time in Wall is a happy one.

My thanks are due to Mr & Mrs George Benson of Brunton House for allowing me to look around the house. This visit reminded me of much that I had forgotten and has greatly helped in the writing of these notes.

BRUNTON POLICE HOUSE - Joan Proudlock

Brunton Police House probably dates back to somewhere in the late 1930s. In Ray Craig's book of photographs there are two photographs taken from the same place, on the east side of Chollerford Bridge. One is dated 1920s and the other 1930s. There is no house visible in the first one, but in the second it is seen quite clearly. I have tried to acquire more accurate records from the Northumbria Police Estate Archives but without success. From Ray's photographic record we also have a print of PC Wilson standing beside the old farmhouse on the crossroads dated again 1930s, however this could be the end of the thirties and into wartime. The house was built because the nearest policeman lived at Fourstones, and if there was an incident in the Wall area he had to cycle across: even then Brunton cross-roads had become an accident black-spot. The building is quite a distinctive shape and is built from either Black Pasture or Frankham sandstone. Over many years as a police house and police station it was a landmark.

Now it is in the private ownership of Jackie and Keith Lewis, both of whom have served in the police force. From information they have on their original documents it appears that the land was bought by Thomas Lee of Low Brunton farm in 1929 during The Chesters sale. Following his death on 16 January 1930 it passed to Annie Lee and Kit Heslop. In 1935 it changed hands again this time into the ownership of Northumberland County Council, possibly as part of an overall plan for Brunton crossroad improvement, with a police house 'on the spot', so we may possibly assume this to be the time in the1930s when this uniquely shaped house was built. On entering the front door and to the left was positioned the police office, and the rest of the accommodation worked around this. Brunton crossroads were eventually altered by NCC to improve visibility, and the original Low Brunton Farm house was removed with a new farmhouse built to the south of the crossroads. The B6318, Military Road is the main road and takes precedent over the A6079, which over the years has led to many accidents in front of the police house. Highly visible signage has now brought some improvements but it remains a dangerous crossroads as many bikers and motorists continue to travel down Brunton banks at speeds which are unsuitable for the road conditions.

Positioned on the crossroads it was almost central to both Humshaugh and Wall and originally patrols would have been on foot or by bicycle.

Frank Stubbs and his family lived in the house from 1980 and he met Jimmy Wilson (PC Wilson). One of the stories he was told was that PC Wilson had to travel to the farthest point of his beat along the Military Road, to where the old repeater station, now a bunk house and café stands at the junction of the road to Grindon. If he was on night duty he was due there at 1am to meet his sergeant, and if he was a minute late his pay for a day or two could be withheld. When off-duty he needed permission to leave his area and go to Hexham!

Some of the names connected with Brunton Police House are, PCs Wilson, Middleton, Crowe, Storey, Young, Stubbs and Lewis. There may be others but we do not have their names.

PC Middleton must have lived there during the 1950s as his daughter, Valerie Middleton, was at Hexham Grammar School with Pat Stewart, Muriel Horne and me. She became a teacher and worked at Humshaugh School. After the Middleton's moved Willie Crowe took up residence and is remembered for his prize winning police house garden. In 1968 Bert and Eunice Storey arrived with their two boys.

The family grew when they had a daughter before they eventually moved to Hexham. Eunice remembers how on arriving they were immediately invited to a coffee morning in the school and how warmly they were welcomed. Bert was well known and respected and Eunice has fond memories of their time living in Wall. In 1974 they left to live in Hexham and after a long illness Bert sadly passed away in 1994. PC Alan Young lived in the house when it needed some repair work due to dampness and after he left it was two years before Frank and Louise Stubbs arrived in 1980 and their twins were born. Louise taught at Humshaugh School until she retired and saw many local children pass through her class. While Keith was a serving policeman he and Jackie came next in 1993, and with Prince their German Shepherd dog they finally bought the house in 2000. Now retired from police work, Keith drives coaches for Jewitts of Chollerford.

STAGSHAW WIRELESS TRANSMITTER STATION - David Brookman

In the far east corner of Wall Parish, beside Beukley Farm, is one of our least known, but most obvious landmarks. Opened in 1937 by the BBC as a medium wave transmitter, broadcasting, (or in WT speak), 'radiating' regional programmes to the borders.

During the Second World War, Stagshaw radiated American programmes during the day for the American Broadcast Service in Europe from 1944 – 1945, when it started radiating BBC European services, soon switching to BBC Home Service in the north.

After a long, and heated, Parliamentary Debate in 1952, on Regional Transmitters, Stagshaw lost out to Pontop Pike in being updated to TV transmission. With the advent of BBC local radio in the 1970s, Stagshaw radiated the service until 1973, when it had to surrender the frequency. Today it radiates Radio Five Live on medium wave.

Originally the site was staffed with an Engineer in Charge, Antenna Staff, and vitally, a cook. With automation and re-engineering in the late 1970s the site was de-staffed. At the same time the station was demolished and a more modern building constructed. The BBC coat of arms – carved in stone – was removed from the brickwork and preserved as a feature as you drive into the site, on the left, overgrown but still legible.

Some features of the original building survive in the form of the box guttering and downpipes, the rainwater hoppers still having the date 1937 on them. In the field, the building at the bottom of the mast has the same features and retains the original large dark wooden internal doors. The site has its own on-site generator, in case of mains failure.

With the privatisation of the BBC transmitter engineering department in 1997 the site came into the ownership of an American company called Crown Castle, who sold on the business a few years later to National Grid Wireless, who in turn, sold it on to its current owner, Arqiva.

All you really need to know is that the main mast is 482 feet high, and the base is 650 feet above sea-level.

GEORGE V SILVER JUBILEE WALL WIRELESS RELAY 11 MAY 1935

The broadcast thanksgiving service from St Paul's Cathedral was listened to by the residents of Wall, who attended a relay in Wall Parish Church.

The actual service was held on 6 May but this report was published on 11 May.

1930s. Brunton Crossroads with the new Brunton Police House

CHAPTER THREE
OUR COMMUNITY

FAMILIES - Mary Herdman

Over the years we have welcomed people from elsewhere into our village. They have helped to add a rich diversity to our community. There are some families whose ancestors have lived here before them. They too were once incomers, but many generations ago. The number is dwindling and will continue to do so as most of their children move on to pastures new.

The census of 1881 lists Charltons, Herdmans, Heslops, Mitchells and Proudlocks: names still to be found among us. An 1886 directory, gives fewer such names, but shows occupations: James Herdman (engineer), Christopher Albert and William Heslop (farmers), Michael Lamb (market gardener) and James Proudlock (joiner). Some of the old names are still with us. Some ladies have changed their names through marriage, but can trace their ancestry to them. Many were born here whose families do not go quite so far back, but whose names are well known, for example the Masons.

As has always happened, 'incomers' settle and become part of the community. Many stay and start their own dynasties. Others move on. Whether they remain with us permanently, or for a brief period, they leave their mark and play their role in the life of our parish. Everyone has a place with us!

VILLAGE BUNTING - Tish Easby

In 2007 Jemima Westle acquired a bolt of plain ecru fabric and suggested we might use it to make some village bunting. As a result a note was included in the Newsletter inviting all families and households to design and make a pennant with a heraldic, family or household emblem. A triangular template was made and we cut the fabric pennants.

The design could be in any medium, e.g. fabric paints or pens, embroidery or appliqué and should include the family or house name. Jemima then joined the pennants together in groups of five in time for the village fête. Now they are hung in the village hall each fête day and on 'high days and holidays' for village celebrations; we have experienced too many wet days to chance hanging them outside!

Every time someone new moves into the village they are asked to make a pennant and we now have 47 completed and the names are: **Lamb, Bilner, Waddell, Swan, Elliott, Lundy, Turnbull, Westle, Say, Herdman, Yeoman, Slack, Lewis Family, Rogstad, Lowther, Herdman, Iveson, Hutton, Mason, Miller, Henson, Gillespie, Price, Horne, Bell, Peel, Harrison, Garden House, Duployen, Proudlock Family, Walton, Mitchell D&S, White, Begley, Gallagher, Jones, Corcoran, Easby, Watson, Stanton, Taylor, Emerson, Proud, Greer, Cattermole, Simpson, Cooper.**

ADULT OCCUPATIONS

The occupations of yesteryear were centred upon the rural community of the parish. A directory of 1828 listed, in addition to farmers, cartwrights, millwrights, a blacksmith, grocers, a butcher, a bleacher and dyer, a weaver, shoemakers, a tailor, a corn miller, a carrier and a schoolmaster.

The census of Wall taken in the first week of April in 1881 listed the details of the families more fully, giving the relationships, occupations and birthplaces of all the members of each household. This recorded more occupations. In addition to those of 1828 there were coal miners, lead miners, a stationmaster, railway workers, an engine driver, a railway clerk, a postmistress, a post messenger, a postman, dressmakers, a gamekeeper, a market gardener and an innkeeper. There were also a number of domestic servants. There would surely have been servants back in 1828, but they were not listed then.

The birthplaces revealed that most people were locally born in Wall or St John Lee. Wives were often from Wall or nearby. Agricultural labourers, who would be hired by the year, hailed from Wall or the immediate area, and from Bellingham, Simonburn, Newbrough or Gunnerton. The same applied to most domestic servants.

There were some retirees from further afield. The most notable was George Waddilove, a retired army major living at Brunton House, who was born in Ripon. He employed seven domestic servants (six were female). Only one was from Wall. Of the others, three were from Yorkshire, one from Germany, one from Scotland and one from Alnwick. The 1901 census showed his widow as still living at Brunton House with a similar number of servants, again mainly from outside Wall.

An 1886 topography revealed that further additional occupations included a fish dealer, a joiner, a coal agent, a victualler and horse dealer, a baker cum shopkeeper, an Irish hawker and, last but not least, a vicar. The 1901 census saw quarrymen added. This was when the two men Johnson and Mason came from Longtown. They were specialist stone dressers and were needed to work in the local quarries. Their move then established their names as now being recognised as old Wall names.

On the whole the same surnames appear on these lists. The occupations of the families had passed down through the generations. They were local people, locally employed in work for the local community.

How very different is the picture today. There is no school here now. The children mix in a wider community and discover a world with much more to offer. They no longer want to 'follow in father's footsteps'. Most leave the village for university or in search of employment. Many of the old jobs are no longer available.

In 2013 we still have our farmers, but fewer farm labourers. Domestic service is no longer a common occupation. The mines, lead-mines and quarries have closed down. We no longer have shops, a post office or a railway. The mills and the engineering works have closed. There are no longer cartwrights or a blacksmith as over many years the garage catered for the modern mode of transport, the car.

The latest industry to thrive is tourism. Having Hadrian's Wall and St Oswald's Way in the parish is a great draw for both walkers and motorists. Here is an opportunity for those who let rooms for bed and breakfast. We have the Hadrian Hotel which gives accommodation and caters for visitors passing through. St Oswald's Tearoom is on the line of the wall itself. It is also handy for visitors to Heavenfield. This tearoom is open from Easter to November and offers much more than tea.

Most of the older families who have lived and worked in Wall for generations are now represented by those whose children have left them and are scattered far and wide. Many people from elsewhere have been attracted by our lovely village and some have chosen to retire here. Younger people who commute to work elsewhere have been tempted to join our community, especially as there is such easy access to areas north and south of the Tyne via the A69. The new houses built on the farmyards and engineering works have been an attraction too. We are lucky in having a vibrant community, but how times have changed! What will the future hold?

ARTISTS, MUSICIANS AND WRITERS

Wall has its place in the world of visual art. Over the years many have portrayed aspects of Wall, and still do. We are a popular venue for local art clubs. On a fine summer's day it is not unusual to see groups of painters dotted round the green. Once I "Mary Herdman" looked out of my window to see schoolchildren all over the place, painting away. There were about fifty of them. I could not resist it. I went out and had a talk with the master in charge. They were a party from Parkwood Junior School, Scunthorpe, on a school trip to the Roman Wall. Their headmaster had discovered Wall during a private holiday and rightly thought it to be an attractive and safe place for his budding artists.

We can also lay claim to associations with many more artists.

John Pattinson Gibson 1832-1912 was a chemist and archaeologist. He inherited and ran the chemist's shop in Fore Street, Hexham (now Poundstretchers). He was a pioneer of photography and prolific in his work around the north east. The main period of his work was 1880-1900. We are thankful to him for many fine photographs of Wall and its environs.

*Ralph Hedley, RBA, 1848-1913 was a famous north country artist. His painting Dr Parker's First Sermon was exhibited in 1903. This depicted Dr Joseph Parker who preached his first sermon at the age of eighteen from Herdman's sawpit on the village green. Hedley made this the subject of two of his paintings. Joseph Parker (1830-1902) was born in St Mary's Chare, Hexham. He became a renowned Congregationalist preacher who founded and was minister of the City Temple in London. He also published numerous popular religious books.

*Frederick Charles Davison RBA 1902-1989 (Fred) was born in Consett, but lived his final years in Wall and died here. He became President of the Tynedale Art Club (Hexham Art Club). He was a well-known landscape painter in watercolour and an art teacher. He exhibited at the Laing Art Gallery, the Royal Society of British Artists, the New English Art Club and the Shipley Art Gallery.

Phyllis Evetts (née Dobson) 1926-2012 was a great, great, great niece of John Dobson, the Newcastle architect and the granddaughter of John Wardle who built the house known as Bibury. She was one of an artistic family living, until 1970, at High Brunton. Phyl's gift lay in painting and pottery. She gained a degree in art, which led into teaching. Ridley, one of her brothers, was a talented musician and conductor of the Northumberland Orchestra. Both her sisters were choral singers. Following her death in 1987 Pat Rowell's cottage became available at High Brunton and Phyl was able to return to Wall. In that same year she married Leonard Evetts. Leon's home and studio were in Woolsington, but Pat's Cottage, as they named it, became their country retreat. Her cottage garden gave her the inspiration for her many flower paintings. Together they enjoyed sketching, and painting around Wall. They staged three joint exhibitions of their work in the Queen's Hall Gallery, Hexham.

*__Leonard Charles Evetts, ARCA 1909-1997__ was born in Newport, Monmouthshire. Leonard's main work was in ecclesiastical stained glass design. In 1938 he published a book on the Roman alphabet and this combined with his study of heraldry led to many commissioned works countrywide. He was a landscape painter in watercolour with several exhibitions to his name. Design was of major concern to him in all he undertook and, following on from four years teaching at Edinburgh College of Art, in 1937 he became Head of the School of Design in King's College Durham (now Newcastle University). Throughout his 37 years at King's College he also practised as a stained glass designer. Most of his church windows are in the British Isles but two are in Timaru, New Zealand and Apia, Samoa. An outstanding example is the set of 46 windows of St Nicholas' Church, Bishopwearmouth, Sunderland. His miscellaneous work ranges from the design for the lighting in St. George's Church, Wall, a stained glass window in a kitchen at High Brunton, the design for The Journal's best kept village in Northumberland award,(won by Wall), the Barclays Bank eagle logo and milk cartons for the Milk Marketing Board's "Drink a pint of Milk a day" campaign.

*Ralph Hedley, Fred Davison and Leonard Evetts all feature in the art dictionary with the title: 'THE ARTISTS OF NORTHUMBRIA'.

North Tyne Studios have housed many artists. From 1997 to 2000, three participated in Tynedale Artists' Network annual open studios event, The Art Tour, in which members welcome the public into their workplaces. They were Kathleen Sisterson, Paul Connell, Diane Hart and Mary Herdman.

Kathleen Sisterson was a founder member of the Network. She lives in Hexham, but helped to establish the studios where she worked for fourteen years. She has exhibited widely, in both group and solo exhibitions, organized painting holidays and taught in adult education. She painted a mural in the children's waiting area at Dryburn Hospital and did the artwork for two publications: The Chantry Chapel of Prior Leschman and The Darkness Seeping. She has been artist in residence at Hexham Racecourse. Kathleen has become well-known to us in Wall, especially through her design for the millennium wall hanging in the hall.

Paul Connell and **Diane Hart** made up the partnership of **Connell/Hart**. They did not live in Wall but rented their studio from 1993 to 2001. Their work is in Pate de Verre. This is a technique in which glass of different colours is fused together. They produce decorative hangings, jewellery and clocks. They currently sell their work at Kirkharle.

Mary Herdman has often sketched scenes of Wall and its environs. Through membership of both Hexham Art Club and Tynedale Artists' Network she has exhibited and sold work, and taken part in exhibitions in many places. These include

Hexham, Newcastle Central Library, Gateshead Metrocentre, Gateshead Central Library, Bellingham Heritage Centre, Riding Mill Water Transfer Station and Metzingen (Hexham's twin town in Germany). The Parish Map which hangs in the village hall is her work.

Jenny Harrington, who is a member of both Tynedale Artists' Network and Hexham Art Club, over several years has opened up her home and displayed her paintings for the Art Tours. Jenny has served as chairman of Wall Village Society.

Jill Brookman NDD was born in Crouch End, North London in 1934. After school she spent five years at Hornsey College of Art, London, studying graphic art and specialising in stage design. As there was little work for women set designers, none at all for cinema and TV work, she started her first job at Unicorn Head Visual Aids Ltd, producing educational film strips on subjects such as 'The History of Cheese.' After a year in an advertising agency she joined an animated film studio in 1957 where she worked for the next thirty years designing and producing art work for films on many subjects from 'The Birth of a Baby' to 'Theseus and the Minotaur'. The advent of computer animation saw the end of most traditional animation studios and Jill moved on in 1987 to work, for nearly ten years, in the art studio of The Building Research Establishment at Garston, Watford. She produced art work and books for scientists, working on everything from dams to refurbishing old buildings and those in danger of radon gas leakage. Finally retiring to the north east, she has taken up painting for herself and for commissions, as well as teaching art locally. She has exhibited and sold paintings in several galleries, mainly in the north east.

Jemima and David Westle are both graduates in the visual arts, and practising artists. When his mother Ella ran the village post office in the 1970s David produced postcards for her to sell. These were from his ink drawings of local views. Both Jemima and David have drawn illustrations for published books and it is Jemima's work which is on the title page of this book. Their skills are of great value in the restoration work which they now do in their antiques business

Ruth Hicken, who is Mrs Chris Jones, does spinning weaving and dyeing, both ancient and modern. She has a studio at The Hearth Arts centre in Horsley and works under the name of Textiles through Time. She is an experienced weaver and textile specialist giving demonstrations and workshops.

William Pym and **Claudia Rankin,** his wife, both sculptors, were early arrivals at the North Tyne Studios. They bought a house in Wall and were married at St Oswald's. They were founder members of Tynedale Artists' Network. Finding himself in a studio containing a forge and an anvil, Will developed an interest in metal work, using it for fine art and practical items. He went on to exhibit widely and to produce many public works. Examples of his work can be seen in the seats and gates of Tyneside parks. Will and Claudia moved on to Hallington. It was here, and later at Langley, that they too participated in the Art Tours. Whilst living in Wall, Will and Claudia played an active part in village life. Will's legacy to Wall is the ornamental steel 'lantern' above the church gate.

Wall has had a history of people playing and singing music, and we are fortunate that is so today, as we have several accomplished musicians in our midst continuing the tradition.

Jimmy Carr, who lived in Ivy Cottage, was a keen and talented musician. Before the Second World War he formed his own dance band which ran for 42 years. Touring under his name, the five-piece band played in halls in Tynedale, Consett and even as far as Barnard Castle. The band was usually out performing four or five nights a week with a repertoire including all the hits of the 1940s.

Wall Ladies Choir played a lively part in the village from 1964 to 2002. The arrival of Mrs Ella Westle in Wall gave the choir new life and membership grew. They are featured in the chapter on our clubs and societies.

Ray Sloan gave Wall strong connections with the Northumbrian smallpipes. In 1979 he made instruments here, for which he has won an international reputation. From 1997 to 2001 he had a workshop in part of the North Tyne Implement Works. He is a fine player himself, who has been a judge, given talks and workshops. He has also been piper to the Mayor of Hexham.

Rob and **Alison Say** Rob is a skilful player of the Northumbrian smallpipes who has given tuition to others in the village hall. He gives talks, demonstrations and performances with his favourite instrument, often playing solo for us on village occasions. In 2010 he made a CD featuring his music. He is also accomplished on the concertina and is a member of the Wall Star Village Band. Rob is joined in the band by his wife, Alison, as a fiddler. She also plays the fiddle for the Singing Babies. This involves introducing infants to the joys of music.

Ernie and **Margaret Bainbridge** Ernie entertains with his accordion, playing regularly at the Three Churches Fête. He has been playing for more than 20 years and is a member of the Tynedale Accordion and Fiddle Club. Margaret followed an arts course at King's College, Newcastle and whilst living in Greece designed and executed a five metre sculptured plaques for two ships. On coming to Wall she was encouraged to develop her singing by Ella Westle who was the conductor of Wall Ladies Choir. Margaret became a regular soloist at choir concerts in the area and also joined the Hexham Orpheus Choir.

June Gallagher is an exponent of the ukulele, who plays with The Ukes of Northumberland. This band plays at functions throughout the area, including a fund-raising event for Wall's celebrations for the Queen's Golden Jubilee.

Chris Jones sings and plays the guitar for the band Canny Crack. The other band members are Anne Dolphin, pipes, Minnie Fraser, fiddle, and Bill Toy, percussion. Together, and as solos, they play and sing Northumbrian and Celtic music. Chris is a story teller of traditional stories as well as writing songs, ("The Lambing Storm" being one of them). It is a tribute to Northumbrian shepherds and their faithful dogs. He has won the storytelling section at The Morpeth Gathering three years running, but has been banned for the year 2013! The band plays at events and also for the National Trust at Cherryburn and Gibside. They have published a CD, 'Canny Crack - Piece of Cake'.

James Gillespie, along with his brother Sam, has lived in Wall since the early 1990s. Throughout their growing up, not only visually, but in their hearts, they have come to know the natural environment and countryside in and around Wall. This is now reflected in their music and Wall had a recent sample of this during the Spring

Music Evening in April 2013 when James accompanied by his guitar sang for us. This is his writing and he speaks for Sam too.

James Gillespie Wall has been the cradle of a secret music, and by Wall I mean Wall Fell as well as the village. The green tracks leading off from the gates of the village, up there where the may blossom dazzles the mind or where autumn mists dance with crow's wings and ash keys, up there, is as much part of my home here as the hearth of our house itself.

The music came to us strongly when we were in our later school years, in longing, and in flight from the restriction of school rooms and the compartmentalisation of the mind inflicted by schooling. Yes, and we were running towards something too. We were moving towards a meeting with the hills, the plants, trees and animals, and with ourselves. We took ourselves to the hills on summer evenings, spring mornings, winter nights, the secret named corners and glades, dells, and sheltered quiet places. Perhaps you know them too; perhaps you have different names for them. We took ourselves to the wild, and we, children of the North Tyne valley, found joy and communion and music. And we found the shadows of illusion and confusion, and smelled the destruction of wars and ecocide across the seas. Wall Fell held all of this for us with love. And the music we listened to then, lots of folk music from the 60s and music drawn from roots all over the world, and the music we sang and played was the beginning of a new language for us - or a rediscovery of a very old one. There is something in the wild that wants to communicate with us, that wants to be honoured by the village; we sang out of gratitude for that wilderness. And I sing now in the passion that we can open up our hearts and hearths to the wilderness again and find ourselves there, and that our love can flow out into the wild once more; that human heart and wilderness can mutually enrich one another, and find fulfilment there in the mirror of the other.

Elva Mason is another singer well-known for her association with the Hexham Amateur Stage Society. For the November 2005 production of "Call Me Madam" she took the starring and exacting role of Mrs Sally Adams, the Hostess with the Mostes. Elva has played on stage in a number of smaller roles and also as a soloist in the Stage Society concerts. She also has worked as Associate Director for the productions of The Wizard of Oz, The Music Man, Oliver, Carousel, (when she also took the role of The Heavenly Friend), Guys and Dolls and Annie.

Wall has also had writers living in the village and surrounding areas.

Jasper Rootham lived at Crag House during the 1970s. He was a classical scholar at St John's College Cambridge and followed this with a Civil Service career working in the Treasury and 10 Downing Street before in 1940 serving in the army in the Middle East, France and Germany. Among his publications are:-

Prose Miss Fire (Chatto,1946), Demi-Paradise (Chatto,1960).

Poetry Verses 1928-72 (Rampant Lions,1973), The Celestial City (Two Jays Press, 1975)

Reflections from a Crag (Unit Offset Ltd 1978).

This last book has a cover designed by Phyllis Dobson and contains 72 poems with many relating to our locality and the surrounding countryside.

Julia and **Alan Grint** They lived for a time in the village and their 'Writing on the Wall' gatherings became very popular, bringing authors of note to the village hall to speak on their writings. They owned Cogito Books, the shop in St Mary's Chare in Hexham now run by their daughter, who has also continued her parents' book functions in the village hall. Both Julia and Alan were writers, having books published by their own company, Ergo Press.

The Faith and Fire Within: In Memory of the men of Hexham Who Fell in the Great War by Alan Isaac Grint.

In Silent Fortitude: In Memory of the Men of the North Tyne Who Fell in the Great War by Alan Isaac Grint and Julia Grint.

Bastles: An Introduction to the Bastle Houses of Northumberland by Julia Grint, Chloe Rodham, Rachel Pearson and Alan Isaac Grint.

Barry Unsworth was 'Visiting Literary Fellow' at Durham and Newcastle Universities and came to live for nearly three years at Owl Cottage, High Brunton. His first novel,

The Partnership, was published in 1966, followed by at least fourteen more, one of which was Pascali's Island. It was nominated for the Booker Prize and then made into a film in 1988, starring Ben Kingsley and Helen Mirren. In 1992 Barry won the Booker Prize for his novel, Sacred Hunger. It was the only time that the Booker Prize has been jointly won. Barry shared the prize with Michael Ondaatje's, The English Patient. Whilst living in Owl Cottage Barry wrote The Rage of the Vulture. A solitary man, he became a friend of the Proudlock family, all of them enjoying his company and taking him out on trips to discover Northumberland. He loved Wall and the surrounding area, always walking over Fallowfield Fell to catch the train from Hexham station to Newcastle or Durham. Having spent two years here he moved to Liverpool University as 'Writer in Residence' for one year, but like a returning bird, came back again to Owl Cottage and the area he loved, to start writing his next book, A Stone Virgin.

Barry died in 2012, having lived in Italy for many years, but he will always be a part of the story of High Brunton, Wall.

YOUNG PEOPLE - Mary Herdman and Joan Proudlock

When we oldies have trouble understanding our computers, we turn to our youngsters for help. They are brought up with them, from primary school onwards, if not before. Today's kids enjoy video games and have a wide variety of programmes on television. They can communicate easily with their friends through mobile phones or Facebook. They have so many indoor attractions which were not available to us.

Many parents these days have become nervous of letting their children out of their sight. Children are also discouraged from many activities such as climbing trees or playing conkers on the grounds of health and safety. It is small wonder that today's children do not enjoy as much outdoor freedom as those some half a century or more ago.

Yesterday's children had less to keep them indoors. They enjoyed playing cricket, football and rounders on the back green, and tennis on a court where a new house now stands across the road from the Hadrian Hotel. The inner green was a popular place to play hide and seek. Playing fox and hounds set them further afield. The 'fox' was set loose. He would lead the pack to Fallowfield, to Wall Mill, the 'Sandy Planting' or the 'Houp' (the field adjacent to Halton Grange). They would play stoolball, build dens and take home tadpoles in jam jars which somehow never grew up to be frogs. They climbed on the machinery at Herdman's workshop. This would be considered dangerous today but somehow they came to no great harm. Marbles were a popular pastime. Skipping, hopscotch, picking flowers and making daisy chains were enjoyed by the girls. The school organized the collection of rose hips in the autumn. The children were paid 3d (three old pence) per pound, and they were taken away to be made into rose hip syrup. During the war school treats would consist of sports in the local fields, and then later, trips by steam train took them to Edinburgh and to York. After the war came the annual Sunday school trips by bus to Whitley Bay. There was eagerness to be the first to spot the sea. The day would be spent on the beach, rounded off by fish and chips and a trip to the fun fair delights of the Spanish City. In my memory, the sun always shone.

Some entertainments were laid on for the children. Mr Robinson, the schoolmaster in the 1940s and 1950s, was very good with them; he organised the School Camps, for a short time a Young Farmers Club and a Youth Club, and also was responsible for games like snap or snakes and ladders in the Parish Hall.

The advent of television brought children indoors more, although football, cricket, rounders and hide and seek remained popular. I remember watching a group of boys playing cricket. Then one of the boys shouted: "It's half past six" The game was abandoned as they all rushed into my house to watch 'Dr Who'. Half an hour later, play was resumed.

Through the generations the first flake of snow brought out the sledges. In days gone by youngsters would use the 'Houp' or the Chare. Nowadays the Chare is more dangerous because of the increase of traffic. Creating a slippery slope on a public road is also hazardous for elderly pedestrians. Salt and grit is spread. The sledgers now gather on the back green where there is a short but reasonably steep slope. Now the back green sports goalposts and swings. Football or rounders are still seen, but with the younger children a parent is usually around, either watching or joining in.

Schooling has changed too. In days gone by those who did not pass the grading exam at the age of eleven would stay on at the village school. Their lives would be centred on Wall and its environs. On leaving school at fourteen they would go into employment, leaving teenagers within the village with less leisure time. Now we have no school. There is no grading exam. Children are transported out for their education: first to Humshaugh, then to Hexham. They form friendships beyond the village. They have the opportunity to enjoy team sports and social activities such as rugby, rowing or swimming. Until they learn to drive, parents are called upon as chauffeurs to take them to clubs or sleepovers. Then they want to borrow the car.

What will tomorrow's children play? Football and cricket get much publicity on television. The top players are seen as heroes. I see those games staying popular.

Cricket certainly became popular with one resident of Wall, who after almost fifty years is still deeply involved in the game.

David Mason has his own cricket story, showing how an interest inspired by Wall headmaster Bobby Wood, eventually led on to him coaching juniors at Tynedale Sports Club. From 1964 and still on-going David has been associated with Tynedale Cricket Club, both as a player and as an administrator. As a regular cricketer he played in teams which included West Indian international legends, Clairmont Depieza, Courtney Walsh and Ian Bishop, all of whom played as professionals for Tynedale. In addition he came up against many other international stars representing other clubs, both in league and cup competitions. He has said the highlight of his career came in the 1975 season (The Year of Victories) when he was part of the Tynedale team who won their league, plus three north east cup competitions, and the records show that he ended the season in third position in the league batting averages. Having been a member of the Governing Board of Tynedale Sports Club, then its Chairman, David is now Chairman of Tynedale Cricket Club, a position he holds with the awareness of how many hours of pleasure the club gave to him when he was younger.

In 2010 two of our young ladies made the news. **Nicole** and **Georgina Lamb** are twins, born to a farming family who have lived in Wall for several generations. The Queen Elizabeth High School in Hexham stimulated their interest in rowing. At the age of seventeen, Nicole represented Great Britain in the Coupe de la Jeunesse in Hazewinkel, Belgium, in both the women's eight and the women's four rowing teams, winning silver and bronze medals. In 2011 she won a silver medal as part of a coxless four in the World Junior Rowing Championships in London. The championships were held at Eton Dorney – the course which hosted the 2012 Olympic rowing events. Nicole is currently studying biology at Newcastle University and continues to row for Newcastle University Boat Club. She participated at Henley Women's Regatta 2012, winning in a senior eight. Always ambitious she has her sights set on the next Olympics and to this end has been selected and participated in the Youth Olympics 2013 in Sydney, Australia. Nicole rowed in the pairs, the fours and the eights. As this is being written news has come that she won a silver medal in the pairs followed by, on her twentieth birthday, gold in the fours and bronze in the eights.

"Winning the bronze in the eight was a good result to finish our regatta and it meant I got a medal in each colour," said Nicole.

Georgina's interest is rugby. She has played for, and captained the local Tynedale Panthers at county level for Northumberland and regionally for the north east of England. Gina was captain of the North of England U18 rugby squad and a member of the England Sevens squad at the Youth Commonwealth Games. She also took up rowing at the high school and was successful in 2010 representing England at the Home Countries International Regatta in Cork, Ireland. Gina has now taken up a place at Harper Adams University studying agriculture with a view to taking over Town Farm if her dad ever retires! She continues to play rugby and has recently been elected Women's Captain for Harper Adams.

Well done girls and well done to Queen Elizabeth High School, Hexham for encouraging enthusiastic sportswomen.

Sons and daughters of Wall have left to live and find work in many parts of the world.

Ernest Proud and George Leadbeater went to New Zealand, Eddie Robinson to America, Shirley Mitchell, Margaret Seaby, Jennifer and Dick Rudd, Bobby and Elizabeth Bowman and Trevor Holliday to Canada, his brother Brian to Australia and also Peter Allcock to Australia. These are the names we know but there may be others.

It is in the nature of life that young people strike out on their own, and so they have done from Wall. Here we make note of just a few of those we have heard about who have spent their childhood and teenage years in Wall or its environs, and have gone on to do interesting or challenging things in their lives.

Shirley Mitchell (née Coats) In 1953, as a 21st birthday present, Shirley's aunt in Canada sponsored her to stay with her in Toronto for a year. She sailed from Liverpool and arrived in Montreal, where her Aunt Minnie was waiting. Very quickly she found a job in the prestigious department store, Eaton's. A year later she returned to Wall but so loved her life in Canada that she went back and stayed, working again in Eaton's in their picture framing department. After six years in 1960, due to her mother needing her, she sailed home on the Queen Mary leaving her friends behind, and a year later married John Mitchell whom she had known since their days in Wall school.

Margaret Seaby went out to Canada in the 1950s and became a teacher at a Native Indian residential school deep in Inuit country. She met her husband there and eventually moved to New Brunswick on the eastern seaboard of Canada.

Ella Hill (née Wardle) went to King's College (Newcastle University) and left with a degree in biology. Having parents who farmed at Planetrees and therefore a background in farming, she wrote to The Institute for Animal Health, (now The Pirbright Institute), Surrey to see if there was a job for a biology graduate . There was, so in 1951 Ella moved to Surrey and began work on research into foot and mouth disease, so using her knowledge of farm animals and her degree in a very practical way.

Fred Thompson, Billy Marran, Neil Scholes and **Calum Bruce**, the last now serving in Gibraltar, are policemen who have come from Wall, whilst other ex-police officers over the years have come to retire here.

Ivor Gray MBE. Ivor lived for a short time in the 1950s in Wall, where his parents worked, and still has happy memories of that time and the lifelong friends he made in the village. Ivor won the fell race for the Queen's Coronation and has maintained his interest in running having completed twenty Great North Runs. For the last thirty years all his spare time has been used in the organisation and administration of various Tynedale Youth Football Leagues. It is for his services to youth football that he was awarded the MBE in the Queen's New Year Honours List 2007.

David Stewart studied geography at Aberdeen University followed by engineering qualifications which led to him working for the council on traffic management. He moved to Perth and then to London as, Operations Manager for the Central London Roads Network, and to add to this more recently, with Special Responsibility for Delivering the Olympic Road Network.

Jill Stewart went to Leeds University and gained an English degree. This was followed by some time working in a merchant bank in London before returning north. For a number of years she has built up her own business designing and creating jewellery and clocks from metal. Jill is based at The Hearth in Horsley.

Stuart Proudlock, after A levels went to Russia to teach English for a year before going on to university to study International Relations. From there he went to the University in Guangzhou, China to study Mandarin. He did more teaching and travelling and also volunteer work in the Newcastle Oxfam finance office. He returned to China and is now Corporate Services Manager at the Consulate in Shanghai.

Andrew, Stuart's brother, worked at the Hadrian Hotel in the village then went to work in a beach hotel on the Costa del Sol. Having returned home he is now Food and Beverage Manager at The Battlesteads Hotel, Wark.

Lisa Proudlock, not related but sharing the same surname, spent three months in Tanzania in the coastal forest area, collecting biologic specimens for the University of Dar-es-Salaam. The work, of which she was part, eventually contributed to a book, The Coastal Forests of Eastern Africa. She followed this, working for six months and living with the people in a hillside village, Tujulom Grande, in Guatamala. Using her experience in environmental water management, along with a fellow graduate and working with the local people, they were designing and setting up a piped and tapped water supply to this remote village.

Young people, who have grown up living in and around the village, go on to work in many ways. We wish they will have fulfilment in whatever they choose to do, and perhaps sometimes remember that place, once home, called Wall.

RECOLLECTIONS OF VILLAGE LIFE - Daphne Bannister (née Huddleston)
A daughter's tribute to a loving mother and a happy childhood in Wall
Audrey Huddleston

Being the eldest of three, my two brothers Geoffrey, Gerald and I lived with our devoted parents Audrey and Matt in the oldest house in Wall, Greenhead House, which was built in 1631. Dad had lived in Wall all his life. Mum, whose father was a farm worker, had lived in different locations in the surrounding area such as Planetrees and Fallowfield, before eventually coming to live in Wall where she met dad. Eventually they married and moved into Greenhead House.

Mum was a very industrious person and she made many of our clothes when we were children. On the occasion of one Sunday School Anniversary at the chapel, my younger brother Gerald, having recited his piece, looked up at the Minister and said "Do you like my new shirt? My mammy made it." The Minister replied "Yes Gerald I do like your new shirt and I think there will be many people here today who wish they had someone who could make new shirts for them".

During the long winter nights our family was kept busy making a "proggy mat". This consisted of stretching a piece of strong hessian over a wooden frame. Then pieces of thick material, old coats, skirts, etc in as many different colours as possible were cut into strips of equal length. When mum thought sufficient strips had been cut we would all sit around the mat frame and "poke" these through the hessian with a "progger". Looking back it seemed almost like a small factory and we all looked forward to seeing the new mat on the floor, this could however take many weeks to complete.

During autumn and winter, particularly after the storms, the family regularly went into the surrounding woods looking for firewood. Fallen branches were trailed home where they would be sawn up by dad to help keep the fires burning.

To go ferreting with dad, who was a real countryman, was to my brothers and myself a very exciting event. Now as I look back this seems so terribly cruel, however times were hard and people did their best to be self-sufficient. Dad carried the ferret in a box which hung from his shoulder on a strap. On reaching the place, often down by the river where there were rabbit holes, dad produced a net which he placed over the holes, meanwhile we three would sit on the bankside and watch. Taking the ferret from its box dad put it down one of the holes and in a short while one or more rabbits would come bounding out of the burrows and become tangled up in the net. Dad would quickly kill the rabbits, catch the ferret and pop it back in its box then head for home, where mum would prepare a tasty rabbit pie.

Each year during the rose hip season the school organised the collection of rose hips. Most children would pick these and there were no exceptions. It became a regular Sunday afternoon event, to go out picking rose hips with mum and dad. We generally headed for the riverside and we always hoped to pick a vast quantity. On a Monday morning the hips were taken to school where they were weighed and we were paid three (old) pence per pound picked. They were eventually turned into rose-hip syrup which was 'full of goodness for young children'. It was always a great challenge to collect the 24lb in order to receive a badge. That badge took a great deal of working for and resulted in scratched arms and legs and it was not unusual to get nettled. Mum and dad frequently had to administer the age old remedy for being nettled, a little human spit on a docken leaf rubbed on to the affected area. It was imperative you got that badge.

A very special tender memory I have is of walking up the New Lane by myself on numerous Mothering Sundays and collecting snowdrops from the wood, then belonging to Mr Wood. It may be coincidence but the best ones always seemed to be growing on the other side of the stream and out of reach. Having picked a generous handful I would then collect a few ivy leaves and make a collar to arrange around the outside of the snowdrops, which I proudly took home for mum.

As children we felt secure in our own little village. On summer evenings my brothers along with other youngsters would often play the game of fox and hounds, running up and down the fell and as far afield as down by the riverside. Young boys can quickly become hungry when expending a lot of energy and it wasn't unknown for them to raid Bob Bell's orchard. Attending Wall School and running through the wood at playtimes I became familiar with every part of it. In springtime and in particular on Saturday mornings I would go into the wood and collect deep mauve and white violets to take home for mum. I would also collect sticks and carry these home in my small wheelbarrow to help out with firewood. I also have vivid recollections of picking primroses on the riverbank along with my brothers.

Summer in the village was a happy time particularly when haymaking was in progress at Mr Ripley's farm. Riding back to the farm with my brothers on top of a bogey load of hay was very exciting. We also enjoyed helping to carry baskets of food and hot tea in milk cans prepared by Mrs Ripley to the men working in the fields.

Most people grew their own vegetables. My brothers and I would help dad set our vegetable garden each spring. As he dug the trenches and put manure in the bottom we would follow him and place potatoes at regular intervals along each row. Peas were also grown and to give support to the young plants we would go up the fell and collect pea sticks. These were pushed into the ground when the plants reached a certain height. When the peas were ready we would pop up the garden and quietly sample a few!

On the arrival of autumn thoughts turned again to food as this was the season for picking brambles and we went out as a family to gather these. One had to be careful when picking some of the bushes as it was easy to put one or even both feet down a rabbit hole. The brambles when picked were made into jam or jelly by mum, this was always very tasty.

On Thursday evenings in the winter months of the mid 1950s a weekly dance was held in the village hall. These were organised by the village schoolmaster (Jimmy Robinson) and were well attended by the village teenagers. A record player provided the music and everyone enjoyed themselves so much that the following week couldn't come along soon enough. Fancy dress competitions were also part of village entertainment and lots of people, both adults and children loved to take part in these. I remember on one occasion my mum dressing up as a rabbit catcher, complete with ferret in a box slung over her shoulder. On arriving at the hall many people wouldn't believe that she actually had a ferret with her, whereupon she put on a stout leather glove and produced it from out of the box. The sight of Audrey with a real live ferret produced a lot of squeals.

Every season in the village brought wonderful sights and sounds of nature. I well remember in March/April each year climbing the fell with Geoffrey and Gerald to where there was a small pond surrounded by rocks. We would lie 'belly flappers' on the ground and scoop frog spawn in our hands and put it in a jam jar to take home. We would then wait for what seemed like forever for tadpoles to develop. Each spring we would eagerly await the arrival of the swallows which would sit on the power lines in front of Greenhead House for a rest. Since I left the village to live in Hexham mum would telephone each year to let me know they were back once again.

Summer being strawberry time brought with it many happy times when as a family we would walk along the railway embankment and pick delicious wild strawberries, stopping occasionally to wave at a passing train on its journey from Hexham to Kielder. This was a daily service used by people living in the North Tyne valley. Many were the evenings when I lay in bed and listened to the sound of an engine shunting at Wall station.

The fell featured largely in the lives of the village youngsters many of whom at one time or another would play roly-poly from top to bottom. Also once each year there was an organised fell race which many of the older lads took part in. At the top of the fell are some large rocks which over the years have had the initials of many of the village lads painstakingly carved on them. On summer days these rocks were a popular place to sit and gaze down on the whole village and the surrounding area. If we were up there and mum wanted us down for any reason, she would stand on the village green waving her handkerchief and call us. On special occasions over the years a bonfire has been lit on top of the fell.

Looking back on my childhood days I find myself awash with precious memories recalling the simple way of life and the pleasures that living in the village of Wall brought to me and my family.

MEMORIES AND THOUGHTS ON WALL VILLAGE – OCTOBER 2011
David Mason (Aged 65)

Some memories of my childhood living in Wall are those of being able to walk or play almost anywhere in the immediate area, up the fell and down by the river. There never seemed to be any need for the parental concerns which have become necessary in the modern world.

Before my parents moved back into the village in 1953 we lived at Low Barns for a while and I can remember as a child walking down to the railway with my dad after a train had gone up the North Tyne line and collecting a few pieces of coal spilled from the fully laden tender which had just been filled up at Hexham.

As youngsters living in the village we would walk along the river bank anywhere from Chollerford to the meeting of the waters near Acomb observing nature or just innocently messing about. This is something neither youngsters nor adults can do today. I recall going for a walk with friends one Sunday morning after church without getting changed from my Sunday best. We walked down past the station and along by the old mill. Somehow I managed to fall, fully clothed, into the mill race but fortunately there wasn't a large amount of water and I managed to climb out easily. Needless to say, the others seemed to find this quite amusing but as someone who never felt comfortable even in a dry woollen suit, walking back home in a soaking wet one was not one of life's more uplifting experiences. Any comments or actions from my parents when I returned seem to escape my memory.

Everyone who was around at the time of the Coronation celebrations can remember how wet it was but as a child I remember two other things. The first was my mam dressing me as a page boy in an outfit which I know now had taken her countless hours to make. I hated dressing up and somewhere up in our loft is a photo of me wearing not only the costume but a very large 'pet lip'. Strangely I am reluctant to hunt it out for public viewing. The second thing I remember about the Coronation was my dad running in the fell race which along with other events was held at a slightly later date due to the weather. Dad would be about 38 at the time but was an officer in the Royal Marines during the second world war (something of which he was justifiably very proud) and was still very fit but as one of the organisers of the celebrations I don't think he had intended to take part because I remember him throwing down his jacket after the start and tagging on at the back of the field. There is some uncertainty about the outcome of that race but it became something of a coincidence when 25 years on at the Silver Jubilee celebrations, I took part in, and won, the fell race under almost identical circumstances. I can't recall dad being so totally exhausted afterwards but I can recall my mam telling me that dad won the fell race at the Coronation celebrations, presumably at the time of the 1937 Coronation when he would be about 21.

I remember during my teens spending almost complete weekends in the Reading Room playing table tennis. Sometimes John Elliott (the younger) and I would slog out 70 or 80 games against each other from Friday night to Sunday night only occasionally stopping for meals it seemed. All this practice must have done us some good because both of us became members of a Wall team which included John Proudlock, Raymond Craig and occasionally Neil Scholes, which won the Hexham and district league during several consecutive seasons.

I was packed off to boarding school for a couple of years when I was thirteen and then I attended college at Ashington and then Newcastle. During this time I only came home during holidays and at weekends so for a period of about eight years, mostly as a teenager, I feel I missed out a little on village life.

Some of my fondest memories however are those of my schooldays at Wall C of E County Primary School and sometimes when I venture through the 'school wood' whilst out walking I feel I can almost hear the children's voices around me playing happily amongst the trees, rocks and bushes. It all seems so much smaller now but that wood was much more than a play area, it was a complete and different world of fun and adventure (and the occasional mishap). Those days are long past and it saddens me a little that we no longer have a village school and that kids are prevented from climbing trees because of the great god 'Health & Safety'. I am also sad that we no longer have village shops – there were three in the village when I was a boy. That other great god 'The Supermarket' put a final nail in that particular coffin.

I am inherently somewhat resistant to change, but I have come to accept that for better or worse it is part of life. What I think has been most difficult over the past 50 years or so is that the pace of change as been so great. As a village, Wall changed significantly during a time when I was privileged to be chairman of the Parish Council. Overall the number of dwellings in the village increased by around 30% through both conversion of mostly old and redundant farm building and new-build houses in disused farmyards. This all happened in a relatively short period of time. As a Parish Councillor, trying to strike a balance between the views of existing residents and those of developers and planners during that period became something of a nightmare which ultimately and regretfully resulted in three members of the Parish Council, including myself, plus the Parish Clerk, resigning.

At the time of writing (October 2011) I have served as a Parish Councillor once again for several years and thankfully things are much quieter and more settled. Life as a Parish Councillor in a small village is largely quite mundane with some of the issues to be dealt with being – additional children's play equipment, maintenance of the 'pant', ensuring seats are in a good state of repair and deciding which charities should benefit from the annual precept. As in many walks of life today it has become increasingly difficult to get anyone to volunteer to serve on Parish Councils and in some villages it has ceased to exist. Whether this is because of indifference or due to the pace of life is a subject which has become much debated.

I feel that we are quite lucky in Wall because organised events, almost without exception, seem to be well supported by both visitors and residents from the surrounding area. This can be anything from a coffee morning organised in support of a charity or organisation, to the millennium or jubilee celebrations. In addition, despite the often inclement weather the popularity of the annual fête never ceases to amaze. My feeling is that the success and popularity of these events is due, in no small part, to the participation over the years of many of those, whom some of us who have lived here since childhood, may have referred to as 'newcomers'. Many of these residents have come and gone but many have lived in the village for quite a long time and one of the most significant things which some of them have brought about is the presence of children in the community. Contrary to a widely held belief, not everyone who moves into every small rural village is retired or about to retire. There was a period of time some years ago when the sight and sound of children playing around the village had almost disappeared and this perhaps gave the impression that the community was falling into decline. Now we once again have a mix of ages and backgrounds which hopefully will continue long into the future.

My personal fear is that with our ever increasing dependency on the motor car and the decline of rural public transport combined with the escalation of fuel costs, communities like Wall may be forced into further decline. Let us hope that for those who do continue to live here, that other great god 'the computer' doesn't persuade them to stay indoors during their leisure time and thus miss out on the joys of living in this wonderfully picturesque village of ours.

GROWING UP IN WALL IN THE 1950S - Pat Stewart

Wall school headmaster was Jimmy Robinson, the teacher Miss Robertson (later Isabelle Everatt); my favourite teacher. Occasionally we had temporary teachers who I did not like and I did not want to go to school. I remember the relief when my mother told me Miss Robertson was back.

The school was a wonderful place to be at that age, with all the wide open spaces and woods to run around in, blackberries and rose hips to pick, trees to swing on and the playground to play games and skip.

When we were a bit older Mr Robinson organised a camping trip week (or maybe a fortnight). We went to such places as Alnmouth, Budle Bay, Grange-over-Sands or Glenluce. We loved it!

Mr Robinson also persuaded some of us to join the church choir, with the promise of 1d (one old penny) each time we went – I don't remember ever getting 1d, but some of us remained in the choir for a long time. Mr Robinson also ran the Church Sunday School. I remember every Sunday going to C of E Sunday School and the Methodist Sunday School which was run by Margaret Ripley and Ella and Isobel Wardle.

There was a Sunday school trip to Whitley Bay on the first Monday of the summer holidays. This was very much looked forward to, as we didn't go very far in those days. I think we were all given 2d to spend.

Wall was a wonderful place to grow up in. We used to wander around all day during school holidays, up the fell, along the lanes, down the river – only going home for lunch (sometimes) and at dark. When we were a bit older we used to congregate at the lamp post at the top of the green at night to decide what to do and where to go in the dark. When we were older still we could go into the Reading Room to play snooker and billiards.

A CHILD IN THE 1970S - Jill Stewart

It's 1974. I'm eight. I am wearing yellow and purple crimplene trousers, of which I am very proud. Wall is a great place to be a child. I am aware that I am living in an idyllic place. Sometimes I'm swayed by how exotic towns and suburbs seem on TV but I like the countryside, I like to see the fell.

We live in a tiny rented cottage. The toilet is outside, the bath is in the kitchen, there's a coal fire for heating, but friends and relatives who live in the country have the same arrangements. There are large gardens and I am always outside anyway.

Next door is Bowman's shop. It is dark and seems old, it sells sweets and iced lollies, newspapers, comics, there must be other things too but I don't notice. We play outside in the back of Bowman's, in the fantastic jungle of old cars and nettles.

When I was small there was a Post Office at the top of the village, in a house by the fell steps, run by Mrs Seaby. Now there is a wooden chalet halfway up the Chare run by Mrs Westle. It smells nicely of creosote and the Post Office part has a wire grille. There's a bacon slicer and a wire for slicing cheese. You can get your 3d stamp, an Old Jamaica, a Curlywurly or an Icebreaker.

I used to go to the village school. I was just there for a year when it closed and Mrs Reed our teacher came with us to Humshaugh. I remember painting and spelling mostly. There was a stove, a tray of tiny milk bottles that froze in winter, beanbags and hoops, the smell of pencil shavings and brown plasticine. We ran in the wood and made dens in the hollow. Assembly was in Mr Wood's room, singing 'Summer Suns are glowing' from a scented purple printed sheet.

Out of school I mostly play on the green in front of Herdman's; cricket in season, football all the rest of the time, although there are only three of us. Herdman's is full of men welding and drilling. We can hear them from our house on Front Street; it's the background noise.

There are three working farms in the village. I've never been in Lamb's, but we go to Fred Henderson's or Ripley's to 'help' with the milking, getting feed and cowcake. The cows come across the main road from the back fields at milking time and stop the traffic.

Sometimes people will just sit on a seat and watch cars go by. We walk down the fields all the time to the river, and pick primroses in the spring, hazelnuts in autumn. My grandma posts primroses to her sisters in towns.

There is church and chapel Sunday school, both of which I'm sent to. Everyone has a garden and most grow food. The Garden Fête and the Leek Show are village highlights of the year. I know everyone. My grandma is everywhere and in everything.

It will be many years before I think it strange for a roomful of men to be comparing the size of their leeks!

Jill Stewart is the daughter of Pat and John giving us two generations in one family of impressions of growing up in Wall.

A VERY PERSONAL VIEW - 1970-2011 - Joan Proudlock

I came to Wall 41 years ago and married John Proudlock the next year. John had grown up in Wall as his parents first lived in Stable Cottage and then moved into his mother's family home, Bibury. John therefore was used to village life as he and his friends had attended the village school as children. My home village was Stocksfield, a large area that was primarily residential. There were leafy, tree lined roads and large detached houses. Many of the residents commuted daily to business in Newcastle.

Coming to Wall I found the perfect country village almost still in a time warp. There it was all snuggled around the village green with the main road to Hexham by-passing the real core of Wall. I discovered later that many people in the area had no idea of the hidden treasure they passed by. Wall to them was the main street.

In 1970 there were three farms bordering the green, Herdman's engineering works spilled out of their work yard, Mrs Seaby's post office and shop, in Garden House, was opposite St George's church and overlooking the back green was John Proudlock's garage, a large corrugated metal shed. Alongside the main road where it still stands, was the Hadrian Hotel, famous throughout the north as the place for a celebration meal, and a little further up, Mrs Bowman's shop. Below the fell and above the village green sat Wall Church of England village school and the voices of the children at playtime rang out over the village as they played their games. All too soon after my arrival the school closed, but I did have the pleasure of making a cine-film of the last sports day on the village green.

When school was out and work over the Reading Room was open for recreation. This sets the scene when I found Wall forty years ago. These were the buildings but it was and still is the people who have made and make Wall the special place in which to live.

Mrs Seaby in the post office, and her husband Jack, a church warden, very quickly knew of anyone or anything which related to Wall. It was not long therefore, before the news went round that John and I were 'intended'! I can still remember the lovely clean smell of polish as I went into her shop and, when chatting over the counter with Peggy found out all the latest news.

Mrs Bowman's shop on Front Street was the sort of shop which sold everything and if it wasn't there it soon would be. Eva her daughter delivered the newspapers and I remember her coming up Bibury drive each morning, papers in hand. Every autumn Eva picked blackberries from the fells surrounding the village and sold them to anyone who wanted to make jam. Eva still has a special place in my heart; she was accepting of the way she was and did whatever she could to help others, taking dogs for walks, cleaning, looking after children and always going to evening service. She lived life simply and she left it too early.

There were three milking herds belonging to the farms in the village when I first came. If it was four o'clock Fred Henderson was leading his cows across the green for milking. It was animal power over vehicle power when Eddie Ripley and George Lamb brought their beasts across the main road. The flow of vehicles on the North Tyne route was temporarily halted twice daily. Cow muck, along with wandering hens, ducks and geese around the village green was part of country living but those are all long since gone.

John and I married in St George's church in April 1971. Everyone in the village who had daffodils in flower brought them to the church and village hall so I could decorate. As we came out of the church we found the gates tied and most of the village children waiting outside for the traditional throwing of the money which was done by our best man, Neil Scholes, who lived in a small bungalow in the field which now contains Mithras Court. Bridal transport for the wedding came courtesy of Norman Doyle who lived in the bungalow next to the school who lent us his car, a white Hillman, the back shelf decorated with flowers and driven by one of John's workers from the garage. It was a country village wedding with the reception held in the village hall. John and I walked across the green, followed by wedding guests. No-one had warned them that a young farmer with a gun would let off a round of shot to welcome the newly married couple to the hall! That was the fun of a village wedding, followed by us finding the caravan we had so carefully hidden having been completely covered in confetti pasted down by water, all crafted by two Wall lasses who will forever remain anonymous! After the reception the guests were welcomed at Bibury and while we were away, as tradition dictated, village folk were invited one evening to have wedding cake and see the presents. So that was the beginning of my forty years in Wall.

During that time so many changes have taken place. It is in the nature of progress that new people with new ideas come along and that when the economy drives, property will change hands and new properties will be built. So it was with Wall. The three farms diversified, capitalised on their assets and when the building "boom" arrived became small groups of houses bringing more residents. The farming continued but in a different way. The milking cows were no longer seen on the village green and the wandering hens and ducks disappeared. Eventually North Farm came to an end following the death of Fred Henderson. West Farm's land is used by others in the family but Eddie Ripley still maintains an active interest in farming life. Town Farm has relocated all the working buildings and the machinery yard to a site below the Hadrian Hotel. John Lamb carries on the family tradition of farming and it seems that one of his daughters, Georgina, may in the future take on that role.

With the building of Mithras Court a group of long time residents of Wall felt it would be good to welcome this new, and in many cases younger, life into the village. This very successfully happened using the village hall as the focus. Quite soon those who felt an affinity with the existing village 'goings on' were producing ideas of their own, joining in on planning and committees, which proved, later on, to be useful when it came to the millennium.

Throughout the 1990s a new spirit crept into the village as we slowly moved forward to the millennium. This was a time which brought so many villagers together as we planned the various projects and events. Through all the concerts, fêtes, countrywide royal celebrations and particular events in the church and chapel, the millennium celebrations are the ones which will long be remembered for bringing the village of Wall together as a lively, creative and imaginative community of folk whose hearts were in village living. Here it is my opportunity to express for all time my gratitude and admiration for all those wonderful women who took part every week for over two years stitching the wall hanging. Along with the children from our school who came to contribute to the book, who are now eleven years older, they, and all the many helpers made a dream become reality. Together in Wall, we showed then the real and twenty-first century community spirit of how village life should be in the co-operation of all ages and walks of life for the good of the community in which they live.

In the life of Wall village through the years, forty years hardly counts. There are others who have lived long life times in the village. Within those forty years there have been so many changes in the structure and demographics of Wall. I so hope that as we travel the twenty-first century, long may the enriching spirit of community last, for it is those who live in and out-bye who make this special place called Wall. It's my home!

THE WATSONS - Angela and David

Four Watsons arrived in the village on 23 December 1990. They moved into their new house within Mithras Court. Soon after their arrival a large amount of snow fell and a coffee morning was arranged for newcomers to the village to meet their neighbours. It was a great start.

At the time Chris Allcock was parish chairman and he asked David to help organise some wood clearing in front of, and to the side of the old school house. A meeting was held and a large number of able bodied men and women volunteered their services. Chopping, sawing, gathering, burning and carting were the order of a number of Saturday mornings. Each session ended with a few cans of the sparkling stuff!

That was nearly twenty years ago. The land is now well wooded, some would say overgrown, but nevertheless a site of lovely memories where people joined in a common purpose and amid good natured banter got on and did something worthwhile for the community – thanks to Roy, Staughans, Brian, Chris, John, Fred, Duggans, Pyms, Ali, Chris and Peter Orton (RIP) – many have moved, some have passed away but fond memories linger.

Meanwhile on Sunday mornings a very young Louise was honing her equestrian skills under the wayward eye of two cowboys: Fred and John who would ride out on the fell, bareback and only flat caps – playing cowboys and Indians – pretending to shoot from under the horses' necks – (remember the grey, Lucky, tethered on the back green – a long rope allowing free access to grazing) a couple of seventy year old school boys!

The said land bordering the old school house was a favourite haunt of our son Phil and David Harding. Rachel and Maurice Lowther enjoyed seeing them build tree houses or just play 'in the countryside' – not exactly woodcraft but freedom with a little risk! If a bee sting was suffered, a jar of honey was soon delivered.

It was Fred and Chris who taught David a little about leek growing – Fred and Chris wanted to win the annual show. Much to everyone's surprise David got third prize one year. Then he had to 'give up the leeks' after just three seasons. His beloved trench was dismantled and 'spread' by Angela within minutes or more accurately the time it took David to walk down to the Letch to explain to Charlie Proud that his work had got in the way and so he would have to withdraw from the thriving club – consequently the soil in our garden is rich and very deep!

In those early days we had a couple of Mithras barbecues with no other aim than to feed and water the neighbours and to dance a vigorous Drops of Brandy from No 7 down to No 2 and back again.

Of course there have been many, many other gatherings which have brought us together including fund-raising events at Querns and in the village hall, and those wonderful progressive suppers, as well as the annual village fête. Perhaps the millennium celebration was a significant marker for many of us. For Angela, a lasting thought and mental picture will be of her mother ringing the church bell with Jill Taylor's mother to announce the turn of the century.

Just some happy memories of our family growing, being included and nurtured by the people and environment that is Wall.

Village Life - Mary Lascelles

Not here the hurly burly of city life
But village peace, free from strife.
Not here busy streets, oh so plain
But evening strolls down winding lane.
Not here traffic jams for miles and miles
But meadow paths with gates and stiles.
Here the air stays fresh and clean,
No fumes or smog in fields of green.
Here snowdrops, violets, bluebells grow
No bottles, papers that people throw.
Here the colours entrance us all;
No rubbish tipped by scribbled wall.

Not here people rushing on pavements flat
But time to wave, time to chat.
Not here crowded shops or tubes so hot
But pub and green where ponies trot.
Not here lonely days behind closed doors
But village life with friends galore.

INCOMERS TO WALL - Tish and David Easby feel that this poem by Mary Lascelles sums up beautifully their live in Wall.

When our work took us to London we knew that we would come back to the North of England to retire. After 23 years we had the opportunity to return before retirement. After the frantic pace of life around London, we decided that somewhere rural would suit us for the rest of our days. When we learnt that a cow byre was available for conversion in Wall, and saw the location overlooking one of the greens, we knew that it was definitely for us.

It took six months to turn it into the home we now live in, and it was worth all the anxious moments and sleepless nights! John Lamb the farmer (who had lived in Town Farm for most of his life) and his wife and daughters all made us feel most welcome, but warned us that we would never be classed as 'villagers', but always 'incomers'. We now realize that you have to be born and bred in Wall to be a proper villager!

I was still working full time in Newcastle when we moved in. David chose to work from home for a while and soon got to know many of the locals who had lived here most of their lives. They told stories about the village and surrounding areas, and passed on lovely tales that were probably never written down anywhere.

Once we had settled in, after about six months, we decided to join in some of the social activities. David started to play Carpet Bowls and I joined the Women's Institute and went to services at St George's Church. We both joined the Wall Local History Society. Through this we met many more local people and became involved with the community – David is now *Chairman of the Trustees of the Village Hall; I am secretary of the Parochial Church Council.

We have been here for 14 years and certainly feel part of the village. We are both retired now.

After a number of years David has now resigned as Chairman and the role has been taken on by David Watson with David still on the committee and alongside for help if needed.

COMING TO WALL - Tony and Irene Cattermole

In January 2000 I was working in Ilford, Greater London, and had been there for five years, when I had a heart attack. I was 62 years old and the medics said I should forget about working ever again. My job was Housing manager, looking after a sheltered housing complex, and had a flat with the job. My boss said that as I would not be working again I would have to vacate my flat, but not to worry, I could have a three bedroom flat in a tower block in Hackney belonging to the firm!!! I declined this offer, and suggested that I might avail myself of the reciprocal arrangements that all housing associations have around the UK for retiring staff, and look for a home elsewhere. This was agreed and our Housing Officer was asked to come up with a home in my chosen area of Northumberland, preferably in the Hexham area.

My wife and I had discovered the beautiful north, and in particular the Hexham area on our holidays, and when visiting our son at Newcastle University. Within a few weeks we were offered a bungalow in a place called Wall, which was made to sound like somewhere in outer space! We had seen the village some years before and thought what a lovely village it was, and how nice it would be to live there. We accepted the offer immediately, sight unseen!

We moved in to our lovely little home, with views across open countryside, with sheep and cattle in the field immediately behind the house, in May 2000. After a year of recuperation my health improved in leaps and bounds, and we became involved in village activities. So far, the Queen's Golden Jubilee and Diamond Jubilee, The Village Society, the yearly Village Fête to name but a few, plus involvement in the village church of which I have been Churchwarden for the last five years. We both love the village, its friendly people, and the wonderful scenery all around us. We consider it a privilege to live here and never want to leave.

WE CAME, WE SAW, WE CONQUERED - Jill and David Brookman

We first came to Wall, on holiday, in July 1987, a Thursday. By Saturday we were running a hoopla stall at our first Three Churches Fête. Don't know how that happened, maybe the forecast, but the original stall holder was suddenly unavailable. True to form it tipped down for most of the afternoon. Still, we enjoyed ourselves and couldn't help be moved by the fact that we were made so welcome. So we came back for more, and in subsequent years ran the skittles and the kick the football attractions and I think it rained on them too. We also helped on the bric-a-brac stall.

Eventually, after several years of renting Owl Cottage at High Brunton for our holidays, sometimes going on to Scotland, sometimes getting no further than Northumberland, we were faced with a life changing decision. In 1997 we were both made redundant, for the second time in our lives, and, in our sixties, had our futures to consider. In June a phone call out of the blue changed everything. Joan Proudlock phoned to say that the cottage next to Owl Cottage, 'Restharrow' was up for long-term rental, were we interested? After a prolonged period of agonising- all of twenty minutes! We called Joan back to say "We are coming".

On 4 October we moved from St Albans in Hertfordshire to High Brunton. We retained our house in Herts. For some years and after four happy years at High Brunton, having looked at and missed out on several properties in Wall itself, one too small, one too expensive and one gazumping, we moved to our current home in Humshaugh. We still however feel a part of Wall village life through our involvement with the Village Society, Carpet Bowls, the Soup Lunch and now the new Book of Wall.

While still at 'Restharrow' and not ready to retire, and wishing to put something back into the community, we got involved with the charity ADAPT. At first I was driving one or other of their fleet of mini-buses, transporting various disabled folk to school, clinic, respite care and hospices. After a year or so of this voluntary work I was asked if I would turn 'Professional' and operate a regular school run and occasional bus-service and soon Jill joined me on the staff as an escort/carer and this we did for several years, at the same time developing our own company 'Wall to Wall Explorer' with the initial aim of transporting tourists around the National Park and Heritage sites, giving them time to browse the various sites at their leisure without the restriction of catching buses, trains or taxis after their visit. As it worked out we ended up taking mainly local folk out and about, far and wide. Thirteen trips to the 'Dead Sea Scrolls' exhibition in Glasgow, and ten to the Royal Yacht Britannia in Edinburgh are etched in my mind, as is the terrible trip to the Tall Ships at Greenock (some of you may recall this with a shudder) when the departing schooners, brigs and clippers were making faster progress down the Ayrshire coast than we were, due to the terrible traffic jams, on one of the hottest days of the summer. Do you also remember the aborted trip to the ballet at the Sands Centre, Carlisle, when we broke down two miles west of Hexham and we had to commission friends and relatives and a fleet of taxis to complete the journey? And these were the days before mobile phones were commonplace. What touched us was that nobody would accept a refund instead they were full of goodwill for us and our venture and continued to support us.

After a year or so we were able to buy a more reliable vehicle and it is this maroon Peugeot people mover that most people will have been familiar with. Finally, in our seventies and due to a massive increase in public liability insurance we ceased trading and retired properly and are busily enjoying that retirement surrounded by our many, many, friends.

A WELCOME TO WALL - Judy Yeoman

My husband Campbell and I had visited Wall in our youth, but we never thought that one day we would be living here. A friend of a friend of ours, an old lady, had come to Wall for twenty years to stay with Audrey Huddleston for her holidays, and she described Wall as 'Heaven on Earth'. When it came to retirement the pull back to Northumberland was great.

We had enjoyed living in a village in our working days. We started to look for a house near Hexham, preferably in a small hamlet. We have been so fortunate to find this village again and a home in the midst of it.

What a welcome we received! We moved here at the beginning of March 1998 after having had the most glorious sunny February in living memory. We moved on a wet, slushy, snowy morning and our removal van got thoroughly embedded in the green. Not a good start!

Doris Herdman, aged about ninety, came to greet us with open arms. She was one of Wall's real characters, and is still a great miss. All our neighbours were extremely caring and kind. We settled to life here very quickly.

We had brought our hens with us but they had to be put in a leaky shed. Fred Henderson and John Mitchell got together and made the most marvellous henhouse for them. We had very contented Black Rock hens and one lived until she was eight years old. Fred Henderson was a retired farmer and another lovely old Wall character, also greatly missed.

We were invited to coffee mornings, bowls, WI, evening activities, church activities: we found everyone we met in Wall kind, caring and enthusiastic.

WATERAID - Maurice Lowther

I have lived in Wall since 1978 but many years ago as a young 19 year old Army officer I was posted to the Gold Coast (now Ghana). In my time there I saw how the people lived – in a totally unhealthy situation. There were many very young lovely African children but I soon learnt that the majority would not live beyond the age of five – mainly due to contaminated water and insanitary conditions.

These images stayed with me for many years until I found something to do about it in 1980. During the year before there had been a UN conference in Rio de Janeiro when governments pledged to ensure that safe drinking water would be universally available. I discussed this with some of the chairmen of water authorities whether politicians would actually do what they said – to which we all gave a resounding "no". And so WaterAid was formed. The National Water Council agreed with our proposals and the water authority chairmen went back and formed WaterAid units which were involved in fund-raising efforts including climbing mountains, swimming rivers and running marathons.

After WaterAid had been in existence for a few years I was invited to talk about it in the village hall. Afterwards Dorothy Charlton was so enthused that for many, many years she made a doll and raffled it at Christmas time making about £100 each year for WaterAid. More recently I was asked to speak to six and seven year olds in a Hexham school and was impressed that many of them already knew of some of the work of WaterAid.

WaterAid has grown from £25,000 in its first year to £56 million in 2012, helped substantially by more than 300,000 individual contributors in the UK, and now includes the provision of sanitation as well as water supply – always making sure that the community is fully involved so that they can keep everything functional. I still maintain my involvement and have for many years been vice-president.

CHAPTER FOUR

THE NATURAL HISTORY OF WALL PARISH

Starling

BIRDS - John Proudlock, Ray Craig, Joan Proudlock

Wall Village nestles at the foot of a fell which runs from St Oswald's across to Fallowfield and down to Acomb. Much of this fell is covered in scrub gorse, brambles and trees which over the years have grown to be of considerable height and spread. To the west runs the North Tyne. Between the river and the village lie the old railway lines, now disused, and a swathe of agricultural land running from Low Barns Farm to Brunton Crossroads. This land is in the ownership of several farmers and is therefore private. To the north of the village lie the remains of three quarries, more wooded areas and farmed fields. It is generally recognised that over the last sixty years farming practices have undergone many changes. Those who have lived in Wall, or its environs, for at least that number of years, will have witnessed it at first hand. These changes have influenced the natural history of our area. Farmers are business people, and in order to survive must move with the times. When a more mechanised way of working and the advent of the combine harvester and other labour saving equipment occurred, it was natural that the farming year was speeded up and so followed changes.

At this point it is interesting to take a step back in time and see Wall through the eyes of Ray Craig and John Proudlock, both young boys in the 1940s and 1950s then, as now, deeply interested in bird watching and all other aspects of natural history. It is to their memories and knowledge I have turned, using what they have told me and under their supervision, that I have written this chapter on the natural history.

The three village farms, West, North and Town Farm had dairy herds which twice daily came into the milking parlours, en route bringing their cow muck onto the roads and village greens. This attracted flies, multitudes in the summer, but they were food for the nesting summer birds inhabiting the barns and out buildings. The farmyards had barns with hay, thus mice and rats. These were ready meals for hungry owls and passing raptors. Corn was cut and stooked in the fields. The droppings from the thresher were soon cleaned up by the resident sparrows. Following the corn cutting the fields were left, often over winter as stubble, until ploughing began in spring. This resting time allowed birds such as finches and buntings to find food, along with many of those we refer to as 'garden birds', which now come to our bird tables and feeders. Around Wall were hay meadows with meadow flowers, providing nesting sites for corncrakes and sky-larks. The fields that were sown were left untouched following ploughing and rolling for lapwings to nest and rear their chicks before harvesting took place. On the village green were wandering ducks, geese and hens. In autumn children picked rose hips and blackberries and helped to harvest 'snannies' (turnips) and potatoes. Wild flowers grew in the verges, on the back green and along the road sides; there for the butterflies and other insects to find in summer, and more bird food, this time on the wing! Fields then had more boundary hedges giving ideal nesting places for many small birds.

Lapwing

In and around Wall was a natural world, but gradually changes came. Mechanisation gave that faster turn-around of the land and soon housing developments replaced farmyards. The roadside verges were cut and neatly trimmed, as were the village greens. Farmyards and farm muck through the village became a thing of the past. Hedges were removed and fields enlarged. Changes came not only to farming but also in 1958 to the railway and the river. The railway line through Wall and up the valley was closed. The farmers who owned the land bordering it took the option to buy the ground and extend down to the river banks. In May 1982 the Queen opened Kielder reservoir. River levels became managed. On the stretch from Chollerford Bridge to Acomb some levels are now higher than before the reservoir was made. Nine inches may not seem much, but to nesting river birds it is critical. The flat rocks, which were exposed during a dry summer, are now permanently covered with water. The bushes which overhung the river banks, providing cover for birds, are now managed to allow anglers more access to their sport of fishing.

As boys and then young men Ray and John would roam down to the river, walk along the railway track, wander the fell and the local woods, always looking for and identifying birds. They looked for nests, not to take eggs, rather to learn about the habits of each bird and where they could be found. In later years they were able to use this knowledge and instinct, to begin taking photographs.

Depending on the time of year a walk by the river could bring results.

Mallard, the common River Tyne duck; heron, often to be spotted fishing; kingfisher, scarce in the fifties and sixties with numbers increasing in the seventies and eighties but now declining again; grey wagtail, sometimes seen on the rocks; goosander, occasionally breeding with small groups being seen on the river in winter; moorhen, which in the past was a resident breeder but the changes in habitat have brought a decline; sand martins, whose numbers have decreased but with a quick eye may

Heron in flight

still be seen in summer; common sandpiper, which was common in the past but is now a scarce summer visitor; cormorant, these can often be spotted flying low along the river; oyster catcher, there are no suitable shingle beds left but these birds have been able to adapt to other bare sites for nesting.

The railway embankments and the cutting provided habitat for many small bird species, especially during the period following the rail closure. whitethroats, blackcaps, garden warblers and tree pipits were among the birds that found nesting sites courtesy of the disused railway, The tree pipit sadly is no longer a breeding bird in the area.

Whitethroat

Above Wall are the fields on the side of the fell. Circling Wall is the swathe of agricultural land reaching down to the river. In days past corncrakes nested and bred successfully there but due to the changing practices in agriculture this no longer happens. The call of the curlew is sometimes heard on the fell or in the hayfields, but again they are not breeding. In summers past we waited to hear the cuckoo's voice, now no longer reaching this area. The lapwing is another rare breeder here, though happily they can still be seen most of the year. Pheasants are plentiful due to the breeding programme in and around the village. When released by the shooting syndicate their numbers decline, but always a few linger and with their bright colours are a welcome sight in a winter garden. A national decline in the numbers of grey partridge is reflected around Wall.

None of the woodland in the Wall area is of any great size, but it does provide a mix of conifers and deciduous trees, encouraging perhaps some of the following birds. Common rooks fly above us but there is only one large rookery left now at Black Pasture Quarry.

Woodpecker

On bird feeders it is now much more common to see great spotted woodpecker previously readily found in woodland, whilst the green woodpecker, no longer a resident breeder, can still be heard but is seldom seen. Magpies are more common now and have become much bolder. With their cackling call they scour the hedgerows in nesting time and are predators to all eggs and young birds. Jays with their flash of blue feathers and their harsh call often fly over the fell and the High Brunton area. Our intrepid birders, Ray and John have over the years provided nest boxes for pied flycatchers and other species too. At one time there was successful breeding of this species but in recent years, there has been almost nil occupancy. As mentioned previously the tree pipit has gone and also the wood warbler. A winter visitor is the woodcock, which formerly was a resident breeding bird. Nuthatches, once mainly located in woodland, have now found bird feeders and provide entertainment as they feed head down. Two raptors, the buzzard and the sparrowhawk, can be found in woods around wall, but whilst buzzards are frequently seen overhead, it is the sparrowhawk which flies low over the garden seeking to take out any unsuspecting small bird as an easy "takeaway" meal. These birds are now nesting, after being almost eliminated in the 1960s, due to pesticides.

One of the success stories of ornithology during the last ten years has been the spread of the buzzard around Wall. On any bright sunny day they can be seen whirling and circling on the thermals. Their 'mewing' cry is heard, particularly when the young fly in summer. Already mentioned, sparrowhawks too are birds of prey. Kestrels can often be seen hovering over the fields or sitting on a telegraph post, weighing up the potential for a meal, before dropping onto a moving mouse. Occasionally for those with a good eye or binoculars, a passing osprey, peregrine or red kite may be spotted. At night the hooting of the tawny owl is often heard, and for those who are fortunate to see it, the white ghostly form of the barn owl might be seen over some of the fields in the area.

Buzzard

Garden centres now provide an enormous range of bird feeders and bird foods. Due to this provision and subsequent, widespread use of nuts, fat balls and seeds, a wider variety of birds have been encouraged into gardens. We see great, blue, coal, long-tailed tits, and rarely a marsh tit. There are blackbirds and thrushes, though not as many as in the past, chaffinches, greenfinches, goldfinches, siskins, starlings, robins, house sparrows, dunnocks, nuthatches, collared doves, pigeons, woodpeckers and occasionally a tree creeper. Great spotted woodpeckers, nuthatches and collared doves are recent arrivals into gardens, but easy meals have made them less timid, and they are attractive sightings. Attitudes to birds and bird watching have altered during the last forty years, due in part to television programmes such as BBC Autumn and Spring Watch, and the arrival, in media reports, of twitchers in their hundreds travelling the length of the British Isles to see a rare bird.

During the months of autumn and winter, fieldfares and redwings, part of the thrush family, arrive to find food on the berried bushes in gardens and

Swallows

hedgerows. In recent winters there has been an influx of waxwings in both Wall and the Humshaugh area. These brightly coloured winter visitors make a most attractive display as they work their way steadily through a feast of berries. Regarding summer visitors, it is generally accepted through most of the country that populations of many are declining. This is the case in our area too. Many factors are contributing to this; climate change in Sub-Saharan Africa could be one of them, along with weather and farming changes in the UK. There are fewer swallows, swifts and house martins due partly to a lack of nesting sites. The sound of the cuckoo call, once common, seems to have gone from the fell. Spotted flycatchers, redstarts, wheatears, tree pipits, whitethroats and wood warblers, which all nested locally either no longer do so or very rarely.

It may seem that farming practices have been responsible for many of the changes in bird life in and around our village. As we know, that is certainly not the sole reason, rather just one factor among many. There may not be cuckoos, corncrakes or skylarks, but there are buzzards, collared doves, nuthatches and chiff-chaffs. In the last sixty years when bird habitats and life have been observed by Ray and John, there have been many changes, but that will always be so. Birds are, even now, many and varied around us. For those who are interested, they play a large part in our natural history, with the early spring birdsong and the summer evening song of the thrush being so evocative of the countryside in which we live.

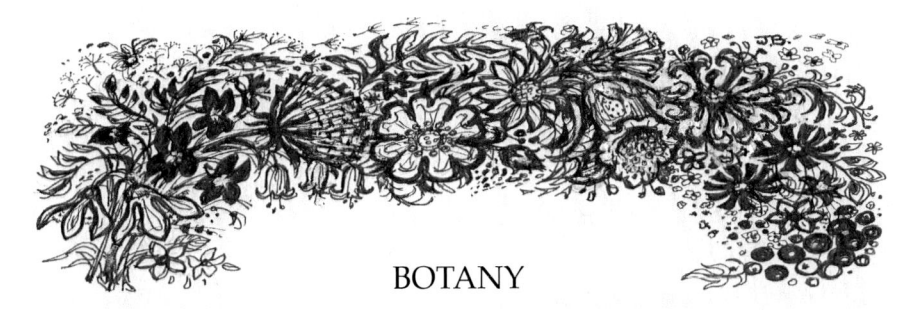

BOTANY

The areas surrounding Wall village are essentially fields, fells and woodland, therefore there is a potential for a variety of wildflowers to grow and flourish. In the past the greens and roadside verges were not as regularly cut and trimmed as they are today. Hay meadows were allowed to stand for a while in summer so allowing a rich crop of meadow flowers. Despite the changes which have come for the walker with an eye for them, there are still places where the flowering sights of spring and summer can be enjoyed.

SNOWDROPS - Patricia Gillespie

A sense of snow
hangs in the folds
of winter clothes,
in the elbow crease
of bleached reeds -
as the husk of a life
might be.

There's your green face
on the other side
of the mirror:
braids of chickweed
and bitter cress
in the well of spring water -
a pulse of recognition
in the centre of your palm.
As we pass along the way,
we meet you
by the light of elm flowers,
in the drift of willow fronds.

At the souk of El Khamadier,
they roll out bales
of Damascene silk.
A carpet of snowdrops
in the Roman wood
is the only garment you have -
legions of pearls and deep green bling.
Such a haunting in the sound
of this embroidery.

There is no stopping their advance.
They are up on their knees,
tugging your skirts of
gorse and daffodil,
begging you to dance.

Looking at things another way:
isn't it strange
how life always brings you
simple gifts, when you
just seem to need a dash
of polka?

> When we lie like Lilliputians
> on the earth
> we gaze into a galaxy
> of lime green stars.

A walk in the New Lane in early spring brings the delightful sight of snowdrops, a carpet under the woodland which edges the lane, followed later by delicate wood anemones. A memory which lingers from 1970 is of long time Wall residents Peggy and Jack Seaby. Jack, being a churchwarden, collecting the rich green moss which grows on the stone walls of the New Lane, to make the Easter Garden for St George's church. The hedges in spring give the first sight of blackthorn blossom followed later by may blossom. In early summer the New Lane verges produce a riot of drifting white as queen anne's lace dances and wafts in the breeze, and for the fortunate person, with sharp eyes, there is a patch of field scabious hidden amongst it, a reminder of how many of our country roadside verges used to be. The Hadrian's Wall Trail now passes down the New Lane. For those of us who just enjoy wandering along its length, it seems the walkers are often more intent on reaching their destination than stopping to listen to the gushing water or gaze over a wall at wild flowers.

The Old Lane offers another delightful walk, less used as a vehicle short cut than the New Lane, it allows more uninterrupted time to just stand and stare at the verges, the fell and the view from the seat looking down to Chollerford bridge and the river. It is a good place to rest and enjoy the peace of a lane walked and brambled by so many, over the years. As the name suggests, this was the original lane used by residents of St Oswald's and the surrounding area, to reach the village and the school, and also by the villagers attending church at St Oswald's long before St George's church was built. One of the later residents of Planetrees Cottage, the cottage at the top of the Old Lane, was the Ballantyne family.

Mr Ballantyne was manager for Planetrees Farm and within the family there was a deep love of nature and the countryside in which they lived and worked. It is entirely due to that love of nature that we have an amazing record of the flora of the Old Lane as it was thirty years ago. Mrs Connie Ballantyne* and her daughter Heather often walked the lane with their dog. During these walks in spring and summer they collected wild flowers and pressed them, and Heather still has that book with the flowers and their names. It is a truly wonderful record of the plants that grew and flourished along the verges of the Old Lane. Following is the list as Heather gave it to me.

Coltsfoot, crosswort, cowslip, buttercup, primrose, fat hen, sorrel, forget-me-not, thistle, tufted vetch, purple dead nettle, lady's smock, agrimony, white and red clover, dog rose, cow parsley, daisy, ox-eye daisy, ground elder, meadow sweet, yarrow, stitchwort, chickweed, goose grass, white dead nettle, solomon's seal, bindweed, lady's tresses, poppy, dandelion, ferns, nettles, dock, milkwort, bladderwort, ragged robin, shepherd's purse, red campion, snowdrop, celandine, foxglove, brambles, gorse, broom, rose, for rose hips, a rhododendron bush at the top of the lane and finally the gooseberry bush which probably arrived courtesy of a passing bird, or perhaps it was just put there, for village babies to be found underneath! There may have been more, but this is an extensive list and was made before farming land and verges were managed, in the way they are now. Wild flowers were there in plenty and a hand-picked bunch in a vase on the table brought the countryside into the house, and spoke of summer. Just one of those things that can't be done now! I leave it to the reader to wander the Old Lane and see what is left from 30 years ago. Sadly the overflowing stream probably washed some species away so the list may not be quite so extensive.

The fells overlooking the village grow gorse. Along Spouty Lonnen in spring, violets peep, and in the late summer bettony and later brambles can be found. In autumn time a familiar sight in the village was Eva Bowman coming back with her gathering of blackberries, which she had collected for someone in the village. She knew where to find the biggest and the best.

Moving towards the lower fields on the river side of Wall, there is Primrose Hill, named by villagers for very obvious reasons. Sadly it is no longer accessible as it forms part of grazing and farm land, but it must have been a pretty sight in springtime. When the railway came through the valley the embankments provided a rich habitat for wild flowers. Following the closure of the line the old track area supported red campion, cow parsley, speedwell, wild strawberry, willow herb, buttercup, groundsel, dock, nettles, clover, wild rose, vetch and bedstraw, to name but a few. Gradually as the track has become more overgrown with bushes, or in some places more used as farm land, the quantity and variety of flowers has decreased.

April into May is the time to pass through Wall on the A6079. Approaching the village from the north, the back village green is awash with a host of golden daffodils which sweep down towards the centre of the village. At the back of the green was a wild flower area planted as one of the millennium projects, now no longer. In spring a carpet of white snowdrops line the track to the old school. A memory held dear by Daphne, a past Wall school pupil, is that of gathering a posy of wild purple and white violets from the school wood to take home for her mother. They are still in the wood for bright eyes to see!

Parallel with Brunton Bank the Hadrian's Wall Trail runs through the coppice which was once part of Fred Henderson's farm land. Pat Rowell lived on the other side of the road, and for those who remember, she was a dedicated gardener. She planted the roadside verges every year, causing motorists to slow down and view the spectacle of colour she produced. Whatever was left over, or later in the season was pulled out, she threw over the wall on the other side of the road. That was long before the walkers passed through the wood. Now it is possible to find dormant seeds popping up, and a variety of unexpected flowers appearing, so giving a mix of garden and woodland flowers growing in harmony. In spring walkers are greeted with a woodland display of snowdrops.

Opposite the Hadrian Hotel clouds of pink blossom float on the cherry trees, and should the wind blow, a carpet of pink covers the ground. At each end of the village a stone plant trough and sign tells the traveller they are entering and passing through Wall. The troughs are planted and maintained by the Parish Council and those who volunteer to help, providing an attractive and cheerful focal point for Wall. Lately the pant in the village, now no longer a supply of water, has been turned into a floral display.

Perhaps it is that these days in our more managed way of living in the country, there is a longing for the flowers that not only 'bloom in the spring', but in the summer too, and if they are not in wild abundance, then the answer is to choose to cultivate. In summer hedgerow and garden flowers welcome the bees and butterflies of the insect world. It is due to a lifetime of observation by Ray Craig, that there is some record of the butterflies that were in the Wall area and of those that are the newcomers.

*Jasper Rootham was a neighbour of Connie Ballantyne and wrote this poem between 1975 and 1978. It adds another flower into the list of wild flowers in the Old Lane.

CONNIE
>Good as bread
>true as steel
>slow to wound
>and quick to heal.
>
>Brave as any lioness
>should some ruffian threaten dread.
>Wife and nannie,
>mother, grannie,
>prop and stay to all she knows.
>
>I lift my glass to bonnie Connie
>thornless sweet Northumbrian rose.

BUTTERFLIES AND BEES

Fragile they may look, but butterflies are survivors, for some varieties travel many hundreds of miles to their breeding or feeding grounds. Food and climate change are the two main factors which have altered the behaviour of some of our British butterflies. For many butterflies there are specific plants which they need as a food source, and if there is a disturbance in that particular plant, or tree, then the cycle of that butterfly will fail. This was most noticeable during the time of severe Dutch elm disease.

White letter hairstreak and comma butterflies need elm leaves for their larvae. Fortunately with elms recovering, these butterfly populations now have a chance of growing. Dark green fritillary caterpillars begin to feed on the leaves of violets in March, the chrysalis develops at the base of the violet plant in June and the butterfly hatches out during July, living for about six weeks. During this short time its main source of food are thistle flowers. There are still violets growing in the school wood but the old railway line and embankments with wild violets growing alongside thistle plants gave the ideal place to find the dark green fritillary butterfly, flitting from thistle head to thistle head. Again changes have come to their habitat and as in many parts of the country, this species has gone. The fate of the meadow brown, the butterfly of meadow and roadside verges, hangs in the balance due to the silage harvest and council verge trimming.

The old quarries provided good butterfly habitat before they became overgrown. The Low Brunton limestone was carpeted with bird's foot trefoil and held one of the largest colonies of dingy skippers in the county, as well as common blue, wall brown and small copper. The latter three species can still be seen in the area in small numbers. All is not pessimistic however, for with climate change more species are moving north and so butterflies, which once were rare, are now part of the summer scene in and around Wall. Along the river, the riverside oaks host colonies of purple hairstreak.

Newcomers over the last twenty years are peacock, comma, white letter hairstreak, speckled wood, orange tip, large and small skipper, holly blue and ringlet, and gradually the spread of these has grown further north to join with the migrant red admiral and painted lady. The small tortoiseshell, large, small and green veined whites are probably our local, most familiar butterflies, the large white's larvae bringing destruction in the vegetable garden, the vegetable gardener's menace!

Many butterflies rely on wild flowers which possess a good supply of nectar, so areas where wild field scabious, knapweed, thistle, ox-eye daisy, clover, vetch, wild carrot and meadowsweet grow, will attract these visitors. So many of these areas which flourished around Wall have now gone. The good news is that nettles flourish and these provide the leaves on which the migrating red admirals lay their eggs in spring. Later in June the hairy caterpillars of the peacock will feed on nettle leaves and later still in the year small tortoiseshell often find a roosting place on the underside of a nettle leaf. Though considered a 'weed' the nettle is a valuable plant to be encouraged rather than sprayed or mown. For the gardener wishing to attract butterflies there is no better sight than a buddleia bush on a sunny, summer day with a host of red admirals, peacocks, small tortoiseshells and any other passing butterfly that is attracted to the nectar possibilities.

Butterflies enhance the countryside and gardens and though now there are not the areas, remembered by older Wall residents, that grew wild flowers in abundance, there are still two lanes, some wooded areas, some field edges, the fell and several private individuals who are actively encouraging insects of all varieties into their gardens and farms by the selective planting of insect friendly plants. Like birds, the population of butterflies and other insects is an indication of how rich the natural environment in and around Wall is in providing the best habitats to support these species.

There are many insects which we see in and around our homes and gardens. Flies, due possibly to the changes in farming, seem to have decreased. In the past in summer, when out for a walk, it was always useful to have a stick or branch to swot away the flies which continually buzzed around the head; however, one of the delights of that season must be to welcome bees into our gardens. There is something fascinating in watching a bumble bee carefully move from flower head to flower head until it finds exactly the right one. There are several varieties of bumble bee and these are determined by size and markings, but all of them have that rounded furry body which looks so comfortable resting on a flower. The worker bees, however, come from the beehives that are in and around the village. From times past until now, local people have kept bees, but the most notable person was Dr Rachel Lowther of The Old School House. Rachel began keeping bees in a hive on the roof of her home in Jesmond before she, and her husband Maurice, moved into their new home in Wall. Here there was a garden and woods offering more space, and the number of hives eventually increased to fourteen. With Wall gardens, and those of the surrounding area full of flowers, the bees were able to find all the nectar they needed, supplemented once a year, by the hives being taken to the heather around Bellingham.

OLD SCHOOL HOUSE
HONEY
1lb
454g
FROM THE APIARY OF LOWTHER, OLD SCHOOL HOUSE, WALL, NORTHUMBERLAND.

The production of honey became a business for Rachel and was sold under the title of Old School House Honey from the Apiary of Lowther, Old School House, Wall, Northumberland. Not only was this a local business, but Rachel's interest and love of bees led her to become Chairman of the Hexham Beekeepers Association. Following her death, there has been held in October in Wall Village Hall, an annual Rachel Lowther Memorial Lecture. In 1999 when the children from our school in Humshaugh were working on the wall hanging and visiting places of interest in and around Wall, they spent an afternoon learning 'in situ' about the old school. Maurice, on their departure, gave each child a jar of Old School House honey. Sadly those hives and bees have now gone but the interest in bees is still there, as there are hives in the Brunton area, on Fallowfield Fell and a new resident of the Brunton area has been attending a bee-keeping course prior to keeping hives. There has been some concern over the decrease in the numbers of bees, but by growing the flora that attracts both bees and butterflies, and allowing the hedgerows and waysides to flourish, perhaps there will be a change for the better.

TREES AND WOODS

Surrounding Wall Village are areas of wooded land set amongst the fields and also trees growing on the sites of the old quarries. Wherever the eyes look trees will be seen, some planted, and others self sown. Woods appear on the Ordnance Survey map with particular names, or none, but some are known to Wall villagers by local names and names that have been created by young village children as they roamed, played and had adventures in them, back in the times when it was safe to do such things.

It is hard to imagine that until about the 1960s the fell behind the village had very few trees. The children played on the rocks and there are several stories of how mothers waved white handkerchiefs from their doorways as far away as the main road .The appropriate child would then know they were supposed to return home! That could not happen now as it is impossible to have a view of the village in the way it used to be.

Travelling down Brunton Bank, the old Black Pasture sandstone quarry and the Brunton limestone quarry are home to ash, sycamore, birch and an occasional poplar and pine. Following the closure of these quarries most of the trees to be found there have seeded themselves and are an indication that they are comfortable in those situations. Black Pasture quarry has been through a programme of reclamation following more recent quarrying and more planting has taken place. Both Black Pasture and Brunton quarries are in private ownership.

Running alongside Brunton Bank is the long coppice of mixed trees through which the Hadrian's Wall Trail passes. This wood contained many elms, but when Dutch elm disease was rife they were felled. During the Second World War it was a hiding place for the storage of ammunition. Recently an army ordnance team closed off the trail and began a search for any remaining buried weaponry, which they placed in the adjacent field. Most of the metal retrieved was scrap, which the army took away, but there were two items which were detonated in the field, one giving a very loud explosion! The trees offer a canopy for the walkers and there are some interesting tree roots which need to be negotiated, crossing the path.

The houses which border the new lane have many trees on their private land. Oak, beech, sycamore, ash, horse chestnut and firs all make up these mixed woodlands, some with long branches reaching across the lane and forming an archway with those on the other side.

North of the A6079 lies the disused Cocklaw quarry, and close by below it, is the Way Wood. This name seems to be a local one, and perhaps happened because there was a rail track from the nearby quarry down to the A6079. The wood consisted mainly of firs but, approximately twenty years ago felling took place in part of it, and the replanting was of a more varied nature.

East of Wall Village, and running down from Crag House on Fallowfield Fell is The Long Plantation. It was mainly a silver birch wood until in the last ten years some trees were felled and replanted with conifers. A village memory is of rhododendron bushes flowering in this wood.

The Scroggs lies between the south end of Wall and High Barns. The name is derived from Middle English and means 'Brushwood' and is a name associated with Northumberland. Could it have been that in times, long past, wood and twigs were collected from here to make 'Broom besoms'? Now it is a wood of oak trees, and not far away across the A6079, are more oaks in the locally known Pit Wood. On the Ordnance Survey map this is marked as Folly Plantation. The story goes that it was bought from the sale of The Chesters Estate in 1929, by a person unknown who planned to build a house on the land. He cut out the centre of the wood but the house was never built, hence it was a folly.

Upstream from Wall station and the mill is the wood known as the Sandy Plantation. It contains oak trees which have been coppiced and are remembered as just small trees in the 1950s. On this stretch of river to Chollerford Bridge there are two other small wooded areas. On the north west side of the A6079 leaving Wall there was another old quarry and lime kilns. After these were worked out self-sown trees grew, and the children of Wall found it an adventure playground. When Fred Thompson and his friends saw a roe deer in the wood it became known amongst the children as the Deer Wood.

These then are the main woodlands within the parish, and over many years they may have reformed, but the main varieties of trees has remained the same. Silver birch, ash, oak, beech, sycamore and now once again some elms are beginning to flourish. In and around the village are many single trees which have been planted. When the Clayton family lived at The Chesters and owned most of the surrounding countryside many beech trees were planted along the river banks, in the hedgerows and along the Hexham road out of Wall. Most of them have now gone, having died or been felled as unsafe. In the field on the west side, next to the Hadrian Hotel, were four large, mature horse chestnut trees giving a park like appearance to the field. Now only half of one remains the others having succumbed to old age. They were the climbing and conker trees for the children. In memory of their parents, Bill and Nancy Armstrong, who lived for many years along Warden View, their family have planted copper beech trees. They are on either side of the road approaching the village from the south. When fully mature they will give a colourful and large, leaf canopy, providing a most attractive approach to the village, thus replacing the trees that were felled. In some of the fields it is still possible to see solitary trees and these are limes, oaks, beech, yews and ash. Along the edge of the back green are five trees which seem to have grown rapidly during the last few years. There are four beech trees, one ash and also a young rowan.

So far no account has been given of the specially planted trees of which there are several. One oak which stands a little more than halfway up the Old Lane is known as Alex's Tree and appears on the Millennium Map produced by Mary Herdman.

Alex Mason was a neighbour of Joan Proudlock. One Wednesday in the early 1990s they both went to the village lunch. On the way home, going up the Old Lane, Alex asked Joan to stop the car. He pointed to an oak tree and told the story of how as a young boy he used the Old Lane to and from St Oswald's and Wall school. One day he had some acorns in his pocket. On the way home he took one out of his pocket and planted it, just to see if it would grow. It did, and for most of his ninety-two years he watched it grow. That tree is now over one hundred years old.

Quietly growing amongst the wild vegetation on the north east corner of the back green is another tree carrying the memory of a long time village resident. It is an oak, grown first as a sapling by Chris Allcock, then planted there, to remember the life of John Mitchell who went to school in the village, and who cared deeply about Wall where he lived and served the community in many ways, until his death in 2001.

The Coronation tree stands in the centre of the village. The original tree was an oak planted by the village to celebrate Queen Elizabeth's Coronation. Sadly the oak died and was replaced by another which also died. The third and present tree is a beech which has grown and spread, giving a canopy over the circular wooden seat which surrounds its girth. This seat is a memorial to the brother of a village resident. He died aged thirty-one following the terrorist attack on the Twin Towers in New York. Carved into the back of the seat on six panels is the following inscription, *"Steve Morris 1970-2001."* Honouring the life of someone very special who will always be remembered.

Near to the play area on the back green is a young flourishing copper beech, which is now thirteen years old. A plaque mounted on an adjacent post carries these words.

Wall Millennium Tree.
MM
Planted by the People of Wall within the First Moments of the New Millennium
MM
1 January 2000.

Chris Allcock, who served for several years as Chairman of the Parish Council was on top of the fell, waiting to hear the church bell ring out, before lighting the bonfire.

Chris composed this short poem. It seems appropriate to end Trees and Woods with his verse.

Young copper beech grow proud and tall
Look kindly on the folk of Wall.
We in our turn will care for thee
Our precious New Millennium Tree.

Chris Allcock 31 December 1999

WALL FIELD NAMES

Whilst researching the natural history of Wall some old field names were mentioned. These have now been added to. Many will only be known to long-time Wall residents.

Sandy Planting, The Houp, once known as The Hope, but local dialect has brought a change. 'Gannin doon the houp'! The Bog, The Flat Field, The Front Field, The Gate Field, The Back Field, The Far Field, The High Station, The Station Field, Chestnut Tree Field, Long Planting, Horse Pasture, Happy Valley, Barns Close, The Gallop, Fell Field, White Riggs, Bull Pasture, Little Bull Pasture, Crow Parks, Primrose Hill.

Adults and children walked and worked in these fields and so they gained the nicknames of association, Happy Valley being one. Could this bring some interesting memories to the surface!

MAMMALS

Squirrel

The word mammal encompasses many species ranging from farm animals through pets to large wild animals, small mammals and even the exotic alpacas of Fallowfield Fell. Wall and its environs are home to many animals but, like in the other areas of natural history, changes have come here too.

FARM ANIMALS

Farming has its own section in more detail elsewhere in the book and the changes in stock over the years has been recorded. Going back to 1929 and on into the war years Jack Wardle's farm, Planetrees, probably represents how most farms were, with regard to livestock. He kept cattle which were fattened for sale, four or five milking cows from which milk came for the home and the neighbours, along with some butter too. There were pigs which were housed in a big shed in the field behind the hayshed and house. Two of these were killed each year for home consumption whilst the rest went at about six to nine months, as fat pigs, for slaughter. There were a few sheep but Jack wasn't keen on keeping many. That was then. Now generally it seems that the milking herds have gone and any cattle to be seen are, as Jack's were, probably being grown on for meat. Sheep seem to be in the majority and are to be seen in many of the fields in and around Wall. In springtime a great attraction at St Oswald's Farm and Tearoom is for visitors to see the new-born lambs in the farm shed and John Reay caring for them.

Nick Robinson who farms out of East Cocklaw and has fields bordering both the New Lane and the Military Road has both sheep and cattle as do John Lamb and Peter Heslop.

Looking at the sheep in the fields around Wall, there are Blackface and Swaledale mule crosses, Blue Face Leicesters, Texel crosses and Suffolk crosses. Holstein, Charolais, Aberdeen Angus, Limousin and Belgian Blues. These make up most of the cattle on the local farms. It may appear there is more emphasis now on crops than in the past and this will undoubtedly be down to the particular terrain, financial productivity, and ultimately the choices available to the farmer in order to keep the small farms viable in difficult times. Nevertheless there is much to be said for the sight of a field full of sheep and lambs or cattle and calves and around Wall they are still there.

PET ANIMALS

Before moving on to wild animals there must be a place in this to record three notable village pets. There were cats, dogs, rabbits, guinea pigs, budgies, goldfish and horses, all belonging through time to village residents. George Lamb had a collection of show rabbits, but when it came to designing the Millennium Wall Hanging, now in the village hall, the three animals to represent the pets of Wall could only be Ziggy, Sam and Lucky.

Ziggy was a black labrador who came to the Herdman family when he was thirteen months old. This was his third home and he was a nervous dog. He joined Ben, an elderly yellow labrador, who soon settled him in to the ways of life in both his new home and Wall Village. Soon Ziggy became a familiar sight as he went for walks and accustomed himself to living on the green. Whilst out walking one day he met Sam and from then on a canine relationship developed as they lived on opposite sides of the village green. It was based on a respect for each other's territorial rights!

Sam was a westie whose grandmother had been a champion at Crufts. He belonged to the Mitchell family who lived on the east side of the green opposite the church. John Mitchell travelled to Jesmond for his work. Often he passed an old couple with a little white dog which John stroked and jokingly said, "Whenever you don't want him, give him to me". One day they did, and Sam arrived in Wall. The green near his home became Sam's territory and he was known to grumble at folk he didn't like when they encroached on it. He followed John wherever he went and that included the church and he 'sang' loudly whenever the church bell rang. Ziggy, a large black dog, and Sam, a small white one were easily recognised in the village and became favourites to be seen on most days. They both lived out their lives as loved family members, fore-runners of the many dogs which live in Wall today.

Lucky was a white pony that came to Wall and became well known and loved. This is her story as told by Lorraine Bewley (neé Henderson) of North Farm.

In 1977 John Huddleston arrived back from a pony sale at Hexham Auction Mart with a little scrap of a grey foal, very young. She wasn't much bigger than a German Shepherd dog. John brought her to North Farm where my Dad, Fred, was milking cows and told us the story of how he had really wanted to buy the mare and foal as the mother was a nice type, but he was outbid by a dealer who was buying up ponies to fill a lorry to go to the continent for horse meat. John tried his best to buy the mare and foal from the dealer at his lorry but he wouldn't sell him the mare but he did manage to rescue the foal. There followed a big discussion as to how to feed the foal which was only used to drinking milk from its mother. I offered to wean my foal William, who had for a year been using his mother Violet Elizabeth, as a milk-bar. We could then try to get the young foal, which already we had named Lucky, to try and drink from Violet Elizabeth; quite a stretch for the little foal as her new mother was taller than her birth mother. I will always remember the look on Violet's face when she saw this tiny creature taking milk from her. She was not amused, it was not love at first sight, but after a few days and with persuasion Violet accepted the way things were going to be. Lucky thrived and eventually was put out to grass on the green where she was tethered on a long line and 'mowed' the grass. When the time came she was broken in for riding and became a firm favourite of village folk and local children, the latter sometimes fortunate to have a ride!"

LARGE WILD MAMMALS

When using the word large, the largest mammal in the Wall area is a deer. Roe deer inhabit the more wooded areas surrounding the village but can often be seen as they move around the fell, occasionally coming into a garden. St Oswald's and the areas around Black Pasture quarry coming further down to the old Brunton quarry are again places where roe deer can be seen.

Badgers, which once used to be a rarity, now have sets in the out-by secluded places and seem to be flourishing whilst the debate between cattle farmers and naturalists goes on. Those who have watched the TV programmes, Spring and Autumn Watch, will know how entertaining a badger watch can be. Many years ago an American naturalist friend of a village family longed to see badgers, and was able to spend an evening in the locality with them watching these creatures. She took a very special memory back home of badgers, both young and mature at their set.

Badger

On down to the river, and there is always the possibility of seeing that wonderful line of bubbles, which indicates the presence of an otter. Otters are there, but only the lucky few have seen them. Due to them working the river there has been a definite decrease in the number of mink which roamed the river banks causing destruction to fish and wildlife.

Stoats, weasels, hares and rabbits are the commonest of the smaller mammals in this group. It seems that most people's gardens suffer at some time from the rampant rabbit population. Two natural enemies of the rabbit are the fox and the stoat but it seems even they cannot keep down the numbers of rabbits which live and breed in the area.

Lamping controls some of the population. For many people rabbits were, and are a good source of real country food. To others they are the greedy garden eaters that we enjoy 'MacGregorising'(Beatrix Potter, The Tale of Peter Rabbit. Pub Warne).

The mention of fox is always controversial, but there is no disputing this is a proud, sleek and beautifully coloured animal. In times past the Tynedale Hunt met at St Oswald's and on the back green in Wall, and had a number of followers from the village who would trail the hunt in cars. Time has brought changes to this country sport. To the owner of hens and other poultry, a fox can cause devastation in a very short time. There certainly are foxes around the Brunton and quarry areas and along the fell, and it is left now to those with the means, to deal with them, when necessary.

Stoat

Stoats roam about too and can be an entertaining sight as recounted by this resident. She happened to look out of her window and there was a stoat with four young playing on the gravel and in the flower beds. As she watched the adult stoat left the youngsters to play. They were jumping from wire netting protecting a large, round stone planter onto the tall stem of a foxglove plant, swinging around on the stem, losing their grip and falling backwards onto the gravel. Each stoat was taking turns whilst chasing each other under and around a log pile. It was obvious they were so excited by this new 'play park'until mother returned and collected them to continue their travels. This fascinating episode lasted for at least fifteen minutes, and it can only be assumed that mother stoat had found a nearby bush under which to snooze and have a rest from her very boisterous family!

When writing about mammals mention must be made of the demise of the red squirrel. Leading up to the millennium there was a significant population of these endearing animals in the area of the New Lane and Brunton Bank. They came to garden bird feeders and gave great pleasure to those watching their antics. The ladies of the Wall Hanging group met at Joan Proudlock's home, Blossom Hill, during February and March of 2000 and enjoyed up to five red squirrels running along the garden wall to feed. On the celebration day when the Wall Hanging was unveiled Joan was able to announce the arrival that morning of baby reds brought to the feeders for the first time by their mother. Sadly this did not last, for in the next few years the red squirrels disappeared and the greys have now taken their place. Despite efforts to curtail the numbers of the introduced greys, there are only now rare sightings of our beautiful and natural residents.

SMALL MAMMALS

The small mammals list is, mice, bats, voles, shrews, rats, hedgehogs and moles. Most of these are to be found in our gardens, buildings or hedgerows. We see the evidence of mole activity in the grassy areas approached from the north into Wall. From time to time war is waged upon these intruders. However unwelcome this activity is, in gardens they do turn the earth and produce fine soil!

A small mammal Capture and Release evening session, in a local garden, established that wood mice, bank voles and common shrews were abundant, and this could be assumed to be the same in any garden bordering on fields and woodland. Rats, as we know, live within reach of us all, and are not often seen, but when found to be present are a concern; then the answer is the local pest controller. Hedgehogs are to be welcomed and encouraged into gardens and it is a privilege to find them as residents, as they are useful eaters of many garden pests. Leaving piles of sticks and leaves in autumn provides a good hibernation site for these prickly but engaging mammals. To many people bats are just bats, associated with Hallowe'en and therefore scary. Fortunately, at the present time, there is an expert on bats living in our area.

Tina Wiffen has supplied the following valuable information which gives an assessment of bat activity likely to be found in Wall and its environs.

'There are records for a large common pipistrelle and a large soprano pipistrelle roost in Wall. Common pipistrelle bats are probably the most frequently seen locally. I know of roosts in Humshaugh, Chollerford, Low Brunton, Acomb and Warden. Soprano pipistrelle are widespread too, and there is a big roost at Chollerford. Daubenton's bats feed low over water and though I don't know of any roosts locally, I have regularly seen them at Chollerford, and there is a record of a dead one at Waterside Farm which was sent to VLA (Veterinary Laboratories Agency for DEFRA) for analysis, possibly indicating there is an undiscovered roost in the vicinity. Noctule bats also feed over the river at Chollerford and have been recorded at Walwick. I would expect them over Wall, on the river, over pastureland and any where with big beetles. They especially like cockchafers and dung beetles. Whiskered bats and Brandt's bats are hard to tell apart. I have taken in a downed, whiskered bat from Humshaugh and there is a record of a dead one sent to VLA also from Humshaugh. Natterer's bats are supposed to roost in Humshaugh church but will also be in the wider area whilst brown long-eared bats roost at Chollerford and in Warden church. These bats are hard to detect in flight but are known to be widespread and common in rural areas'.

Bats

Tina's research and knowledge has given for the first time an overview of what species of bat might be found in and around Wall for those who might go out at dusk on a bat hunt. As a final note, a resident of High Brunton, living in a house with a small stone porch, experienced a bat encounter.

One summer evening she was sitting on her bedroom windowsill, with the window open, reading. All at once she heard noises; shuffle shuffle PLOP, shuffle

shuffle PLOP. Out, from between two stones in the porch wall came bats one after the other. When at a later date she counted them from the start of their evening flight, she counted one hundred and thirty seven. They hung, tightly packed, along the walls of the porch and as each one moved and shuffled along and plopped out of the crack, it made room for the next. They were identified as common pipistrelle bats. During all the activity associated with a porch and front door they were never seen during the day, and they caused no disturbance.

To conclude this chapter, it would seem, that despite the many changes which have taken place, it is encouraging to discover that our village and the rural areas surrounding it, are still able to provide an environment where wildlife of all descriptions can flourish, giving us, and hopefully those to come pleasure and enjoyment.

CHAPTER FIVE
OUR INDUSTRIES TRADES SHOPS AND SERVICES

For many years the most prominent industry in the parish of Wall was quarrying. Many of the village men worked in the local quarries of Black Pasture, Brunton and Cocklaw and also in the mine on Fallowfield. In and around Wall there were the farms, all requiring workers. The large houses in the area needed staff, cooks, maids, gardeners and certainly some of Wall's residents, such as Ella Mason and Dorothy Charlton filled those roles. Herdman's North Tyne Implement Works employed staff, local men worked at Wall Station and when Willie Proudlock started up his garage in 1929 local men were employed there too. Then there were the shops, many and varied. There was not much that couldn't be bought in Wall, in past times.

In this chapter we look back but also see how Wall's working life has changed and developed into a more locally tourist led industry. The hospitality that Audrey Huddleston first demonstrated with her bed and breakfast has expanded into a growing capitalisation on the asset, integral both to our village name and our surrounding area, Hadrian's Wall.

THE GEOLOGY AND WORKINGS OF OUR QUARRIES AND MINES
Chris Allcock

The strata beneath Wall in its surrounding area are sedimentary rocks typical of the western edge of the great North East coalfield. They belong to the Lower Carboniferous period of 345-280 milllion years ago when England lay nearer to the equator and comprised warm shallow waters, huge river deltas, swamps and rain forests.

Rainwater and floods carried debris from older high ground where it settled and compressed in the calmer water conditions, the depth varying as the earth's surface rose and fell under the action of continuous volcanic periods. The earth's crust moved inexorably but continuously as Europe gradually wandered further northward. In the ice ages, ending a mere 10,000 years ago, glacial and river erosion scoured away huge depths of overlying strata, leaving our landscape much as we see it today.

A diagonal 'knife-cut' through the strata would reveal a multi-layered sandwich of freestone (sandstone), limestone, shale and, in our vicinity, thin seams of coal, all tilted eastwards. Of these, mainly the freestone and limestone were exploited by our ancestors and the scars of many old workings are still visible throughout the area.

FREESTONE QUARRIES

The parish landscape must have hundreds of sites where freestone has been extracted but the small indentations go unnoticed, long since concealed by nature. From early man, through the Bronze and Iron Ages and through to the present, stone has been quarried to build shelter and protection, boundary wall and homes. It was extracted as close to (and preferably from higher ground) the structure as possible to minimise transport effort. Larger settlements and improved road transport demanded larger excavations and the creation of quarrying as an industry. Masons became skilled at shaping the stone.

Around Wall, two bands of particularly substantial rock, free from shale bands and capable of yielding large blocks, have been quarried for over 2,000 years; the upper band covers the tops of Wall and Fallowfield Fells, outcropping most obviously over the higher ground. The Romans obtained much stone from this source – Written Crag is clear evidence thanks to Flavius Carantinus whose carved name is now in the Chesters Museum. The lower, thicker freestone band is found in Black Pasture Quarry on Brunton Bank and as the exposed crag at the top of the Old Lane. It, too, was quarried by the Romans for their constructions down to the Tyne.

BLACK PASTURE QUARRY

This stone matches material down to and at the side of the Chesters Bridge Abutment. With the departure of the Romans the quarry would be generally dormant until the expansion of the Chesters Estate. Their masons worked the stone for local use until it became in greater demand through the 18th and 19th centuries. In about 1900, Herbertsons of Galashiels acquired the quarry and greatly expanded the site.

The stone was blasted with black powder, a gentler explosive which would not cause shattering. The aim was to obtain large blocks of well over one ton but there was a huge amount of unsuitable stone, evidenced by large waste heaps. Much of the stone had small iron-stone inclusions which limited its use in the most prestigious buildings but it nevertheless was very sound and used extensively in local villages and towns. A great deal of the best stone was transported to Scotland by rail. Amazingly, the North British Railway trucks were hauled by steam engines along a full width track which zigzagged from the main line sidings at Cocklaw Kilns up into the quarry. Legend has it that there were a number of 'incidents'!

Some of the large blocks were cut and dressed where there was ample waterflow at The Saws, on one of the shunting sites below Brunton Limestone Quarry. There the 'back and forth' method was used with long saw blades of hardened steel, which were regularly re-sharpened at North Tyne Implement Works in Wall. Some of these old blades could still be seen at the works until its closure in 1998.

In addition to workers from Wall and local farms, many came from Acomb where the Fallowfield mining was declining. They established the footpath via the Craig and past the front of Planetrees Farm; ultimately the route became a public footpath. At its peak about 120 men were employed but the workforce declined rapidly around 1914 – many of the men enlisted for the 'adventure' of the Great War. The quarry effectively closed in 1919, until the late 1930s when the Air Ministry contractors removed thousands of tons of quarry waste for the construction of Ouston Aerodrome now Albermarle Barracks.

Small-scale occasional working resumed in 1990 when large blocks were mechanically eased out and transported by road to Scotland – raw material for matching originally-used stone in restoration work. Black Pasture Quarry has now been returned to woodland. The old quarry woodland and all access to it is privately owned.

PLANETREES QUARRY

This is a freestone quarry about half a mile from Black Pasture. It is believed to have been worked by Hexham RDC in conjunction with the underlying Cocklaw limestone quarry. Transport of stone was by self-acting incline. Using gravity, a 'set' of loaded tubs pulled up the empties by means of a long wire cable; there was an automatic passing place half-way and control was by a large hand-operated brake drum at the top. This was mainly used by the limestone quarry.

THE ROMAN WALL (AS A QUARRY)

It is almost inevitable that, shortly after the Romans left Britain, the Wall began to be plundered for building stone and in effect became a quarry. The uniform dimensions of the facing stones were ideal for the construction of houses and farm buildings and examples can be seen to this day. Locally, St Oswald's Farm is comprised of many such stones and old photographs show that heather-thatched cottages in Wall (demolished when St George's Church was built) were built almost entirely from this source. Remote sections of the Wall were saved from plundering because of the difficulty of transport and because there was little habitation. Milecastles, turrets and forts were rich sources of large and intricately-carved stones. The historical value of the Wall was not appreciated until late in the 18th century when early historians endeavoured to start protecting what remained of it.

LIMESTONE QUARRIES

A bed of 30-40ft of the Great Limestone outcrops extensively across Wall Parish. It rises gradually from the North Tyne (below Walwick Grange), crosses the A6079 beside the lay-by north of Wall, along the line of the New Lane to High Brunton and onward to Stagshaw and beyond. Quarry workings occur almost continuously along this outcrop, evidenced by the lime kilns, many of which have disappeared. One very fine large example exists in its entirety near Brunton Quarry; another, smaller and more typical, is at Cocklaw Quarry.

There is little doubt that the Romans were the first to exploit this stone to produce burnt lime for use as lime mortar, a strong durable bonding agent, in building the Wall, turrets, etc. It is probable that the New Lane was created by progressive workings of the easily-won outcrop.

BRUNTON QUARRY

The quarry face of early workings can be seen running northward from the buildings at High Brunton. The Alston Limestone Company leased and developed the quarry in 1922 and purchased it in the Chesters sale in 1929. They developed the quarry extensively, first burning the stone in kilns beside The Saws (see above); the lime was delivered in tubs down a self-acting incline straight downhill to a main line siding north of the cricket field. The kiln complex near Brunton Quarry was also used for transport of lime by road.

In 1926 an aerial ropeway was installed to take crushed stone to the extensive Cocklaw siding complex of kilns, crushing and milling plant and tarmacadam plant.

Thus the finished products were loaded directly into the North British Railway trucks for delivery throughout south Northumberland.

The handsome triple lime kilns at Cocklaw sidings were built in the late 1800s and used until about 1912. They were reopened in 1939 to produce burnt lime for fertilizer. For air raid precaution reasons they were screened by the erection of a corrugated iron structure. Planners decreed that the kilns be screened from view. Sadly they can no longer be seen from the road.

About 21 men were employed – 15 at the quarry and 6 at Cocklaw sidings – most coming from Wall and the immediate area. The quarry was closed in 1966 when the then owners, Amalgamated Roadstone Corporation, transferred the workforce to the newly opened limestone quarry at Mootlaw near Ryal. For a short time Hexham RDC used the quarry void for landfill but they were evicted for wrongly tipping household waste which continually burned and attracted vermin. Thereafter it was used by Mr Nicholson for charcoal burning, a timber works and as a small-holding.

Kiln Rigg Cottage was originally a pair of quarrymen's cottages built in the early 1800s. Left to decay in the mid 1960s, they were resurrected as a home in 1979.

COCKLAW QUARRY

An extensive deep cut into the hillside directly uphill from Cocklaw Kilns, it was worked by Hexham RDC for the production of roadstone and tarmacadam. They were the original operators of the coating plant. Stone was brought downhill on a self-acting incline. The large brake drum at the top is still in situ in the 21st century. It was closed in the late 1930s because of the large depth of overlying shale and competition from large local whinstone quarries.

Mineral rights are owned by Allendale Estates. A recent application to reopen the quarry was acknowledged by Northumberland County Council. Due to a law dating back to 1948 the right to rework the quarry will not cease until 2032.

COLLIERIES

Wall Pit - Wall Pit was a small drift mine (ie tunnel entry) above Spouty Lonnen, which was worked from 1848 to 1855. Very small output from a thin seam; the coal was used and sold locally. The collapsed and overgrown entry can still be seen.

North Tyne Colliery - Sited alongside the railway south of Wall Mill, it was the largest mine near Wall and employed about 20 men. The spoil heap can still be seen from the road, covered in dense silver birch trees. It was operated by Walton & Cowper and closed in 1921.

Wall Mill Drift Mine - About 20 yards south of Wall Mill, this was a drift mine which worked in the late 19th century. Until about 1926 the drift mouth remained open and the decaying timber supports were visible. The spoil heap ran down to the millrace.

St Oswald's Mine - The site of a small mine entry can be seen in a field below St Oswald's Church. There is very little spoil so it was probably a failed venture.

Fallowfield Fell - Across the extensive slope of Fallowfield Fell are about 18 small shafts which led to a honeycomb of coal working driven from Fallowfield Dene. Shaft-head masonry can be seen at only one and all are now merely about 8ft diameter grassed-over depressions. The shafts would have been for mine ventilation, easy access to the workings and for delivery of timber supports. These coal workings were not connected to the lead mines in Fallowfield Dene.

Fallowfield Dene Mineral Mine - Although not within the boundary of Wall, this was an important and extensive lead mine, reaching a depth of some 600ft. When the lead was depleted the mine continued for the extraction of associated minerals, barites and witherite. Both are compounds of lead and were used mainly in paint and the paper-works in Tyneside. The mine closed in the 1930s.

Quarrying and mining were important activities over hundreds of years, providing employment for many local men. The landscape of Wall would have been much more industrial, than now in the 21st century. Restoration was not imposed on, or practised, by any of the operators but happily nature has healed nearly all of the old scars.

FARMING

Ours is a very rural parish. Farming has always been an important industry. It is a mixture of arable with cattle and sheep on the lower ground, and less arable, some cattle and more sheep in the higher areas.

Over the years there have been changes. In the middle of the 20th century, there were several dairy farms, three of them within the boundaries of the village. Dairy farming was intensive work. Cows were brought in and milked twice daily, 365 days a year. And the milk tankers came at eight o'clock in the morning! The dairy farms closed in the 1980s as they were no longer viable. The cattle we see now are for beef production.

Farming methods have also been updated. We no longer see sheaves of corn propped into stooks to be taken on trailers to the stackyard for the straw and grain to be separated by the thresher. Today the combine harvester does the job. Grass was once mowed, left to dry into hay then piled into pikes before being taken on bogies to be stacked in the farmyard. These were superseded by bales of hay. An earlier crop is silage which is now in plastic bags.

Arable farming has changed too. There are still fields of wheat, barley or oats, but gone are the potatoes and the turnips. Instead there is a newer crop. In spring we see the gaudy bright yellow of oilseed rape.

Over many years the people of Wall have enjoyed success in the show ring. After the Second World War, and for many years following, the Robinsons of West Cocklaw had (and still have) quite a reputation for breeding and showing Clydesdale horses and Bluefaced Leicester sheep. They won prizes all over the north east. In 2005 their ewe, Cocklaw Sparky, was supreme champion at the Royal Highland Show, along with their tup which was judged reserve champion. Cocklaw Sparky went on to further successes including being supreme champion at the Great Yorkshire Show. The Robinsons still continue to succeed with both horses and sheep but some of the outbuildings house another business. Suit-a-bility is a menswear hire company run by Kathryn and Elsie which has established itself for weddings and formal occasions. Quite an original and successful way of using farm buildings and diversifying!

George Lamb of Town Farm loved animals. He was a well-known breeder and exhibitor of Suffolk sheep. He started to keep his Suffolks in the 1940s and showed them at agricultural shows, including the County Show at Corbridge where he gained many first prizes. George was one of the early members of the Suffolk Sheep Society. In June 1993 he was awarded a Border Fine Arts Suffolk Sheep replica at the County Show in recognition of his achievements and contributions to the breed during his many years of service to the Suffolk Sheep Breeders' Society. George also bred and showed Dutch rabbits, various bantam hen breeds and modena pigeons. His greatest achievement with small animals was at the National Dutch Rabbit Show at Earl's Court in London where he won runner up to 'best in show' for two years running. Along with his rabbits, bantams, pigeons, ducks and even peacocks frequently featured in his farmyard.

In May 1989 the brother and sister team of Helen and David Woodcock (aged 14 and 17 respectively) of High Barns represented the Northumbrian Holstein Friesian Breeders Club at the Royal Show junior stock judging competition.

In the 1990s Dr Rachel Lowther of the Old School House was secretary of the Northumberland Beekeepers Association and chairman of the Hexham Beekeepers Association. She was a well-known exhibitor of honey and beeswax products.

At the end of the 20th century and into the 21st Mrs Marion McKechnie of Garden House bred British Saanen goats in her adjacent paddock. With her 'Echin Herd' she was often a winner in the Northern show fields. She went on to become secretary for the Northern Goats Society and a show judge. Marion has now left the village. Where her goats used to roam there are now Hebridean sheep. Alpacas are now to be seen at Fallowfield. Mike and Melanie Douglas breed these delightful animals. They are the subject of a separate article in this chapter.

As far as can be seen from the Ordnance Survey map and relying on the memories of local people there may have been as many as 21 farms in the parish. Some have ceased working now whilst others have continued, some having stayed in the same family for several generations. The farms are, Keepwick, East Cocklaw, West Cocklaw, Dunkirk, Low Brunton, North Farm, West Farm, Town Farm, High Barns, Fallowfield Farm, Crag House, Planetrees, St Oswald's Hill Head Farm, Codlaw Hill, Codlaw Dene, Wall Fell Farm, Errington Hill Head, Grottington, Beukley, Errington Red House and Errington.

This poem was written by a young Wall boy about the age of ten for St George's Harvest Festival in September 1996. He had talked with Alex Mason, who was born at St Oswald's Farm Cottage. As a young man Alex worked on farms. Later he followed his father to become a quarryman.

The harvest started in September when the corn was in its prime.

1920s Harvest
Stuart Proudlock
The binder came first to cut the corn
Pulled by two horses
Came out the bundles when it was shorn
Came the golden corn.

Five bundles of corn were needed for a stook
Left out in the September sun
Waiting, standing still.

At the hiring men were bought
For half a year's work.
£15.00 was what they sought
And lodging at the farm.

Horses were bought in
Draught or shire was what they were
From the market at two years old
Big and strong to do the work.

A man came to thresh the corn
With his big machine
Separated the grain and straw
Bags of grain up to sixteen stone
And stacks of straw at sixteen feet.

Sold at market, some of the grain
Sold to the merchants
Merchants of corn.

Reap the fields using a machine
Not the scythe as some believe
One each field, three if big!
Came the reaper, drawn by the horse.

The stalls were lined with produce.
Traditional songs were sung!
All the farmers were present
At the Harvest Home.

The following are the writings of Richard Dodds, his memories of growing up on his parents' farm at East Cocklaw, a lovely insight into farm life in the middle of the 20th century.

EAST COCKLAW - Richard Dodds

Earliest memories begin at the end of the horse era, around the mid 1950s, with my father still planting the turnip seeds with our carthorse Peter in the shafts of the drill and later weeding the rows with the scarifier. In retirement the gentle Clydesdale would often be found standing in the shade of an ancient beech tree, in the typical stance of the heavy horse, with just the tip of a rear hoof resting on the ground. The beech tree, such a feature of the farm for so long, succumbed to a ferocious gale on Boxing Day 1998.

The farm's main enterprise in those days centred around the dairy cows. Ayrshires, these eventually being replaced by British Fresians, which were milked in traditional byres, the milk being carried to the dairy to be cooled and then poured into milk churns ready for collection. Normally very placid animals they could occasionally kick out and my father had a long scar on his forearm to show where the surgeon had plated his broken bones together after one animal caught him with its hoof. Each knew its own stall in the byre and that's where it went for milking, so if one had to be tied up on her wrong side she would invariably cross over which as you might imagine caused problems, not least for the cow tied up beside her. Swedes and mangles supplemented the diet for the animals during the winter months; these were carried in swills between the cows and put in their troughs. To keep the swill out of harm's way, it was necessary to lift it above the height of the animals, which then seemed to take great delight in trapping the hapless carrier between them. The very end stall of the bottom byre was occupied by our last remaining Ayrshire called Rhoda. I do recall she had horns which curved distinctively upwards, maybe dad kept her because he was sad to see the last of the breed disappear having started his farming career at East Cocklaw with the brown and white animals. On the cow byre beams, a collection of red, blue and yellow certificates were displayed, telling of success for our cows in their class at the old Tynedale mart. With the coming of bulk milk collection about to replace the traditional milk churn, it was time for a change and dad decided to disband the dairy herd.

The combine harvester was replacing the binder but I can just recall it in action, producing the sheaves which were then stooked in the field leaving the grain to ripen before being carted and expertly built into weather-proof stacks ready for threshing day. At one time the thresher must have been taken to deal with a stack in our bottom corn field, because I remember it being stuck and there is nothing more exciting than seeing lots of tractors each towing the other, wheels spinning and trying to grip as they struggled to move the steel wheeled machine. Threshing day was an occasion which brought together all our close farming family relatives and workers as it required many hands to supply the thresher with sheaves, carry away the large sacks of grain and deal with the resultant straw and chaff. For the assembled company my mother, Nancy, was the best when it came to making a brown stew which tasted fantastic when mixed with mashed potato. I don't suppose there was much she hadn't gathered from the garden or field, for dad did like his few rows of veg grown in the field, the trouble was the few always seemed a few more the next year until it required a tractor and trailer to bring all the bags and buckets home. Invariably his produce would find its way into many homes and or displays at our harvest festivals. With the veg taken care of in the field my parents could indulge their passion for flowers and the garden would become a marvellously colourful sight when, in the summer months, dahlias and chrysanthemums began to bloom. The vegetables seemed to thrive in the field and dad, being dad, was always generous with the seed. Imagine, therefore, what happened to the carrots which being light are notoriously difficult to sow evenly. It was nothing for them to come up three wide in the row so no wonder we got sackfuls. Peas were another garden to field transfer about which I had serious misgivings; there are only so many mouthfuls you can manage, after that the picking began. A basket was of no use, it needed sacks, big ones, and quite a few. What a daunting prospect! A gardener reaching the end of his row would have only just begun our field one. The fact is that dad and I were probably not much in evidence at this stage, we would be required in some more pressing agricultural activity so it was usually my mother who did the lion's share and we'd come in to find the kitchen table obliterated by a mountain of peas, all to be shelled. I don't know if it was by accident or design but in my later years my parents' holiday always seemed to coincide with the peas being ready. This task I would try to make easier by inviting my family and friends over to help, I thought they might enjoy this form of recreation. The Kenwood food mixer had an ingenious attachment for shelling peas; fed in between two rollers the pods came out one side while the peas dropped into a bowl, effective but slow. I then had this quite brilliant idea to improve on the Kenwood 'one at a time pea popper'. I would engage the mangle on mother's washing machine thereby speeding up the process and doing multiple peas at high speed. Clever eh?! Unfortunately my scheme had one slight unforeseen flaw, there was nothing to deflect the peas down into the tub – consequently there were more peas flying around the room than went into the container. What did go in however, was a very green juice which I'm sure could have set a whole new fashion trend! In green…

Cauliflowers, another product of the field, were an essential ingredient of Nancy's much coveted piccalilli, but the vapours given off during cooking certainly made your eyes water. However, they did have a wonderfully decongestive effect, so much better than Tunes! All the veg offcuts and peelings in those days were boiled in a very large pan, especially kept for the purpose and mixed with crushed oats they became what was known as a crowdie. This was fed to the cock chickens and turkeys being reared ready for Christmas. They really were free range in those days. The trouble was chickens go back to roost in the hen house, turkeys by contrast are clueless…they could go anywhere, even on the cottage roof. How they managed to fly up I don't know but what a job we had to get them down! For me there was no place I would rather have been than at home on Christmas morning, with presents to open and the prospect of a fantastic Christmas dinner at Keepershield with my cousins , at the home of Uncle Fred and Auntie Molly.

Summertime on the farm of my childhood was dominated by hay making, usually beginning in the last week of June. Today we need to differentiate between conventional bales and large round ones which are now the norm but even so the round ones are not new. Only their size, as I discovered when I came across some very old ones in the corner of a shed, and found out these were the product of an Allis Chalmers baler. Dad's assessment of these was that they were almost impregnable – that is very difficult to prise apart and very difficult to stack on a trailer or in the shed, so were consequently abandoned in favour of the rectangular ones produced by our Jones baler, which even produced grooves for the sisal string.

The grass was cut by a semi-mounted mower which was superseded by the trailed one, a type little changed since the horse drawn days only the shafts had been replaced by a draw bar. The two tractors at this time were the Fordson Major and a Turner Diesel named the 'Yeoman of England'. With no hydraulics the diesel had already seen its day but what an amazing top gear it had as I found out on one of my first outings behind the wheel over a rig and furrow field. Once cut, the grass would be allowed dry for a day or two and assuming 'hat weather' turned by the Vicon acrobat, the spiked raking wheels moving two swathes at once. For rowing up prior to bailing two swathes were rowed into one. On level ground it was a very effective machine, on slopes the metal frame carrying the raking wheels, already near the tractor could prove lethal if the tractor turned too quickly and on one occasion ripped the Turner Diesel tyre off its rim. The Cock Pheasant, a later edition to the farm's hay making equipment, lifted two rows of hay over its spinning rotor to help dry it out, its weakness was cocksfoot among course grass, capable of bringing the rotor to a grinding stop as smoke came off the slipping belts. Before the advent of modern bale sledges, boards bolted to wooden skids were trailed behind the baler and the emerging bales were stacked three high and pushed off to make rows which at the end of the day stretched way across the field. That surely had to be one of the noisiest and dustiest jobs on the farm. With no time to be lost, tea would be brought to the field in baskets filled with sandwiches, scones and cakes, made by our mum or by Mary, whose husband Billy Batey worked on the farm. The tea itself came down to the field in tin cans, lids sealed with muslin cloth. In our bottom field, a beautiful cold clear spring quenched many a thirst during hay times and harvest past. This spring feeds a small stream which flows into the Erring Burn and ultimately reaches the North Tyne through the Chollerton viaduct. Bales were stacked onto a trailer roped for security to be led home, 79 per load. Lower layers of the hay 'mows' were stacked relatively easily, how straightforward depended on the condition of the bale. If the hay had been fit to bale it was easy. If the conditions weren't perfect, which was quite often the case, soft banana shaped ones were more tricky to deal with and sometimes required a few props to stabilise a newly built mow. As the layers went higher, either pitch forks or subsequently a bale elevator, which had a somewhat temperamental engine. This wouldn't tolerate too many bales at once or the belt came off. Swallows would build their nests high up in the rafters of the hay shed and if one was still occupied at that time we'd try to leave a flight path in the bales for the birds to use. An extra pair of hands was always welcome at hay time and Adam and George Johnstone would often come up after work or at weekends to help out. Many a time, Adam being a mechanic was very helpful in coaxing the reluctant elevator engine to start.

The blue Fordson Major was replaced by a red David Brown 950, I first caught sight of it pulling the plough when walking up the farm road on my way home from school. I for one still remember the 'where and when', showing how memorable an occasion it was for a young lad. Equally so was the appearing of the David Brown Albion Combine, its 5ft cut maybe not so impressive today as it was then. Being a bagger combine the sacks were filled from grain spouts on a platform and slid down a shoot to be let out when three or four had accumulated. At the end of the day these were loaded onto trailers, carted home and stored in the granary ready to be crushed and used for winter animal feed.

Being bred on the farm, I felt no inclination to leave it and being required for educational purposes was a most unwelcome intrusion into my, up till then, happy way of life. Holidays couldn't come quickly enough and finished much too soon. Easter holidays sometimes coincided with the lambing; a small flock of blue faced Leicesters were kept in the former years. To the uninitiated these are fine woolled thin skinned animals with prominent white heads, noses having a bluish tint. The appeal of these animals to my father was lost on me. Being thin skinned the lambs were prone to feel the lack of heat which is characteristic of Northumberland in early spring and in the days before heat lamps the sight of a shivering lamb lying on a sack in front of the Rayburn was not unusual, always with the possibility that these would become mobile and leave little puddles on the lino as shaky legs skidded on the slippery surface. Leicesters are notoriously prolific often having three or even four lambs without the corresponding number of milk dispensers so we usually had a few pets. After school, when other children were clocking up the homework hours, it wasn't unknown for us to be tending these ewes or feeding a pet lamb. In those days the Leicester had to be white, no brown on any account must be found on its legs or head, such discolouration would render it worthless as a pure bred animal. Today rams with two tone brown markings are in demand as cross-breeding sires – how times and fashions change, whatever next?

To end with one of my most enduring memories is of dad returning home from Hexham mart with a Suffolk ewe and its tup lamb which he'd bought to be my very own sheep. I eventually sold the lamb at the breeding sale for £20. I was on the ladder to success, I would rear Suffolk tups and make lots of money. A succession of ewe lambs exposed the weakness of my scheme. I'm still searching for that elusive fool proof plan with no drawback, I should know by now they don't exist. There again if this rural ramble is ever printed would any reader be interested in buying shares in some pet lambs or a pick your own pea plot?!

Sheep and lambs have an important place in our local farming. The following song composed by Chris Jones, is a tribute to Northumbrian shepherds and their faithful collie dogs. This is what Chris says about the song.

"I do know that when it was first composed I felt it was so sad that I would have difficulty in singing it.

As far as I am aware it is the first song in the English folk tradition to mention a quad bike! A few years ago I entered it in the song writing competition at the annual Morpeth Gathering where it won first prize (which is an absurdly large shield!) ". Here then, is text of that song which Chris sings to the accompaniment of his lap organ.

The Lambing Storm – Chris Jones March 2008
As the dark days of winter turned into springtime,
Just as the snowdrops appeared by the wall,
The lambing storm hit roaring down from the fellside,
Covering the ground in the wind driven snow.
As he crossed the yard away to his fireside,
He missed the shape of old Ben by the wall,
A black and white collie some seventeen summers,
Surely too old to be out in the sna.

Ch And the shepherd was calling, the shepherd was calling,
The shepherd was calling the old collie home.
Since his days as a pup he had lived in the farmyard,
Known only once to come in by the fire,
Spending his time way out with the sheepkind,
Sensing their safety as his toil and his care.
When the storm had abated they stood by the door,
And watched as the moonlight played tricks on the sna,
Way out in the distance they heard a dog calling,
So clear and so mournful they knew they must go.
They set out in the darkness with torchlight a blazing,
As starlight threw shadows on the way they'd to go,
Out on the fell over banks and the ditches,
The snow was too deep for the quad bike to go.
When at last they found them in a wee bit old quarry
A worn out old youe, a dead lamb by her side,
Tucked in by the wall with old Ben beside him,
The flickering of life from a pure – bred tup lamb.
Ch And the shepherd was carrying, the shepherd was carrying,
The shepherd was carrying the old collie home.

It's back to the farmhouse and in by the fireside,
A box by the Aga to keep the lamb warm,
A bottle of milk sets that young tail a wagging,
But when they turned back old Ben's life was gone.
They buried him next morning down in the orchard,
Just where the daffodils peek through the sna,
Where the youes and their lambs would play in the nursery
Surely Ben's shade will look after them now.

And that very same autumn at the pedigree stock sales,
Where a years - worth of labour is forward to sell,
With friends and with neighbours stood there at the ringside,
The lamb took first prize and top price as well.
Ch And the shepherd was carrying, the shepherd was carrying,
The shepherd was carrying a new puppy home.
Ch And the shepherd is calling, the shepherd is calling,
The shepherd is calling a young collie home.

"A Lambing Storm is either a lot of twins/triplets being born overnight and the shepherd finds it almost impossible to sort out the correct mothers the next morning or, a vicious late snowfall that leaves many lambs dead from hypothermia."

FALLOWFIELD ALPACAS - Mike and Melanie Douglas

After noticing alpacas in countryside magazines, we decided to investigate further with several visits to local breeders. We were instantly attracted to these gentle, inquisitive animals and seriously considered purchasing some for Crag House. Our 88 acres are not sufficient for a traditional farming venture but perfect for a sustainable diversification project with minimal effect on the land and environment. We joined the British Alpaca Society and the North East and Border Alpaca Group and purchased four pregnant females in 2006, including two top quality girls from a recent import from Peru.

Alpacas are camelids and are bred for their luxurious fleece, prized by top-end fashion houses such as Max Mara. They eat grass and hay with a small daily mineral supplement and are largely self-sufficient. We fenced off several paddocks and built fairly simple field shelters to provide cover in the worst wet weather but generally the alpacas stay out and are extremely hardy. They are sheared once a year and produce one baby, or cria, per year.

After shearing, the fleeces are skirted by us to remove vegetable matter and coarse hair, then sent to the mill to be processed into extremely soft yarn. This is then either sold as yarn or made into a range of clothing and luxury baby wear.

After five years, both our experience and the quality of our herd continue to increase. The herd now numbers approximately 40 and includes imports of alpacas from Australia and New Zealand. We have had three females in quarantine in New Zealand, which we imported to the UK in spring 2012, as well as two further stud males which came in from the USA in midsummer 2012. These animals broaden our genetics and will further improve the quality of our herd.

We have always taken our alpacas to shows and are now achieving national recognition with several top prizes at both Halter and Fleece shows. The herd profile has been further raised with a new website (www.fallowfieldalpacas.com) which has helped sales. We have recently exported two of our top females to a leading breeder in Scandinavia.

We run regular courses at Fallowfield, from the hugely popular two hour Alpaca Experience to full day courses on husbandry and all aspects of alpaca management. The alpacas have also proved a great draw for our Bed and Breakfast business with many visitors booking because of the alpacas.

Melanie is chief steward of the Alpaca section at the Northumberland County Show and has recently become a committee member of the Tynedale Agricultural Society. She is well known in the alpaca community and is currently training to be a qualified alpaca judge, one of only a dozen in the country.

Our alpacas are well known locally through the public footpath that runs through the paddocks and also through regular appearances at local shows, including the Wall Fête in July.

We continue to get great pleasure from these delightful and friendly animals, making many close friendships along the way. We hope our alpacas will be part of the scenery of Wall for many years to come.

MILLS

Not many of us bake our own bread. Sliced loaves are so handy! When we do bake we can nip to the supermarket for our flour. That was not always the case. Grain was milled locally. Watermills were commonplace throughout the countryside. The ordnance survey map names two on the Erring Burn: Keepwick Mill and Walk Mill.

At the crossroads is Brunton Mill. This was fed from an underground stream ducted from a pond. In the late part of the 19th century a tragedy occurred. Mr Shanks of Low Brunton had gone to oil the mill wheel while it was working. He was crushed to death. Men from Herdman's works were called to release the body and the mill was never used again. In 1989 Border Craft redeveloped the property and the dilapidated mill was dismantled. The grindstones and cogs went to Beamish museum but the wheel was to become a feature. It was taken, in a derelict state, from the mill to Herdman's workshop. Here it was restored, then taken to its present position on the end of a building. The wheel which for years had not been seen is now an interesting sight for all to see.

Wall Mill is by the North Tyne, just below the railway station. The earliest record is that 'William Kell held the mill in 1547 at a rent of ten shillings'. Over the years it was owned or leased by several other well-known local families, Tulip, Rowell and Ripley among them. Edward Rowell who ran the mill in 1853-55 was reputedly proud of his horse, Miller, who could pull a ton of flour up the steep station bank. In 1882 ownership passed to John Clayton of The Chesters. In the sale of 1929 it was bought by Mr Bob Stewart, a local quarryman and rabbit catcher. Ownership passed by marriage via the Rowell family to the Ripley family.

The mill was modified many times in its long history but was always prone to damage when the river flooded. It was last used commercially in about 1900. It became dilapidated until 1922 when William Ripley and Cecil Herdman (of Herdman's) repaired the mechanism and modified it for threshing. Another bad flood caused by snow melt washed away the weir, breached the sluice gate causing final damage to the mill wheel.

NORTH TYNE IMPLEMENT WORKS (J HERDMAN) - Mary Herdman

The North Tyne Implement Works was founded in Wall circa 1800 by James Herdman and at that time employed twelve men. James was a millwright, cartwright, grocer and draper. His work included the making and repair of farm machinery, carts and wagons, farm implements, furniture and coffins. His wife Jane ran the grocery and drapers shop from their home. At first they were tenants then they bought the premises in 1929, the year of the Chesters Estate sale.

Over the years the buildings housed wheelwrights, cabinet makers, blacksmiths, millwrights, fabrication engineers and welders, giving service to the community both through the repair of broken implements and the manufacture of a wide range of products. The firm was widely known in the farming community. Their business grew into a general engineering works which was to dominate the west side of the village green until the 1970s. They made use of the village green outside of their door. Old photographs circa 1890 show a crane made from an old ship's mast, a steam engine, a saw bench and piles of timber. A Ralph Hedley painting depicts their sawpit. In later years the green was gradually cleared. The crane was demolished in the 1970s.

I joined the Herdman family in 1964, when Ron and I were married. At that time the firm was run by Ron's father Cecil and Cecil's brother Edward. After their deaths in the 1980s it passed to Ron. Throughout our married lives we have lived next door to the premises. Life here has had its moments for me. On one occasion I was just setting out for Hexham to do the shopping, when Ron ran in and asked me to draw a Galloway bull on a sheet of steel before I left. It was wanted for a weathercock. At another time I was asked to draw a horse to go on a gate.

A few years into our marriage Ron and his father were discussing difficulties in fulfilling an urgent order on time. I volunteered to paint the equipment in question. They jumped at my offer. As I finished the farmer came for it. It was hitched on to his tractor with the paint still wet. He reckoned it would be dry by the time he reached home! That being done, other items were already lined up. I was to spend many an hour painting gates, with our son Jim sitting watching me in his pushchair. I was still covering everything in sight with red oxide some five years later. It finished when I was pregnant again, and too fat to bend down.

The products of that time were most often connected with farming; gates, trailers, transport boxes, bale carriers, animal feeders: whatever the customers wanted. There were many individual one off orders; dog grates, coffee table legs, wrought iron work etc. If it could be made in steel we would have a go. We were called upon to produce public sculptures to the design of William Pym who had his studio on our premises at that time.

One interesting project was the restoration of a mill wheel. In 1989 this was taken, in a derelict state, from Brunton Mill. This mill had not been used since a man was crushed to death in 1897 while he was lubricating the gear wheels. During and after reconstruction, it made a spectacular sight as it stood in the yard before being taken to its present location back at Brunton Mill, Brunton Crossroads in 1990.

The business remained in the Herdman family until its closure in 1998. Both of our sons had left the village, neither wishing to carry on the business. In November 1998 there was an auction of the remaining products and the contents of the building. Large numbers flocked to the sale. The village was jam-packed with vehicles, some parking as far out as the lay-by. Some buyers took their purchases immediately, whilst others collected them over the next few days. A few goods even went to the Beamish Museum. The yard and half of the building were sold to Border Craft. In 2001 they demolished that part of the building and used the site to build the terrace of three houses known as The Falster.

At that time Ron retained the part which was currently housing North Tyne Studios. They were finally closed in 2003, the building sold, also to Border Craft. They retained it intact and converted it into two flats, Falster Forge, in 2005.

NORTH TYNE STUDIOS 1989-2003 - Kathleen Sisterson

A shock for Wall Village, art had arrived; studios were established above Ron Herdman's workshop. The van of George Bernard Shaw delivered wood panelling from an exhibition in Hexham Abbey, to line the walls and produce hanging space for paintings.

Studio Interior
Shrouded art work line stark white walls,
Ambiguous paint pots
Stacked high, colours unknown,
To glimpse a word
Red, crimson, black,
Bring positive recall.

The vivid contents slide on canvas skin,
Caressed by brush and finger tips,
Create a love child
Secret spirit yet unseen, shrouded,
Against stark white walls
Remain at rest.

Outside, the village green occupied by Lucky, the white horse, while doves hover and land, cattle cross the green for milking at the farm, white goats graze the surrounding hills. An ideal setting for graduates from Newcastle and Sunderland, soon all studio spaces were filled.

At this time I was studying for my MA which entailed entertaining tutors of fellow students in my studios. Unfortunately it was winter. Although the Calor gas heater did its best, snow filtered through the roof tiles, tutors wrapped in fur coats (warned prior to visit) huddled around it, relishing the experience of country life.

Studio-Frosty Air
My breath escapes in vapour clouds,
Coffee cups mushroom like grey atomic shrouds,
In frosty air.
The icy mists creep, dilate and shrink,
Snowflakes hover undecided, float or sink,
The water pant a static crystal winks,
In frosty air.
The drop upon my nose solidifies,
My mind an icy field clarifies,
Words brittle, splinter then petrify,
In frosty air.

The idea for the Artists Network was conceived in these surrounding with the dream of bringing artists together. As everyone knows it has flourished and changed in many ways, but North Tyne Studios, Wall will always be its birthplace. Many exhibitions have been held on these premises with barbecues, weekend schools and the yearly visits from the general public during the Artists Network Open Studios weekends.

Summer was wonderful, but winter would find us sharing the heat from the coke stove in the factory workshop while we enjoyed our lunch. Ziggy, the owner's Labrador dog, would greet us when we arrived and keep an eye on us for the rest of the day. Many exhibitions originated within these walls, and, when leaving the studio large works often became jammed on the staircase. Panic! But as always we resolved the problem in anticipation of their return.

Returned to Studio
Returned -   From exhibition gallery,
             Rows of pictures lie forlorn.
Returned -   The job done
             Their message displayed to the discerning
Returned -   Their heartfelt cry,
             Unheard.
Returned -   To the void,
             Nothingness.
Returned -   To plastic bag and parcel tape
Returned -   To wonder where the painful struggle led
Returned -   To anonymity,
             Stacked against a studio wall.
Returned -   To exhibition gallery
             The cycle now completed,
             Once again recurs.

A memory highlight: 'The Millennium'. The village wanted an event that would be a lasting memory. We felt that the studio should be the centre of this project, and decided upon a 'Wall Hanging' to be displayed in the Village Hall. It would involve the whole village, with many talented people and Joan Proudlock, the best organizer I've ever encountered as the driving force. Once decided, I was asked to design this work: a triptych expressing all the elements of the west, east and central views of Wall and the surrounding areas. This work, with the wonderful 'Parish Map' developed and produced by Mary Herdman, with copies distributed worldwide, can be viewed in the Village Hall.

After a memorable year, the North Tyne Studios experience came to an end when the owner decided to retire and sell the premises - a conclusion to an epic experience and sadness to all who worked there.

The Green Bottle
Dried flowers in a green glass bottle
Gathering dust on a studio window sill,
Kept as a totem and reminder,
Passed on by a friend;
Exams completed, expectations fulfilled,
Bringing luck and success to me in turn,
Now accompany me as baggage
Along my path from studio to gallery
Always there, with colour gone and spikey stalks,
Containing still the mystic of emeralds
In the green glass bottle,
Today holds only faded dreams.

WALL GARAGE - Joan Proudlock

The original garage on the existing site was a corrugated metal hangar. It was bought from the Tyneside Exhibition in 1929 by William Proudlock, whose home was Black Pasture Cottage on Brunton Bank. It was transported by rail from Newcastle to Chollerford Station. Two low loaders were positioned back to back and the structures tied on. Gradually they made their way up to Brunton Crossroads and on to the village. The structures were erected by James (Jimmy) Dickinson, grandfather of James Dickinson of Gunnerton, for the sum of forty pounds to form 'Willie Proudlock's Garage' as it became known throughout the area.

Three pits were dug for working under vehicles and an office and storeroom created overlooking the back green. Steel girders held up the roof. At the back of the garage was a black, pot-bellied stove; the only source of heat for the building, so Willie Proudlock moved his business from a wash house behind the Hadrian to his new premises.

Willie had wagons which led from the local quarry, and a cattle wagon, useful for local farmers. These were eventually sold on to Adair Atkinson of Birtley. As there was much farming in the area, a lot of agricultural and commercial repairs to implements and vehicles were done, particularly for Wards of Wolsingham. The garage also held an agency for Vauxhall cars and Bedford lorries. Petrol was sold from the forecourt, first Pool petrol and then, after the war, National Benzole. Hire cars for holiday makers were also available.

From 1929 until he died in 1959 Willie Proudlock owned and ran the garage. There were many local lads who 'served their time' (had an apprenticeship) at the garage. These were remembered by the late Ted Charlton who worked there too: **Jim Telfer, John Murray, Jimmy Ritson, Bobby Steel, Johnny Steele, Douglas Ross, Robert Blackcock, David Liddle, Alan Thompson, Alec Nixon, Clive Dodd, George Rutherford, Melville Peary and Ted Charlton.** These men represented Wall, Acomb, Humshaugh, Colwell, Simonburn, Wark, Birtley and Keepwick Fell.

Willie's son John was just sixteen when his father died and working as an apprentice fitter and turner at Vickers Armstrong's, so the garage was sold to another Wall man, Billy Armstrong, the father of Maureen Proud. So in 1959 the garage became Thompson Son and Armstrong and remained as that for eight years.

Maureen Proud has recorded the following:

"William Armstrong was the mechanic of the firm. He had three or four apprentices in his time at Wall. I worked in the garage for four years driving the hire car for weddings, christenings, private runs and also school contract work. We collected children from Hallington, Bingfield and Walk Mill to go to Hexham schools, and children from Gunnerton Fell and Chipchase Mill who attended school in Barrasford. I sold the petrol and did the accounts. At that time the garage also sold cigarettes, sweets, torches and batteries".

In 1967 ownership changed again; this time back into the Proudlock name as Willie's son John had finished his Vickers apprenticeship. He followed this by working for a while in Vickers design drawing office, and then for two years worked and gained experience in two garages, Dobsons of Throckley and Fawdingtons of Stagshaw, thus preparing himself for his future working life in his own garage business.

John W Proudlock was the trading name that became part of North Tyne life. At first petrol continued to be sold, National Benzole then Sadler, but as there were other petrol stations close by, the forecourt could be put to a better use. This was to display an all-terrain vehicle manufactured by Steyr Puch, called a Haflinger. The garage became agents for this vehicle which was demonstrated to many farmers in both Cumbria and Northumberland.

In 1990 a new housing development, Mithras Court, forced the demolition of the corrugated metal garage. It was a difficult time as the cheapest option was to move the business out of Wall to a unit in Hexham. The land on which the old garage stood had been rented from North Farm by Willie Proudlock and that agreement was due to be reviewed however it became clear the only way to keep the business in Wall was to buy the land.

The new garage was designed by John and architect Peter Brazell. The metal structures were installed by Scott's of Great Whittington and the stonework by award winning firm Robsons of Hexham. During the course of the building work, machinery was moved and business continued in a barn at Planetrees Farm on Brunton Bank.

A paint spray booth and body shop were part of the new building and instead of pits, hoists were installed. A toilet and staffroom replaced a dash across the green to the public toilets and 'bait' eaten on a metal stool round a pot-bellied stove, crumbs often shared with the mice which came through the gaps in the corrugated metal from Fred Henderson's field and the sparrows which flew in. Two offices, one a reception area, the other for management were at the front of the garage looking onto the forecourt. It was a purpose built garage and the external stone work was built to blend in with the old village houses and used original stone. It was opened by Melville Peary who originally worked for John's father.

Work developed quickly into specialising in Saabs: people came from far and wide for repairs and services. The spray booth and body shop brought work from insurance companies, private customers and the motor trade.

Over thirty five years of trading John W Proudlock was fortunate in having a high calibre of staff: **Davey Mewse, Paul Nicholson, Richard Rudd, David Hogg,** father and son team **Jimmy and Raymond Hanning, Andrew Johnston, Andy Waters** and **Darren Burns.** Jimmy Hanning became the person all the customers met as he was the manager, booking work in and dealing with customer enquiries. Until John retired he earned the trust and respect of all who knew him and when John took a holiday he knew he left it in good and safe hands. In the office, working part time on accounts over the years were, **Edith Thompson, Alwyn Robinson, Peter Mason, Howard Morton, Gilbert Hunter** and **Sally Best** whose bookwork skills John relied on.

There are many stories that could be written of events during thirty five years. Actors Alexandra Bastedo and Anthony Quayle were customers on separate occasions when staying at the Hadrian. The garage hung a banner: 'Wall Welcomes the Queen' when she travelled through, having officially opened Kielder reservoir. Late Wall resident Neil Scholes, as a traffic police sergeant, had the honour of driving the police car in front of the Queen's car which he slowed down on approaching the garage as the Queen waved to those assembled on the forecourt. Royal recognition!

Another change came in 2001 as John Proudlock retired and sold the garage. It became known, under the new ownership as Wall Garage and a sad chapter in its history began, as it closed within three years.

For some time the garage remained closed, then it took on a new lease of life under different ownership, and returned to Wall Garage, a working business. Equipment to start a new MOT station was installed and a regular repairs service was started. Vintage and classic cars became a feature on the forecourt as part of a restoration service for old vehicles and they were displayed at the Three Churches Fête in the summer. At this time of writing part of the garage is closed but the area nearest the A6097 is being used as a vehicle valeting business. Who knows what the future holds for this corner of Wall, but for many people going up the North Tyne valley the site will always be known as Proudlock's Garage.

THE POST OFFICE, THE MAIL TRAIN - Some of Mona Craig's writings

"The mail and newspapers came by the 7.10 train in the morning, it was sorted at the post office. Some papers were stamped and delivered to the 'well to do' who lived 'out-bye' and their prices doubled from 1d to 2d. The mail was delivered on foot in all weathers (no plastic macs or wellies). One sister* went up Brunton Bank, Errington Hill Head, Wall Fell, Codlaw Hill and places in between. It took about three hours, and then she did the cooking and helped in the shop 'open all hours'. Another sister did the village, and then up Spouty Lonnen to Fallowfield, that didn't take quite so long. At night the mail had to be taken in sealed bags and put on the 6.20 train. There was a flat barrow in post office red – used mainly at Christmas – but most of the time a bike did the job, mostly by the master tailor. Another, older sister, was official postmistress. She manned the shop and attended to commercial travellers while the others were out. The mother also lived there. I remember her as an old lady in long black clothes, sitting knitting by the fire, with a shawl round her shoulders. She wasn't allowed to do anything, but I know she used to 'ratch' about in the shop and the pantry on the rare occasions they were all out – I know because I used to sit with her. She died at the age of 73, when I was 21. How times have changed!"

*The sisters mentioned are the Laing Sisters.

Chris Allcock did a presentation for Wall Village Society, when it was a Local History Group, with the title 'Wall's Wandering Post Office'. The information following is taken from his work.

1851 Ward's Directory: the postmaster was Michael Scott, letters arrived at 3.30pm and were despatched at 9.30am. Michael Scott lived in a cottage in Front Street. There had been a letterbox incorporated into the front window. There was also evidence of another (later?) inset into the wall to the right of Bibury gate.

1881 Hexham Courant: 'Villagers of Chollerton and Wall clubbed together to pay for a pony and its winter keep for the local postman, Isaac Maddison'. The Maddison's lived in Hillhead House, so it is probable that Isaac was postman for Michael Scott, or was postmaster himself for a time.

1906 Kelly's Directory: 'Sub office. Wm. Laing, sub-postmaster. Two collections and two deliveries daily. Letters should have Northumberland SO (sorting office?)

added' 'Wall Railway Station is nearest Telegraph Office.' There was a letter box at the station. Population – 380.

1925 – 1959 Miss Phyllis Jane Laing – 'shopkeeper and post office'. Tel. Humshaugh 25. The shop, now Milestone Cottage, was originally run by Mr and Mrs William Laing who had bought the premises in The Chesters sale. Phyllis was one of their seven children. Her sisters Maggie and Kate delivered the post daily plus any telegrams over a wide area: Fallowfield, Errington, Bingfield etc. etc - ON FOOT!

1959 Garden House, owned by Jack and Peggy Seaby became the Post Office as well as a General Store. Peggy had three days training to become a sub-postmistress; she admitted that she "didn't learn much, but picked it up in time by trial-and-error!" Her pay was £206-11s per annum. A letterbox was installed in the side wall. Its position is clearly visible.

Postal Orders and stamps etc were delivered fortnightly from Hexham. The PO had to be open six days per week, and had to be open on most Bank Holidays including Christmas Day, Good Friday etc for telegrams. These had to be delivered ASAP by whatever means possible, anyone available was 'pressed into action'. Because there were very few telephones, telegrams were regularly received and sent. Another duty was to clear cash from the telephone kiosk, then on Front Street outside Milestone Cottage. Peggy could get a 'competent' relief worker to give her occasional time off. Amongst others, John Mitchell acted as stand in. Peggy and Jack retired in 1971.

1971 Lewis Mason lived in 'Thurlestone', one of the two houses built c 1954, just below the Chapel. He erected a handsome wooden shop in his garden and ran a shop and Post Office. Sadly, he died soon afterwards. Elva Mason then ran the business until 1973.

1973 Ella Westle bought the house and continued to run the shop and PO. However, in 1988 it was raided by a limping man wielding a knife. He got no money, and was arrested shortly afterwards whilst attempting a similar raid in Morpeth. Mrs Westle was naturally unnerved and decided to retire.

1988 Sharon Kelly, daughter of the Hadrian landlord, took over the shop but closed it soon afterward – not profitable (probably had not been for some time). The PO business was transferred to the Hadrian.

1989 The PO was run from the bar for a short time, then transferred to a portakabin/steel container in the back yard. This was in operation for only about three months – again not profitable, and probably conflicted with running the pub. So in 1989 Wall was without a Post Office or a shop.

1989 Concerned at the loss of this amenity, Rachel Lowther, Chairman of the Village Hall, led an investigation into the possibility of establishing a Community PO in the Village Hall. There were so many obstacles – security, the need for a separate room, insurance, full commitment by local volunteers etc etc, that the idea was abandoned.

Ali Lloyd Jones, a local resident, was willing to 'have a go' herself, but was unable to find an acceptable room in the village; even the Chapel schoolroom and Church vestry were considered, but the set-up costs and other problems were too formidable.

1991 Maureen Proud had experience of PO procedures, having been a relief worker for Ella Westle, so she decided to set up a part time PO in her own kitchen.

Most transactions could be made, and 'The Letch' became an important centre of village life. Opening hours were 9.00am to noon. Stamps etc were ordered fortnightly from Newcastle. She kept it going for over six years, but eventually decided to close. Bureaucracy, petty-officialdom and coming computerisation made the effort not worthwhile. She was also much involved with hobbies, WI, and travel to New Zealand. It was time to retire. The Post Office was finally closed on 27th July 1997.

We do still have a letterbox on a pole in the middle of the village green! At High Brunton however a new post box has replaced the Victorian one with the V and crown. It was stolen a number of years ago when there was a craze for such items as artistic features in properties in the south of England.

It is a long time since the post was sorted locally. It is now delivered once per day by van from Hexham Sorting Office. Our nearest post office is two miles away, in Acomb.

"Stan's" Story…

Many residents of Wall and out-bye know 'Stan' who has served Wall since 1978. Following Stan sorting his Erring Burn round in the Hexham office he places the mail into two large trays in his van for delivery. A special occasion card from The Queen comes to the office in a special bag and then joins the rest of the mail.

When a postman has been on a particular round for 34 years he knows all his customers and where to leave packets and parcels should they be out. Stan is a trusted friend to many. Sometimes over the years Stan has been able to help someone with lifting a coal bucket, making sure a person on their own is not in difficulties, or simply having a cheery word and chat, as he could be the only person an out-bye resident might see that day. Mobile phones have replaced a trudge to the nearest house with a telephone in the case of a van breakdown. In bygone winters, a farmer and his tractor were the answer to being stuck but now the Post Office policy is, "Don't go."

In the past Stan was responsible for carrying money in his van. Pension money for villages was carried in cash with none of the security arrangements that are now in place for vehicles with large amounts of cash to deliver. The cash was delivered to the post office each week on a particular day so that pensions could be paid over the counter. About ten years ago cash payments ceased so Stan is not as vulnerable to attack as in the past. He did once however succumb to the terrifying advances of a flock of geese when delivering mail to a farm. Most postmen are wary of dogs but on an out-bye round, Beware of the Geese!

For 34 years Stan has been our postman; first in Wall, but now his round includes three industrial estates in Hexham and out-bye around Wall Village and he works a five day week. In all that time he has been cheerful, helpful and dependable. In the history of Wall's postal service and in appreciation of the service he has given while wandering Wall and its environs with the mail, and in 2013 still continuing to do so, he certainly has a place of his own in this book. For all those letters and parcels cheerfully and safely delivered in all weathers ——-Thank You Stan.

SHOPS

In White's Directory of 1828 there are three grocers listed: Mary Ayston, Thomas Hill and Ann Humble. The butcher was William Robson.

The census of 1881 shows the grocers as Mrs Margaret Hewison and Jane Herdman, with John Hudspith as a grocer and general dealer. The butchers were Michael Scott*, Thomas Robson and John Rowell. William Laing appears as a tailor.

Bulmer's Directory of 1886 gives us Michael Robson as butcher (also running a post office), Thomas Hewison and John Hudspith as grocers and William Laing as tailor, draper and grocer.

The 1901 census again gives us Michael Scott* and Thomas Robson as butchers. John Hogg is listed as a grocer. William Laing is referred to as a clothier and grocer. None of these sources give reference to premises.

From 1925 to 1959 Miss Phyllis Jane Laing, aided by her sisters Maggie and Kate, ran a post office and general store. She sold a wide variety of goods, for example: groceries, tobacco and cigarettes, paraffin, candles, paint, wallpaper, sweets, hardware and cotton thread.

Other shops in the village during the 20th century were: Orchard House, Front Street, a general store run by Annie Herdman. She had a horse and trap for local deliveries which were mainly groceries. High House, Front Street, (previously The Bay Horse, then The Temperance Hotel). This was a general store run by Mrs Bowman who took on the newspaper business on the closure of Miss Laing's shop. She also sold vegetables and flowers from the large rear garden. Garden House, opposite to the Church. Mrs Muse ran it with her daughter as a general store from the early 1930s. From about 1934 the house was occupied by Jack and Peggy Seaby, who bought it and took over the post office in 1959. They retired and closed it 1971. The Chare Shop, in the garden of 'Thurlestone.' A general store and post office built by Lewis Mason in 1971 and bought by Mr and Mrs Westle in 1972. Mr Westle died in the early 1980s. Ella Westle retired and closed the business in 1988.

Over the years in the village there have been numerous mobile shops: a grocer and general dealer, a fishmonger, a butcher, a greengrocer, a baker, a coal merchant, ice cream vans and even a chip shop.

At the time of writing we have weekly visits from a greengrocer, plus occasional visits from fish merchants and a coal merchant. The mobile library visits the centre of the village for one hour on alternate Tuesday afternoons but ceased stopping at High Brunton a number of years ago.

Joan Proudlock recalls the visiting vans of High Brunton.

"Every week the baker and general dealer (Tommy Nichol's Van), fish sellers, who came and went, and Malcolm Johnson, of Johnson's of Barrasford, with his mobile shop would visit Brunton Bank. Malcolm was not only a grocer but a trusted friend to all those he served, on his travels up and around Brunton Bank and the Old Lane. He carried shopping baskets, helped his customers in and out of his van and if they could not manage to come out of the house he collected the order and selected the goods himself. If an item was not on the van he made sure the customer got it the next week, or sometimes it was just dropped off. He was also happy to spend time with those who used his travelling shop, because he might be the only person they saw that day, and surely, it was always good to have a chat and pass the news around. Malcolm retired several years ago but he is still missed by the customers who still have memories of those times."

Now, serving all who are able to go there, there is an excellent, award winning, community run shop two miles away, in Humshaugh.

*Found by Ivor Gray in the Hexham Courant dated 4 October 1924 is the following.

Death of Mr Michael Scott - The death has taken place at his residence in Wall, of Mr Michael Scott, one of the most widely known men in the district. Deceased, who had reached the advanced age of 86 years, had been wonderfully well up to the time he contracted a painful disease in the foot. He was one of the earliest workers on the junction length of the North British Railway from Hexham bridge northward, and was also employed by the late Mr John Clayton, of the Chesters. He afterwards commenced business as a butcher, and carried on that trade successfully for a long period of years, retiring some years ago. He was well known at the Hexham markets and also in the wide district over which he travelled. He took no part in public affairs, but had served as an overseer of the parish. Deceased was born in the house in which he died. The funeral will take place at St Oswald's today (Saturday).

PUBLIC TRANSPORT

In earlier times travel was enjoyed by the wealthy, but less so by the working classes who did not stray so far from their place of birth. In the 20th century that changed. People began to look further afield for their work and education. They wished to enjoy their time off and they wanted goods beyond the scope of the village shops. They sought the bright lights of Hexham, with its two cinemas, and the big stores of Newcastle. Youngsters went to the Saturday night hops in Bellingham or perhaps the Fandango in Hexham. Trains and buses performed a vital role in public transport.

Now, in the 21st century we still need transport for employment, school, shopping and enjoying our leisure pursuits so many people own cars. The train service is long gone and the buses today subsequently have fewer passengers.

The Railway

"Why should that out-of-the-way part of the country be opened up by a railway? It would only disturb the game". This opinion expressed by the coal magnate, Sir Matthew White Ridley, did not prevail. The Border Counties Railway went ahead. The line stretched from Hexham to Riccarton Junction, a distance of 42 miles. Wall station was the first on the line. (The next, Chollerford, was in Wall parish, but served Humshaugh. The name of this station was changed to Humshaugh in 1919). It was opened to the public on Easter Monday 5th April 1858 with a regular timetable. The fares from Hexham to Wall were 6d first class, 4½d second and 3d third.

The railway was a single line. In the early days, Wall being one of the smaller stops rated a 'railway agent' rather than a stationmaster, but Bulmer's directory of 1886 lists John Watt as stationmaster. Wall was important as it had a 'passing loop' siding and a weighing machine.

For many years, the line was used for passenger, postal and freight services, but eventually traffic on the line decreased. During the last year of passenger operation only £60 was taken in receipts from Wall station. On 19 September 1955 it closed, long before Dr Beeching wielded his axe. All the remaining stations followed one year later. Freight continued for almost two years more, then that ceased. After a few special trains, total closure came in 1958. The station came into the hands of Mr Edward Ripley who stored his grain in the signal box and fertiliser in the ladies waiting room.

Several events are worthy of note.

On 6 May 1865 John Davidson, the guard on the 5.45 goods train from Hexham was seriously injured by striking his head on the road bridge at Dunkirk. It appears that he was climbing over the wagons of the moving train to speak to the driver.

Local memories include a landslide in 1947, a result of the thaw that followed the harsh winter. This blocked the line between Wall and Humshaugh stations. The line filled up with water. This was near a bend in the line and a northbound train ploughed into the landslide and became stuck in the water. The driver and fireman were injured.

Another incident involved the last train of the day. It stopped at Wark Station. The driver and fireman, as was their wont, nipped into the nearby Chipchase Arms for a swift pint. Two Barrasford lads came across the unattended train and decided to use it to get home. They climbed aboard and set it in motion, then realized that they did not know how to stop it! It passed through Barrasford and Chollerford before it ran out of steam near Wall. The lads fled the scene. The railway company was never able to identify them.

In May 1945 a fire which started in the roof of the station master's house, allegedly by an oil lamp, burnt down the building and part of the station. Only the ladies' waiting room and the signal box survived. The family of nine escaped with nothing but what they stood up in! Thereafter tickets were issued from the waiting room. The house remained a ruin until 1987 when the station was bought by Hexham doctor, Peter Willis. He learned how to lay bricks and worked 16 hour days while living in a caravan to complete a five year restoration project. He then brought in a length of line and a rescued railway carriage to finish off his train buff heaven.

As the railway station was a mile from the village, and Hexham station was not central in the town, buses were usually much more convenient for journeys there.

The Buses

Mona Craig has given us a good description of wartime bus travel:

"The bus company must have made a small fortune during the war, we were mostly packed like sardines. We never expected to get a seat to go to Hexham. Petrol was rationed and there was very little, if any, 'pleasure petrol'. The tankers were running the gauntlet with the U boats to get the oil here, plus the fact that German bombers kept trying to get the refineries. Sometimes there were more standing than sitting on the buses, they were 20 and 32 seaters in those days. Often we would get settled in and the conductor would shout: Acomb and Wall in the other bus please. Then it was all change. If they hadn't a spare bus they crammed them in. They were allowed eight standing, but never left anybody!

Every now and again the police would clamp down on them and the conductors would be fined, paid by the bus company. Once they made them all get out and there were sixty odd! They got over that one though, the driver would say: "Run to the station lads (sometimes the railway bridge), we'll wait for you there" – and they did! The fare was 4d single and 6d return, but when you compare that with 10/- pension, one twentieth, they aren't so bad today after all."

In May 1923 a regular bus service between Bellingham and Hexham was started by Mr Anthony Charlton of Wark. He had a canvas covered vehicle with solid tyres, entered from the back and very dark inside. After Mr Charlton came Cecil Moffitt with his blue buses which became a familiar sight up and down the North Tyne valley. Buses then were basic. Air conditioning had not been thought of and seats were made with wooden slats. As time passed they did improve. Buses with more than forty upholstered seats appeared, some with heaters. In one there were two floor heaters. Regular travellers knew where they were, third from the front at the right hand side, third from the back on the left. Sometimes they worked, especially in the summer when they tended to jam full on.

In 1962 Cecil Moffit sold his company to Jack Charlton of Newbrough. The name was changed to Mid Tyne Transport and this lasted for about nine months. One well known conductress at this time was Kitty Bowman who lived in Wall. On the bus route she took newspapers to some of the remote areas, after first picking them up from the shop in Humshaugh. Mr and Mrs Weir then took over and changed the name to that which we now know: Tyne Valley Coaches. Over the years buses have been modernised. While the blue buses have been well known for many years, white buses have now become familiar.

Over many decades buses ran between Bellingham and Newcastle, enabling shopping trips. They were run by Fosters of Otterburn, then Moffits and finally Tyne Valley Coaches. At first they would go straight up Brunton Bank, but then it was decided that they should turn right at Brunton Crossroads, go from Front Street to the green up the Falster, rejoin the main road at the garage and return to the crossroads. Here they resumed the journey to Newcastle. This service ceased in the mid-1970s.

Tyne Valley Coaches are well known for their school transport and almost every local child who has attended Hexham Middle or Hexham High School will have memories of their days travelling to school. The service for the general public is now much curtailed. The timetable is restricted to day time travel from Monday to Saturday, convenient for shopping in Hexham.

From Easter to October half-term The Hadrian's Wall AD122 bus is in operation. This provides a valuable service during the tourist season for travellers, walkers and locals alike. Timetables for this service are available from Tourist Information points in the area.

Operating a rural transport service is very difficult these days as there are so many different needs. Taxis are used for local journeys more than they were, and even with the bus pass for the elderly still in operation many folk prefer the comfort and ease of the car. How will it be in the future? Who knows!

GREENHEAD HOUSE - Daphne Bannister

I can recall in the early 1950s, with three young children to care for and life being fairly hard, my mum Audrey Huddleston decided that she would like to invite paying guests for full board, which meant mum cooking all the meals. This was to prove to be a lasting success.

In the beginning, when Mum embarked upon the idea, continental holidays for most people were out of the question, so she placed the occasional advert in the Newcastle Journal, which led in turn to several people coming to stay in our pleasant village of Wall. Very often they stayed for two weeks, some with a young family. I imagine some of the children, never having seen farm animals, were fascinated by the three farms which we were fortunate to have. I remember afternoon milking time at Mr Ripley's (West Farm) was simply magic for them when they were taken by me to see the cows being milked.

People came from North and South Shields, Wallsend, Tynemouth and various other towns, from various walks of life. I remember an extremely jolly chap who worked on the slipway at Swan's Shipyard. Shortly after he entered Greenhead House it rang with laughter. Many evenings and early mornings were spent playing cards while three young Huddlestons were tucked up in bed. After visiting for several years, he and his wife became firm friends, as did many other people.

My father, being a keen gardener, played a big part in this. He had a large vegetable garden and was therefore able to grow all the vegetables for the meals. These were lovingly prepared and cooked by Mum. A mobile butcher and a fishmonger came into the village weekly, which enabled Mum to buy both for the meals.

After several years of full board guests, Mum chose to concentrate on B & B only, sometimes providing an evening meal. It was during this time that she opened the house to people from all over the world – America (where a long lasting family friendship was formed), Canada, Australia, New Zealand and many others. All were made welcome by a tray set with tea, scones and biscuits.

I remember one particular incident when a gentleman with a family, who came from Nottingham each year, sat down to breakfast on the morning of their departure. They ate their cereal. At this stage Mum had cooked breakfast and popped it in the oven for a short while to keep warm. In the meantime my Aunt Mary popped into the kitchen to see her, as she did most mornings. After a short while, the family having paid Mum waved goodbye, thanking her for a lovely stay. When she returned to the dining room she looked at the table and was horrified to see the cutlery untouched. She questioned herself momentarily as to how they ate breakfast without using the knives and forks, then realized, upon opening the oven door, she saw four breakfasts looking straight at her. It goes without saying that Mum promptly sent a refund and a letter of apology.

Until the mid '90s the door at Greenhead House was always opened with my Mum's happy smiling face welcoming people into our home, all being given the best of food and being treated perfectly. Lasting friendships formed and continued for many years by people re-visiting Mum and by means of greetings cards. This brought to a close my mum's love and devotion in meeting so many. She was a very special caring hostess.

ST OSWALD'S TEA ROOM - Elizabeth Archer

I was brought up at St Oswald's Farm. In 1997 I had the idea of making a tearoom out of the stable and byre next to the farmhouse, because it was on the line of Hadrian's Wall, and beside the military road, with lots of traffic looking for the Wall. My husband Derek and I enquired about planning, which seemed positive, but it did take a year to get planning permission. Because St Oswald's is right on top of Hadrian's Wall, English Heritage had to be involved with Highways, to improve the entrance.

After we had permission we didn't take long to have building work done inside. Shire Builders did the major work, and all the family helped with other jobs – picking out lime, re-pointing, painting, and clearing outside for the car park. My dad, Ridley Reay, built walls and landscaped the garden area.

I hadn't done anything like this before, but I could cook. I did a business course and a food hygiene course. I went round other tearooms seeking ideas.

The building work started in January 1998 and we opened on the 4 May 1998. It was very nerve racking! My sister Althea Williamson (née Reay) designed the logo for our tearoom.

It took 2-3 years to get established. Foot and Mouth disease hit in 2001, this was a very poor year. 2002 was very busy and the Hadrian's Wall Path opened in 2003, so we have both a steady flow of walkers and people passing in cars. We also have many people who come very regularly. We have been open this year, 2013, for 15 years and are celebrating with bunting in the tea room. It is still hard to predict how busy it is going to be. Now I have a few part time staff, but I still enjoy doing all of the cooking myself. The trade mark of St Oswald's is good home cooked food.

I enjoy meeting and welcoming people who call in at St Oswald's Tea Room. I hope that they find our tearoom a relaxing and pleasant place to be in.

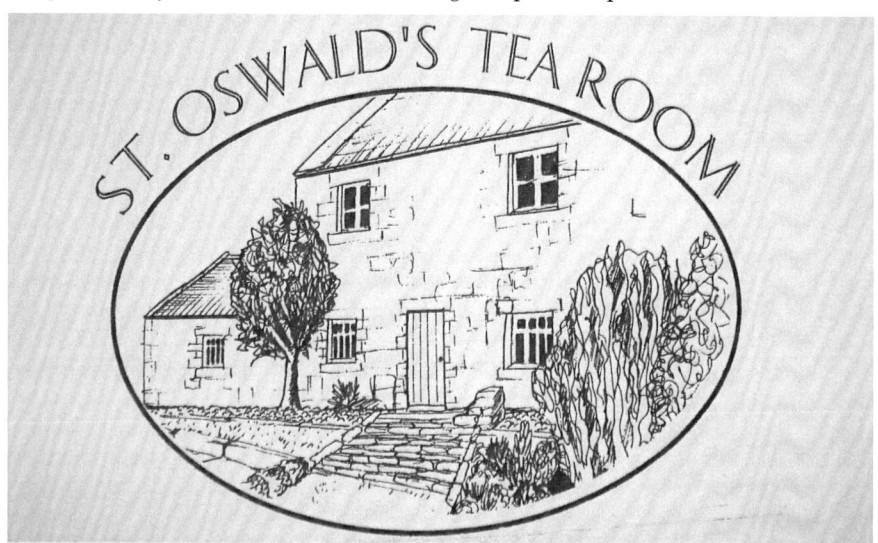

THE HADRIAN HOTEL

The Hadrian began life as the Smith's Inn, so called as a smithy was situated at the rear of the inn. The inn was bought by Mr Clayton of the Chesters Estate in 1829, when the name was changed to the Smith's Arms. In the 1900s the inn was leased to the Purvis family,

Mr Purvis being the smith. Upon Mr and Mrs Purvis's deaths their two daughters ran the inn. At the time of the Chesters Sale in 1929, the tenant of the Smith's Arms was Miss Molly Purvis, on a yearly rental of £19 10s. When the pub was sold as part of the sale the official sale book said:

'The Inn is substantially built of stone and contains bar parlour with small bar, dining room, sitting room, kitchen, scullery, pantry, dairy, beer cellar, five bedrooms, outside WC water laid on. Good garden.'

The new owner was Mr Alf Thompson, owner of the George Hotel, Chollerford. He dug a new cellar, built more bedrooms and added a restaurant on the south-west corner.

Mr Thompson also turned the stables into garages and built an engine-house to generate electricity, which meant that the Smith's Arms had electricity two years before the rest of the village. His final act was to rename the pub. It became The Hadrian Hotel.

At the same sale a Gosforth schoolmaster's wife bought the two houses next to the inn for £240. These cottages are Bastle Houses. After finding that she could neither evict the tenants nor raise their rent, she sold them to the then proprietor of the Smith's Arms. The cottages later became staff accommodation for the hotel.

The pub had many eccentric guests. One older gentleman lodged in the stables at the back of the Hadrian with only a bed, table, chair and oil stove. Another memorable guest, who stayed at the Hadrian in the early 1930s, loved walking around Wall so much that she paid for eight seats to be placed around the village!

The original pub was the front part of the present building, with the entrance being to the side for the rooms letting area, and the public bar entrance at the opposite end. The restaurant and kitchen area were built in the 1930s.

After Mr Thompson came Mr Armstrong, a tripe merchant from Newcastle. He died soon after buying the pub, but his widow stayed into the 1950s. She was followed by Mr Eades and then Mr White, who made the Hadrian a well-known place to go to for business lunches, weddings and parties in the 1960s. At this time it was owned by Vaux Breweries. The Hadrian has been looked after by many people since, including Mrs Mellor, Mr Kevin Kelly, Mr Alex Duncan, Mr Kevin Kelly (again) and the current owner, Mr David Lindsay who retired in 2011, but 2012 saw him back at the helm again.

Whilst giving a brief talk on Wall Village in September 2012, Joan Proudlock had an interesting encounter. Following an invitation from Rev Christine Bull, a group from

St Nicholas Church in Gosforth came for a day visit to Wall and its environs. Some of the visitors went walking on the fell but one lady stayed behind and mentioned she was the granddaughter of the Mr Thompson who had bought the Smith's Arms. As we were all having lunch at the Hadrian Joan brought in her copy of The Chesters sale book and was able to show her he had paid £875. for it, as it was written in pencil in the margin of the sale book by Mr Wardle in 1929. This price was corroborated by David Lindsay, the Hadrian's owner, who produced his copy of the sale book. Our new friend was delighted with this knowledge and we were delighted to meet her.

Wall Mill and Wall Station

CHAPTER SIX
OUR CHURCHES, OUR CHAPEL AND OUR SCHOOL

THE CHURCHES

In 1850 the Parish of St John Lee stretched from Thockrington in the north to the banks of the Tyne at Hexham in the south. It included Hallington, Bingfield, Wall and Acomb. Today the ecclesiastical parish of Wall has three C of E Churches, St Oswald in Lee, Heavenfield, St George's, Wall and St Mary's, Bingfield.

Vicars have come and gone in Wall and each has brought their own way of living in the parish. The following lists a few names. London, Tymms, Westgarth, Porteous, Simpson, Pocklington, Sinfield and our last vicar, Canon Clive Price, who retired in August 2007, the vicarage subsequently being let out. We presently enjoy the services of our Priest in Charge the Rev Christine Bull, whose home is in Bingfield.

St Oswald's

The oldest of the churches is St Oswald in Lee. In 635 AD at the battle of Heavenfield the heathen Cadwalla was defeated by the Christian King Oswald of Northumbria. Before battle commenced Oswald ordered a large wooden cross to be erected, before which he and all his army prayed. The first church, named for St Oswald, was built in the late 7th century. In the 1950s its foundations were discovered by dowsing. In 671 monks came to venerate St Oswald. In the reign of Elizabeth 1 (1583-1603), the decayed first church was rebuilt. By 1737 it was again in a state of disrepair. This time it was rebuilt by the vicar of Hexham. In 1887 it was remodelled by W S Hicks who added the porch and the bellcote to the existing building. This church contains some interesting relics. These include a Roman altar which was found nearby and now serves as a socket for a cross.

Continuing this heritage, St Oswald's remains a place of pilgrimage, with an organised walk taking place annually from Hexham Abbey to St Oswald's. It starts with a short act of worship in the abbey then proceeds to St John Lee for worship and a picnic, and so on to Heavenfield, for closing worship and tea. Finally the AGM of the Friends of St Oswald's takes place. All are welcome to take part in this day which is advertised in the church vestry.

In 1879 the diocese decided to make St Oswald in Lee the parish church for Wall, but a parish church over a mile from the village and up a steep hill was rather inaccessible. In 1894 a new vicarage was constructed in the village. St George's Church was built two years later. The foundation stone was laid in 1895 and the consecration followed in 1897.

St George's

The church stands on the site of a former heather thatched cottage. Due to the limitations of the site unusually it is aligned north/south. The beautiful oak rood beam, cross and altar rails were made in Ralph Hedley's woodcarving workshop. The magnificent north window by Charles Kempe was installed in 1907 behind the altar. The commemoration at the base of the right panel records that the widow and son of Major George Marmaduke Darley Waddilove, who died on 6 March 1887, dedicated the window to his memory: 'in honour of Christ Crucified'. There is a memorial plaque on the east wall which reads: 'To the Glory of God and in loving remembrance of James Herdman, 38 years churchwarden of this parish and builder of this church. Born Nov.18 1827, Died Mar. 2 1907. He rests from his labours'.

The third church for which the Wall incumbent is responsible is St Mary's at Bingfield. This is part of our ecclesiastical parish, but not part of the civil parish. It was dedicated in 1875. It has some medieval masonry and some from the early part of the 18th century. The church has been part of the Parish of St Oswald in Lee with Bingfield since 1879. In a field beside St Mary's is the old 'hearse house' which used to contain a horse-drawn hearse for the use of the parish, when required.

St Mary's

    The Parochial Church Council meets four times a year and had a joint meeting with the Methodist Church Council in November. The service on the fourth Sunday morning of each month is a 'Worship for All' service planned by members of both churches. For the annual Service of Remembrance in November, parishioners gather for 11am at the War Memorial. Those who have been worshipping in St George's church, led by the vicar, join them for the Act of Remembrance when the wreath of poppies is laid. All are then invited back to the church for coffee. Special services for the major festivals are highlights of the year. They include a candlelit Midnight Eucharist at St Oswald's on Christmas Eve and the Epiphany Service, which also marks the birthday of St George's Church. There used to be an evening Epiphany party, now replaced by a family lunch party in the village hall. On Easter day the parish comes together for Eucharist at St Oswald's, when it has become a tradition to decorate a wooden cross, made from the Christmas tree, with flowers. The children enjoy an Easter Egg Hunt around the churchyard afterwards.

    In July every year the Three Churches Fête is held in the heart of the village. There is a marquee on the green for a variety of stalls (white elephant, gifts and tombola), a plant stall selling wares predominantly grown by villagers, second hand books for sale in the church, home-made teas in the hall, a village archives display and alpacas with their owners, Melanie and Mike Douglas, from Fallowfield. Music is provided by Ernie Bainbridge (keyboard), Rob Say and Andrew Davison (both Northumbrian pipes) and singing by Humshaugh First School pupils. Other attractions, which vary from year to year, often include fancy dress, face and nail painting and an obstacle course for children. Police cars, fire engines, and vintage cars arranged by Wall Garage, an ice cream van and pony rides all have contributed to the success of the day. Several years ago, the idea was put forward that a proportion of the proceeds should be given to a specific local charity, to be chosen each year. This has proved a success, but of course, one of the main contributors to the fête is the weather, and we cannot control that!

    In 2007 a group of ladies got together to design and make a banner depicting St Mary's Bingfield, St Oswald's Heavenfield and St George's Wall. This was a part of celebrations in the Deanery, and the resulting needlework banner, in the manner of three stained glass windows, was hung in St Nicholas Cathedral in Newcastle. It is now in the process of being quilted by Tish Easby, present secretary of the Parochial Church Council, and when complete will be displayed in all three churches on different occasions.

The centenary of St George's Church took place in 1996 and was celebrated with a flower festival. Dorothy Charlton, a faithful member of the congregation and our village poet wrote this poem as a permanent record of those who took part.

St George's Church Centenary 1996 - Dorothy Charlton

"St George's Church Centenary, How can we celebrate?" said Reneé
A flower festival - wouldn't that be great?
So Elva ordered flowers – she did pulpits and pedestals too!
Jean did an outside feature in yellow, white and blue.
Angela and her mother and Molly made windows and panelling gay;
Pat climbed about decking the organ (It's broken by the way!)
Dorothy C. conditioned flowers – remarked "It's awfully late"
Then couldn't get home, for Doreen was garlanding the gate.
On Friday, Kathleen and Gwynneth decided two heads were better than one.
The bookcase was a real delight when their task was done.
Meanwhile Dorothy I. and Jill around the font were working;
They did a really splendid job, with never a sign of shirking.
As Sybil and Mary in each choir seat
Placed garlands and posies that looked a real treat.
And Molly, with help from Dorothy C.
Worked at the altar 'till time for tea.
Dorothy C. placed vases on each corner bracket
One came crashing down again - it made such a racket.
Elva brought her candle sticks because the vase had broken!
Dorothy told the Vicar and Roy - not one cross word was spoken.
Then Elva, Jean and Dorothy C. started arranging once more
They finished and while they tidied up, Roy kindly mopped the floor.
As Doreen polished the altar cross and the handle on the door
We felt we'd done a canny job - hope folks would come and see
Said Doreen, "Send folk to the hall for home-made scones and tea."
Sunday morning a family service - our Methodist friends were there
Sang well known hymns and worshipped- it's wonderful to share.
We had a flowery sermon, (If Clive will forgive the pun)
And this is where my saga is very nearly done! But not quite!
Because at ten o'clock that night Roy did a 'Son et Lumière'
Had a really good turn-out - hardly a vacant chair!
The spotlight places shown by Roy brought us all a lot of joy.
Casting its shadow on window and wall
Our old wooden cross with thanks we'll recall.
So we had a happy festival and the bit that made us smile
Were all the lovely comments - they made it all worth-while.

Tony Cattermole, Churchwarden of St George's church, has given the following information, which will aid any readers of this book searching for past records of their family ties with Wall's ecclesiastical and civil parishes.

Church Records for the Parish of St Oswald in Lee
St George's Church, Wall
St Oswald's Church, Heavenfield
St Mary's Church, Bingfield

Some Parish Registers are held in the Parish by the Priest in Charge, the Rev Christine Bull. These are listed below. All other records are held in the Northumberland Archives at Woodhorn Colliery, Queen Elizabeth II Country Park, Ashington, NE63 9YF Tel 01670 528080. www.experiencewoodhorn.com

Registers held in the Parish
St Oswald's Burials From 1884
St George's Burials From 1981
St Oswald's & St. George's Baptisms From 1880
St Oswald's Marriages From 1991
St George's Marriages From 1994
St Mary's Marriages From 1988
St Mary's Baptisms From 1892

When Benjamin John Edward Proudlock was baptised at St Oswald's in 2011, there was great interest in seeing his grandfather and great grandfather's names in the Register of Baptism, giving a sense of continuity. Though the Proudlock side of his family attended St George's church his Wardle ancestors attended the Methodist chapel in the village.

Maureen Proud has given us memories of her role in a nativity play which took place in St George's church. It was put on by Mr Robinson, Mrs Crozier, the scholars and Youth Club members, over two or three nights. Mr Robinson was headmaster of Wall Church of England School from 1941 to 1963. He encouraged strong links between church and school.

"I was Gabriel and had to walk down the aisle towards the altar with my arms outspread, draped in long white pieces of material. One mum was wearing a hat, which my wings removed and carried some distance down the aisle. A lady told me some years later that she had seen an 'apparition' down the side of the church, only to realise later that it was a very solid angel running outside to get into position for the next scene!"

THE METHODIST CHURCH
In the 1800s non-conformity was growing throughout the country and becoming very strong in the Tynedale area. There is a record of a comment from an earnest believer," The spiritual destitution of this village is great, and the erection of a chapel a matter of great urgency". Chapel records show that in 1868 the Chapel trust was made up of fourteen local men of whom three were farmers, three were miners, two were quarrymen and the rest a grocer, a mason, a nurseryman, a gardener, a labourer

and a student. Remembering that Methodism had its origins in the working classes it is not surprising that we don't see a single landowner or gentleman on the list. Methodism was not only 'born in song' but also in honest toil. At that time there was no place of worship of any denomination in the village of Wall.

The foundation stone was laid on Good Friday, 10 April 1868 by Hugh Taylor of Chipchase Castle. In the cavity of the foundation stone was placed a bottle containing the names of the Superintendent Minister, the Rev John Booth, and the original trustees of the Chapel, many with family names we recognise today; Rowell, Johnson, Lamb, Wilkinson, Atkinson and Maughan. The Wesleyan Methodist Chapel was built of freestone procured from Black Pasture Quarry at a cost of £200, of which £110 had already been raised by public subscription. It was officially opened on 19 September of the same year, built in five months! The schoolroom and small kitchen were added in 1898 at a total cost of £324.

By 1954 the Trustees were men with even more familiar names, Dodd, Wardle, Charlton, Armstrong, Henderson, Cresswell, Heslop, Ripley and there was still a Lamb in there as well!

The chapel building contained the Sunday school room and a small kitchen. The partitions between the chapel and the schoolroom could be removed when more seating was required.

Although there is no longer a Chapel Sunday School, it flourished in years gone by. There was a good attendance; classes were held on Sunday mornings.

Maureen Proud has given these memories from when she came to Wall in 1950.

"Mr W Ripley was Sunday School Superintendent in the 1950s, Miss Margaret Wardle was a teacher and in later years Mr W Armstrong, myself and Isobel Wardle, along with

Mr Bilner who helped for a time, also taught and ran a youth club in the school room.

Wall Chapel Sunday School took part in the annual Music and Arts Festival of the Hexham Methodist Circuit, which was held the week before Palm Sunday. Wall competed against others in both individual and team competitions, winning 'The Shield' on a number of occasions. Classes included sewing, knitting, cooking, painting, reciting, sight-reading and singing. The Anniversary involved two services on one Sunday. The children recited poems and sang hymns. The evening service often followed, a booklet of poems, readings and hymns with a special theme. It was always a time of lovely dresses and smart shirts. Many mums would be finishing making dresses on the Saturday night before, as my mum did for Hazel's and mine and as I did for my three girls. The Centenary Anniversary of 1968 was very special and included an exhibition. Sandra Heslop and Jacqueline Proud presented Mrs Grace Lamb and Mrs Davidson with flowers, after the two ladies, our oldest members, had cut the celebration cake."

Members of Wall Chapel were instrumental in forming The North Tyne Youth Fellowship which was launched in 1976 and did a great work amongst the young people. For the past 35 years there has been a tradition of an adult group of carol singers who have helped to make the lead-up to Christmas significant for the village and out-bye.

As this book is being written Wall Methodist Chapel has closed and will be sold. Much of the information recorded here has been given by Peter Burgon*, who wrote and read 'A History of Wall Chapel' at the final service held in the chapel, 2.30pm Easter Sunday 31 March 2013. The title of the service was 'A Celebration of a Work Complete'. It is fitting the records of Wall Chapel should have a place in this book, as we write the passage of time.

*Peter Burgon of Barrasford Chapel and Sandra Heslop of Wall Chapel were married in Wall Chapel in December 1992. Barrasford Chapel is still open for worship.

Wall Methodist Chapel

WALL SCHOOL

Early in the nineteenth century George Chatt wrote a poem called Bonnie Tyneside.
The second verse reads thus:

> Oh! Bonnie Tyneside! Where my infancy pass'd,
> Like a beautiful dream, too happy to last;
> Oh, I'll see the bright hills, where in childhood we strayed,
> And the school green at Wall where so often we played;
> And the schoolmaster still at the village is seen,
> And the schoolchildren still are at play on the green;
> But the classmates I knew they are gone far and wide,
> They have wander'd away from Bonnie Tyneside.

The school building above the back green, was probably first built in the 1850s. The schoolmaster, Robert Elliott, was assisted by his wife, eldest daughter and son. It was rebuilt and enlarged by the owner of the property, John Clayton of the Chesters, in 1882. William Irving took charge as schoolmaster. The new building was considered capable of accommodating 110 children. The attendance was approximately 70. While renovations were carried out lessons took place in a house in the village.

School hours were 9am – 4.20pm. From 13 November 1897 to 1 February 1898, they were changed to 9.00am – 3.50pm with the lunch break cut by half an hour. This was to enable children to walk home before dark.

In 1905 the summer holiday lasted for four weeks, from 20 July to 21 August. During this period the partition was removed between the two classrooms to give the infants more space. A new wood and glass partition was erected. 10 June 1907 saw the closure for one day due to flooding to a depth of five inches. This followed a terrific overnight thunderstorm. A further day closure occurred on 20 May 1910 for the funeral of King Edward V11.

This school became Wall Church of England School on 10 April 1906. The school building went into the ownership of Northumberland County Council at the Chesters Sale in 1929. Sadly it was closed in December 1971. The premises, comprising the school and the schoolmaster's house, were then sold to Mr and Mrs Spooner and converted into a private home.

The last sports day, held in July1971 on the village green with parents and villagers watching, was cine-filmed by Joan Proudlock and that film is still in existence.

SCHOOLDAYS IN WALL SCHOOL - Jean Reed (née Herdman)

September 1938, at last I could start school. I remember that day so well. My father took me that first morning. At that time the ages were from five to fourteen: the infants in the small room, juniors and seniors in the big room, open fires in both.

Some children had long walks to school in all weathers, carrying their lunch. Kathleen, Ernest and Charlie Proud came down from the Craig. In summer often they came over the fell and in bad weather and winter down the Old Lane. The village children went home to eat at lunch time.

Mr Parker was soon replaced by Mr Robinson and Miss Robertson (later Mrs Everatt). Looking back now I realise how much Mr Robinson did in the village: Monday choir practice, Tuesday County Library in the Reading Room, working for the Church and the Parish Council. Later there was a Young Farmers' Club and a Dance Club.

When the war began an army camp appeared on the back green opposite the garage. We walked past the cookhouse on our way to school. Evacuees came next, from North Shields and Willington Quay, where the docks were being bombed. Extra classes were held in the village hall, with more teachers. The children and teachers were billeted in cottages in the village. The Chapel supper room operated as a canteen in the evenings for soldiers and a rota of ladies manned it. Films in the village hall were a highlight of our lives. The Home Guard appeared in uniform and had manoeuvres on Sunday mornings which always finished in the Hadrian at 12 noon. Mr Robinson was an air raid warden too. German bombers flew over Wall on their way to bomb the Clyde.

In the spring of 1945 building work at the school divided the big room to form a kitchen at the end. Mrs Robson was appointed as school cook and after Easter school meals began: no more going home for lunch. We were introduced to raw grated carrot, but the meals were wonderful! I left the school in July 1945, and in September moved on to the Queen Elizabeth Grammar School in Hexham.

September 1966, and now I had returned to Wall School as a teacher with Mr Wood as headmaster. Mrs Huddleston was the cook and we had the best school meals I ever had during my teaching career. Mrs Thompson was our kind and caring dinner nanny and Mrs Marren our hard working caretaker. She had to wrestle with coke stoves which gave off fumes and dust, and with outside toilets which had to have little paraffin lamps in the winter to stop them from freezing, but these were very happy years.

Christmas 1966: we were preparing for our Nativity play which Mr Wood had written. It was intended to be in the village hall, but so many children had flu that we had to cancel.

The outside of the school was wonderful. We had the school wood with its snowdrops, primroses, violets, birds' nests and wild life plus all the greens to play on. Mr Wood had persuaded the Parish Council to lay a concrete cricket pitch before I arrived and it had a great deal of use. Bobby Wood played for Tynedale and many of the boys he taught to love cricket still play. The green by the garage could be hazardous at times as Fred Henderson took his dairy cows across to the fields up the Old Lane. We had to check for 'booby traps' before we used it! The other green was, as now, prone to flooding and a large pond would appear. It was great to paddle in with wellingtons on, but even better when it froze over, to slide on.

The bombshell came early in 1971. Wall School was to close. All the usual things happened, including a village meeting in the hall – all to no avail. Mr Wood was appointed head at Riding Mill, where his wife grew up. I was transferred to Humshaugh with the children. Mr Wood bought a house in Hexham and moved out of the schoolhouse before the school closed.

Christmas 1971 was a sad time for us all, but there were only 25 children in the school so it was inevitable. At that time children stayed until 11 but in 1977 first schools began and children only stayed until they were nine. January 1972 and the bus arrived to pick up the pupils. I travelled on the bus at first, but then I bought my first car and no longer used the bus.

LOCKING OUT - Dorothy Charlton (née Hetherington)

This was a much looked forward to event on the last day of term before breaking up for the Christmas holiday.

After 'big' playtime (dinner hour) we all had to be back early (most of us went home for mid-day lunch), except of course the people who walked from Chollerton, Brunton Corner and Fallowfield, they brought sandwiches. The big boys, thirteen year olds, locked the boys' and girls' porch doors.

When Mr Parker, the headmaster, came back from lunch he was unable to get in. He entered into the spirit of the game and went and got his stick. He then banged on the doors, rattled on the windows, poked the stick under the doors and rattled that. He went back to the house and came back wearing an outdoor coat and hat of Mrs Parker's and pretended he was a visitor wanting to see the headmaster. This pleased the little ones who laughed at Mr Parker, Sir, having Mrs Parker's clothes on! They tried to tell us bigger children that "It isn't Mrs Parker you know, it's really Sir!" Great glee! After some half hour Mr Parker had had enough and announced: "If I'm not allowed in school in two minutes all big boys will be given two of the best."

So the doors were unlocked and we all sat down in our seats as quickly and quietly as possible. Then came the dreaded question: "Who locked the doors?" No-one said a word. "Senior boys out here on the floor," Oh Crikey! Then, "Please Sir, there's someone in the girls' porch Sir"! The door opened and in waddled a little brown duck with an ounce plug of pipe tobacco tied around its neck. "Surprise, surprise Happy Christmas Sir!" End of lessons for that day and sorry for the caretaker with a few duck calling cards left on her clean floor before the duck was removed.

Possibly the duck was purchased from Mr John Davidson of North Farm who kept a lot of poultry, especially at Christmas. This custom was discontinued on Mr Parker getting a new headship.

Mona Craig gives an account of a similar episode, differing in some details. Hers includes a lady teacher. The boys produced a white duck with twenty Players cigarettes, and the girls gave the teacher a doggy nightdress case. She tells us that the nightdress case cost six shillings, the duck (which was bought from North Farm) the same. The cigarettes cost 11½d. The pupils had paid from their meagre pocket money.

A party followed with food provided by Mrs Waddilove from Brunton House and all the old party games: How Green You Are, Old Macdonald's Farm, Spin the Trencher, Postman's Knock.

Miss Robertson (later Mrs Isabelle Everatt) gives an entertaining teacher's perspective on the Lock Out, which is to be found in her section in the book.

Through the years the teachers and pupils have been important in village life. They have enriched the social calendar, organised activities, given concerts and nativity plays. They have participated in war efforts. Three 20th century headmasters have played a major role in all of this.

Mr Parker was headmaster at the start of the Second World War. He and his staff, Miss Robertson and the evacuee teachers, gave much of their time for the benefit of the children. He organised a 'play centre' in the church hall (now the village hall), and began country dancing for the older children, taking it himself. After seven years at Wall, he left in 1941 to be head at Ponteland Coates Endowed School. He was succeeded by Mr Jim Robinson.

Mr Robinson had been head at Bingfield School for three years before coming to Wall. He was keen on games. The boys enjoyed their football and shinty on the green. He was an expert on Rural Science, introducing rabbit-keeping and poultry which became part of the school curriculum, teaching management, responsibility and care to the pupils. He had a well stocked garden. The older children loved it. In the late 1950s he started a Young Farmers' Club which lasted a short while before becoming part of the Hexham Club.

The play centre and dancing continued. Mr Robinson also started and ran a lending library in the Reading Room. In his time a lot of work towards the war effort was motivated from the school. He is fondly remembered for the railway trips he organised in the mid-fifties, to places such as Edinburgh or York.

Then there were the school camps! These are remembered fondly by many past pupils as a time of fun and growing up.

Mr Robinson arranged for these to be held during school holidays from the late 1940s to 1959. As few people had cars it was to give the pupils the chance of a holiday to visit places further afield: Budle Bay, Warkworth, Alnmouth, Glen Luce, Silloth and Grange-Over-Sands. Some of the adults in the village volunteered to help, cook and supervise. Ray Craig remembers Humphrey and Annie Armstrong, Frances Mason, Peggy Robinson and Mrs Leadbeater. When at a coastal site the youngsters collected sea coal from the beach, and cooking was done on an open fire until the arrival of Calor gas. Everyone had duties each day and meals were at a long table in the marquee.

Here again we have the memories of Maureen Proud.

"Olga and Margaret let down the guy ropes on Fred's and Robin's tent then they came into ours to hide, as they couldn't get back to their own. I heard the boys outside looking for two guys, one tall and thin and one short and fat: much to the disgust of the girls. (Olga Purvis and Fred Thompson subsequently married.)

One early camp Charlie was at, the bus boot came open going up a hill and some of the equipment fell out. Another camp was so wet they ended up sleeping in a barn.

Another camp saw Maureen and friends 'shipwrecked' on a log up the river Aln. They were rescued by Mr Robinson!

Mr Robinson retired in 1963, moving to Allendale. He was followed by Mr Wood.

Bobby Wood was enthusiastic about sport, particularly cricket, playing for Tynedale himself. He nurtured a love of games in his pupils. Because of low pupil numbers, he joined forces with Whitley Chapel School to form teams for football and cricket. He it was who instigated the concrete cricket wicket, constructed by Lewis Mason, David Mason, Barney Mitchell, John Elliott and Ray Craig which is still to be found on the back green.

Mr Wood was a member of the Parochial Church Council, and served as its secretary. He also wrote the scripts for the annual nativity plays put on by the school. These were well supported by the people of Wall, both through the making of costumes for the children and attendance at their performance. The last Nativity was given in St George's Church in December 1971. Indeed he found the community very supportive in whatever he did, whether it was sporting events or fund raising for the school.

In August 1995 came the dreadful news that Bobby Wood had died at the age of sixty-two. The Abbey was full for his funeral. Family, friends, teachers, cricketers and many more crowded in.

The three successive headmasters: Mr Parker, Mr Robinson and Mr Wood loved, and were loved by Wall. Each in his turn did so much for the community.

Many people have happy memories of Wall School and this was most evident at the Wall School Reunion which took place in the village hall on Boxing Day evening 1987. The hall was full, as many generations, and teachers, who had passed through the school gathered together to exchange their stories. Sadly for many, Jimmy Robinson, held in great affection had died soon after he left the school, but his son Eddie came from California to meet up again with his school friends. The evening started with a slide show of school and the camps followed by a pie and pea supper and then a dance. It was an evening to remember! The following are some memories of her journey to school from Ella Hill (née Wardle), when she made those journeys each day from Planetrees farm at High Brunton to school and back.

WALKING TO WALL SCHOOL - Ella Hill

When I started school in 1935 most children had to walk to school and that might mean two or three miles each way every day. A girl called Kathleen Tasey used to walk at least a mile and a half before she got to Planetrees. Fortunately for me, Planetrees was only a mile away from school and the Old Lane was a very quiet road so there was no danger from traffic. At first I was taken to school by two older girls called Doris Curry and Winnie Young who both lived quite near. Later, I joined up with my friend, Betty Graham, who lived at The Craig (now Crag House) and Oswald Muse who lived at St Oswald's. Over the years other brothers and sisters joined us. By then, Betty and her family had moved to Wall and the Prouds were at The Craig.

I don't remember being late for school in the morning but I am sure there must have been times when we dawdled. I do remember going home and taking such a long time that we got into trouble for making our parents worry about what we were up to. The Old Lane had lots of ways to distract us with birds' nests in spring, paddling in the stream in summer, picking and eating brambles in autumn (the colour of tongues a giveaway) and playing snowballs in the winter.

The start of the war in 1939 brought an influx of evacuees and made it necessary for the school to be divided into two sections, morning and afternoon. However, this situation did not last for long as many of the children went back home, after their parents decided that the danger of living in the towns was not as great as they had been led to believe.

The other big change that the war brought was that all the lanes were used by the army who stored piles of ammunition all over the verges and in the woods and fields along the sides of the lanes. These were closed to everyone except permit-holders. Children, however, were allowed to go to school without permits. We got to know some of the soldiers quite well, especially those who drove lorries and sometimes gave us lifts home.

Occasionally, my father would be going home from Hexham Mart having taken some pigs there in the trailer and we would climb into this smelly conveyance and be given a lift home. Heaven only knows what our shoes were like by then.

CHAPTER SEVEN
OUR CLUBS AND SOCIETIES

When considering the clubs and societies which happen, or have happened in Wall, some have taken place, due to the fact that we are fortunate in having a village hall. This provides the right facilities and accommodation, for a variety of meetings. Others are outdoor groups and some just work towards one annual event. Some societies, such as the Women's Institute have been in existence in Wall for many years, whilst others are younger, and some have simply come, and gone again when their usefulness has passed.

BONFIRE NIGHT
Just after the foot and mouth epidemic of 2001, Alison and Paul Henson, John Mclelland and Stephen Browell decided to start an annual Guy Fawkes bonfire night. Every November since, bonfires and displays of fireworks have been held either in John Lamb's fields to the south of the village or in Peter Heslop's to the north. They have been followed by celebrations and hospitality, courtesy of David Lindsay in the Hadrian Hotel.

The displays have been paid for by 'Race Meeting' evenings at the Hadrian and collections, both in the village and at the field gate where the occasion is held. The results have always been magnificent. The thanks of the village are due to the team who put in such hard work fund raising, organising the event, building the fire and lighting the fireworks. Thanks too to John and Peter for the use of their fields and to the Parish Council for their support. Long may this fun night continue.

WALL BOWLS CLUB - David Brookman
In January 1984 notices of a meeting about forming an indoor bowls club were posted around the village. This took place in the village hall on Tuesday 10 January. There were 23 folk in attendance'. It was opened by Mrs Ormston, who expressed thanks to Mrs Rachel Lowther for The work she had carried out in pioneering the venture'.

A committee was appointed with Mrs Lowther as Chairman, Mrs McKechnie Secretary, Mrs Proud Treasurer and Messrs McKechnie, J Carr, Armstrong and Henderson as committee members. Mrs Lowther reported that the carpet and bowls were available for a three month free loan period. The Parish Council and Humshaugh Sports Council had offered some financial help, but fund-raising was necessary and suggestions were put forward. Tuesday was to be the 'play' day, with afternoon and evening meetings. The Wall Indoor Bowling Club had come into being.

Minutes of a meeting held at the Garden House on Thursday 19 January 1984 at 7.30pm.

Present: Mesdames Lowther, McKechnie and Proud, Messrs McKechnie, Henderson, Carr and Armstrong.

The minutes of the previous meeting, being somewhat extraordinary were not read.

Mr Bilner had reported that hardboard could be purchased at a price of £22. It was decided to leave this matter pending delivery of the carpet, to ascertain whether it was really necessary. A lengthy discussion took place concerning the constitution of the club, subscriptions, attendance per session and the like. It was agreed that the constitution (in draft form) be presented to Neil Braithwaite, solicitor, to confirm that they were in order.

Mr Carr undertook to create the boxes for the bowls and the diamond for the centre of the carpet. The Chairman reported that Mesdames Mitchell and Ormston would undertake to organise a raffle to raise funds. Mrs Proud had offered to organise a fête and it was agreed that this would take place on Saturday 3 March at 2pm in the village hall. Mrs Proud to book the hall.

Now that the details were finalised, the secretary would arrange to have a notice displayed in the post office giving details of meetings, charges etc. There was some doubt as to whether the name of the club could in fact be Wall Indoor Bowling Club and the Chairman agreed to investigate. The invitation to attend the Newbrough Triples Tournament on Saturday 28 April was warmly received. The Secretary to confirm acceptance, but the actual number of teams to be entered would be confirmed nearer the time. The Secretary would arrange to open an account with Nat West bank. It was decided to arrange that any two signatures from Mesdames Lowther, Proud, Mckechnie to apply. The Chairman reported that the carpet was to be available next week and it was agreed that the first session would take place on Tuesday 24 January at 2.00pm followed at 7.30pm, by the evening session. The Chairman undertook to book the hall. The Chairman reported that Hexham Adult Education officer has looked into the possibility that NCC might pay for the hire of the hall.

Now that it was formally constituted both the Parish Council and Humshaugh and District Sports Association, which organisations had already indicated their willingness to assist financially, would be approached by the Secretary as would Tynedale District Council who might be willing to assist.

The meeting closed at 10.00pm signed R S Lowther 15/5/84.

A great deal was decided at this meeting and it gave the foundations for a club which quickly attracted members. So, in case you missed it the first playing session was at 2. 00pm on Tuesday 26 January 1984.

The next committee meeting was held on Tuesday 15 May and it was reported that; the club had a balance of £200. plus a grant of £150. from Tynedale Council and £50. from Humshaugh Sports Club and that the purchase of a second carpet would soon be possible. A summer social was proposed for July, with a match between the afternoon and evening members, and a barbecue. Not mentioned was a £25. donation from Wall Parish Council.

On Friday 15 June the Hexham Courant had a photograph of Adrian Proud and Doris Herdman the youngest and oldest members of the new Wall Carpet Bowling Club. By the first AGM on Wednesday 6 February 1985 there were 40 members: 31 senior and 9 junior. The club had made remarkable progress. Cups and shields had been purchased to award to both junior and senior winners, visits had been made to other clubs and it was hoped that return visits could be hosted in the near future. In 1986 a change of name came, from Wall Carpet Bowling Club to Wall Carpet Bowls Club.

There were many on-going problems to be faced over the ensuing years. Gradually, largely through their own efforts, the bowlers solved them. The club was, and is, rich in enthusiastic and hard-working members.

There was floor sanding which was completed by Jimmy Carr and his team with the help of Len Common's offer of a planer. Rubber mats were purchased but having been used, were found to be unsatisfactory. Diamond centres were in use until 1992, when after a trial, they were replaced by wooden round ones. The dimensions of wooden blocks at the bowling position caused discussion which was soon resolved. Norman Craig made a new set of bowls trays which took up a lot less storage space than the old ones and were still in use in 2011.

Northumberland Police Federation generously donated a set of four yellow bowls and four blue bowls and a thank you was extended to a member who had acted on the club's behalf.

Equipment had to be obtained, much of it expensive, and it all required storage. Space was lacking, and the piano was in the way. Some problems took years to solve, especially those concerning the floor and space. In 1987 an extension was built on to the hall and the piano then could be moved. Eventually it was placed on the stage, where it remains today. The stage was reduced in size giving more length to the hall.

The floor, which was always a major problem was in need of sanding again to improve on the unevenness of the under-carpet surface, but problems remained. The floor had several very uneven places. In 1991 the cost of a new floor was discussed and the subject of under- carpet boards was again raised. The boards were heavy to lift. Matthew Charlton inspected the floor and reported that renewal was not needed as the floor was made of well-seasoned wood. They recommended patching. In 1996 the Village Hall Committee promised to pay for the repairs. In April 2000 the subject of under-carpet boards was revisited, but it is not until 2001 that it is recorded that the boards acquired from Newbrough CBC (first offered in 1996) had made a big difference and no further mention was made of the floor thereafter you'll be pleased to know, although the second-hand boards were actually showing signs of wear and Len Woodcock had kindly offered new boards to replace them. By March 2003 this was all done.

It is worth noting here that at the 8th AGM on Wednesday 8 April 1992, the Chairman, Norman Doyle, proposed that a new office be created, that of President. This was unanimously accepted, as was his next proposal, that Rachel Lowther should be the first President in recognition of all the work she had done in the founding and establishing of the club. She accepted the office, reminding the meeting that it had all come from an idea born on the day of the first village lunch outing, when she and Billy Armstrong had sat in the sun watching a game of bowls.

In August 1997, the club and indeed the whole village were saddened by the death of the President, Rachel Lowther. As its first Chairman she had progressed it through to its second decade, and under her guidance the club had flourished, gained strength and established itself within the village and beyond. She would be greatly missed.

By 2006 falling membership was a problem, but new members from outside of the village helped to boost the numbers. In 2008 the Secretary reported that of the club's 26 members, only two were aged under 60! It would be good to have some younger players.

Amongst the clubs Wall have played or had contact with over the years are: Acomb, Allendale, Allenheads, Bellingham, Birtley, Cambo, Catton, Corbridge, Dalton, Falstone, Haydon Bridge, Heddon, Kirkwhelpington, Newbrough & Warden, Otterburn, Ovingham, Ponteland Methodist, Riding Mill, Shire, Slaggyford, Slaley, Snods Edge, Stamfordham, Throckley, West End Methodist, Whalton, Whitfield and Wylam.

At the 26th AGM on 6 April 2010 Ella Hill relinquished her role as Secretary, a post she had occupied since 1988. Jean Bilner was elected in her place and David Brookman took on the role of Treasurer, on the understanding that he didn't do audited accounts, which was gratefully approved by the whole meeting. He is already treasurer of the Village Society and said "I hope I can keep the two accounts separate!" (Only joking!). At an informal committee meeting held during the tea-break, it was proposed by David Brookman, seconded by Chris Jones and voted for unanimously by the other eleven players present that the honorary post of President be offered to Ella Hill in recognition of her contribution to the club over the last two decades.

After over quarter of a century, we still meet on Tuesdays and we are still going strong!!!

CHAT AND CRAFTS - Mary Mason

Chat and Crafts commenced in 1995. We were a small group interested in knitting, any craft we could be shown how to do and of course, and most important: 'the chat'. Annette Johnson had had a group of ladies meeting to knit squares for blankets at her home, Bibury. Subsequently she moved away, so these ladies formed Chat and Crafts, meeting in the village hall. From 1997 we joined the workshop for the Wall Hanging Project, and enjoyed working with 'real professionals'. In October 2000 we again became Chat and Crafts.

We began to knit blankets and baby clothes to send to Katanga in the Congo, to a nurse missionary there. By 2006 the government in the Congo would not unload containers from ships containing medical supplies and our goods, so we were unable to send our products. We are still in touch with Mary Rutter the missionary, and hear of the good work going on.

We continue with the knitting and send goods for the Tear Fund (Shoe Box Appeal), Newcastle Cyrenians and Newcastle Soup Kitchen. Also we have knitted Easter chicks which were sold at the St Oswald's Tea Room, the money going to Wall Chapel.

In 2007 some of us helped to make a banner depicting St George's Church, St Oswald's and St Mary's, Bingfield. This was shown in St Nicholas Cathedral in Newcastle, with others from the Deanery. It is being quilted ready for display by Tish Easby.

We still enjoy making items in craft sessions, some tutored by professionals. Each week we make a break for our cup of tea, a time for us to catch up with each other and share news and we are always ready to welcome anyone to come and join us.

HADRIAN LEEK CLUB

The Hadrian Leek Club started in the 1960s with about 36 members, men and women, Shows were held in the village hall every September. The main class in the show was for pairs of pot leeks. These are short and wide. They must be no longer than 6 inches from the bottom to the fast button (the split where the leaves start). The main criterion of a pot leek is its girth.

When the shows were first organised, prizes for the pot leeks took the form of furniture and kitchenalia, which were arranged behind the leeks, every participating member winning a prize. This made for a spectacular display, but involved most members making their way to the suppliers over the ensuing days to exchange goods. Later cash became king.

There were also classes for blanch leeks (a longer, thinner variety), vegetable collections and flowers such as chrysanthemums, dahlias and floral arrangements. More recently cookery and children's classes were introduced.

The evening of the show saw an auction of many of the entries in support of the club, followed by the enjoyment of leek soup at the Hadrian Hotel.

The club was disbanded in 2011.

WALL VILLAGE TODDLER GROUP

The toddler group in some form or another has probably existed in the village for as long as there have been young families who want to get together, whether in people's houses or in the village hall. In the early 1970s as there was no official group in Wall, Joan Proudlock, with two young children, started one in her home at High Brunton. This ran for two mornings each week and catered for eight toddlers at each session.

A more formal group was mentioned in the newsletter in April 1991 when it met on a Monday morning in the hall and advertised for toys for the children to play with. A shed on the hard standing in front of the hall was put up to house the toys. Later, the meetings were changed to Friday mornings

Over the years the running of the group has passed from mum to mum as children grow older and move on, and as new people come along. Activities have included Halloween parties, Christmas visits from Santa, crafts, outdoor play and fund-raising events such as coffee mornings, or the 'Sponsored Toddle' in May 2006 to cover costs and new toys.

As a community it is wonderful to have young families growing up in our village and the surrounding areas. The Toddler Group provides fun and games for the young children and support and friendship for the parents who attend.

At the time of writing, the group is not currently meeting as many of the young children in the village have started pre-school, but this is part of the ebb and flow of family life. I am sure there will be toddler groups meeting in the village in future years.

THE VILLAGE LUNCH - Ella Hill

The first village lunch was held as a Lenten lunch on 9 March 1983 and was such a success that a further Easter lunch was arranged for 16 April. This was equally successful and inspired two ladies in the village to suggest that an organised outing for senior citizens could be paid for by having a regular lunch on the first Wednesday of each month to be held in the village hall at 12 noon at a cost of 50p. So began what is now called the soup lunch.

Doreen Mitchell and Joan Ormston arranged the first trip which was during June 1983 when the bus went to Morpeth then along the coast to Whitley Bay and Tynemouth. It was a lovely day and several people enjoyed a paddle in the sea while others went to the park and watched a game of bowls which was going on there. It made Doris Herdman wonder if Wall could have an opportunity to try their hand at bowls, so with both Rachel Lowther and Billy Armstrong feeling this was a good idea then another village institution – the Bowls Club was set to come into being.

From 1984 onwards the local newsletter gave notice of the lunch dates held on the first Wednesday of every month except June, July and August. The coach trips, organised by Doreen, were usually held in June and much enjoyed by many of the older people in Wall even if the weather was not always ideal. A visit to the Lake District prompted Edna McMillin to write a piece in the July 1984 newsletter to record how much the work of all those who organised the lunches and outings was appreciated. In the following years the coach trips covered many interesting places in Yorkshire, Cumbria, Co. Durham, Northumberland and Scotland. Cities like York (a wet day), Edinburgh, Durham and Carlisle and coastal towns such as Berwick, Whitby, Bamburgh and Seahouses. Then there were houses and gardens to visit, Paxton House, Chillingham Castle, Abbotsford, Sizergh Castle, Floors Castle, Mellerstain, Durham Botanic Garden and Harlow Carr. The outings also covered many market towns, Appleby, Rothbury, Barnard Castle, Ripon, as well as beauty spots such as the Yorkshire Dales, Solway Coast, Teesdale and our own Northumberland coast. Usually the trips ended with a high tea courtesy of the local Women's Institute on the way home, stopping at villages such as Castle Carrock, Bamburgh, Rochester and Romaldkirk. The routes were chosen carefully to give as much variety of scenery as possible, both going to our destinations and returning home.

Setting out and laying of the tables, serving the meal and clearing away needed helpers and originally Rachel Lowther and her team of helpers happily took on the task. From the beginning in 1983 the soup was a homemade vegetable type, very popular with the customers, made by Tony Ormston and Ronnie Westle. Later, John Mitchell and Reg Dodd took over the job which involved an evening's work chopping up the vegetables and cooking the soup ready for the next day's lunch. When Reg moved away from Wall John did it on his own until he died in 2001. Judy and Campbell Yeoman then took over the responsibility and have made delicious soup with frozen mixed vegetables ever since. The dessert course was looked after by the ladies of the village and was usually a sponge or a crumble using fruit from local gardens such as plums, apples and rhubarb, always with custard of course. Lately the dessert has been made by Ella Hill and transported to the hall each month.

Looking back, quite a lot of those who used to be regular lunchers are no longer with us and because the demography of the village has altered there have had to be changes. It now costs £1.50 for lunch which is still very good value for money. The number of those coming for a soup lunch has dropped so that it is necessary to consider whether costs are being covered. The less profitable months have been struck off so that there are now only six lunches from October to March each winter. A raffle is still drawn at each lunch but amounts raised are smaller. 2010 was the first time for 27 years that there was no bus trip because it is now so expensive to hire a bus for a day that the expense could not be justified. Instead any money raised will be donated to local charities.

It is hoped that the soup lunches will continue but it depends on whether there are enough volunteers to make it possible as the older helpers are unable to continue indefinitely. It would be missed by those who enjoy the social opportunity to catch up with news while enjoying a bowl of delicious soup, a dessert and a cup of tea.

Sadly it must be reported that the last Village Lunch was held in March 2013, and here we say a big thank you to all those who, over the years, have helped in any way.

WALL VILLAGE SOCIETY - Mary Herdman and Joan Proudlock

On 11 November 1988 the Parish Council called an open meeting in the village hall to test the interest in the community regarding the founding of a Local History Society. Following this an initial meeting was held the next week. There is a record of those who attended this meeting held on 16 November 1988. Each person following signed to show their support for the idea and proposal, always useful if a grant might be required in the future.

Norman & Mary Doyle, Eddie & Florence Herdman, W Bilner, W Armstrong, Rachel & Maurice Lowther, Nancy & Tommy Potts, Peggy Seaby, John & Joan Proudlock, Renée & Roy Berrill, Drew & Gwynneth Wood, Dr Ridley & Mrs Scott, Raymond Craig, John & Shirley Mitchell, Marjorie Mullins, Prof Wilkes, David Mason, Joan Ormston.

Apologies were received from, Mrs E Westle, Mr & Mrs F Henderson, Mr M Herdman, Mrs Spooner, Mrs Hodges, Mrs P Stewart, Mr A Ormston. It is interesting to see this list of some of the people living in the village at this time. A further meeting was called on 18 January 1989 and a committee was formed that night.

The first talk was in February 1989 when the speaker was David Mason who gave a slide show of Wall. Then, as now, we met on the last Thursday of the month, enjoying talks from either local people or professional speakers. We also enjoyed a variety of conducted walks and outings.

Affiliation to the Association of Northern Local History Societies was proposed at a committee meeting on 9 December 1989. The secretary, Isabelle Everatt, wrote to the association, requesting application forms and a draft constitution for consideration. At the AGM on 25 January 1990, the proposal to join was carried unanimously.

Early in 1995, in an attempt to provide a wider appeal, the society considered broadening the range. Topics of general interest should be introduced. Whilst an interest in history would continue, subjects should include music, art, photography, drama, gardening, natural history, travel or whatever was requested. An appeal was sent out in the village newsletter asking for suggestions for talks and ideas for a new name for the History Society in its new wider role.

At the AGM in 1996 the decision was made to change the name of the society to Wall Village Society. In principle the society was to continue as before, as it does to this day. As well as talks and slideshows covering a very wide range of subjects, outings, quizzes, suppers, displays of our personal collections and antique valuation evenings have been much enjoyed.

In 2010 an idea was put forward for a book about Wall and its parish. This, like the Millennium Wall Hanging, would be a community based project. The Village Society committee felt they could also be the management team for the book, and so they assumed the extra title of Book Group, with the Society and its members backing the project.

For a while there have been dwindling numbers but the year 2012/2013 has shown a rise in numbers attending meetings and new residents of the village have shown interest which is encouraging. A 'Coffee Morning with a Difference' was held in the village hall, the difference being no money was required! The purpose was to invite new residents to come along and for everyone to get to know each other. The hall was full, and all this gives hope for the future. This year the Village Society has also taken on resurrecting the village trip, up-river from Newcastle Quayside to Ryton Willows; and Wall had the 43 seats on the boat fully booked!

WALL WOMEN'S INSTITUTE

Golden Jubilee 1918-1968 - Mrs Frances Mason
Fifty glorious years – how swiftly they go by
From 1918 Wall has had her WI
From small beginnings long ago until the present time
The ladies of the area have produced both rhyme and mime
Sewing, knitting, cookery and the making of good wine
Floral art and gardening and how to make things shine
Have all been shown to members by talk and demonstration
Although at times the follow-up brought feelings of frustration
Music, song and dancing have given endless pleasure
And party nights and outings enjoyed in fullest measure
Our motto 'Home and Country' is dear to one and all
We try to build Jerusalem in green and pleasant Wall.

****

WI Beginnings - Mrs Dorothy Charlton
A simple postcard is our proof
Dated May, nineteen eighteen
Asking 'Ladies of Wall'
(Long skirted – best hatted!)
To meet on the village green
They were used to shortages
War time and rations
Cloche hat, plain skirts, austerity fashions;
But is was unanimous – all were agreed.

A WI is just what we need.
They sang 'Jerusalem' to start each meeting
A hymn for those days which seemed very fitting
Ideas shared for jam, baking and knitting
Followed by tea to alleviate the sitting!
Had lively discussions on everyday topics
Or tales from a traveller back from the tropics.
From old woolly jerseys, pulled out
Thrifty housewives ne'er wasting a clout,
Made hearth rugs – both hooky and proggy;
Then a small competition to enliven each meeting,
Applause for the winner fines for those not competing.
These memories culled from old minute books
Left by founder members long gone
Give us WI traditions - Jam! – Jerusalem!
We carry on!

Wall WI 2013

May 2013 will see the start of the 95th year of Wall WI. At present we have 16 members and meet on the first Thursday of the month at 7.30pm in the village hall. New members are always welcome.

The members enjoy a varied range of demonstrations from Raku Pottery and Chocolate Making to talks on the history of the Grainger Market and the 'Trials and Tribulations of a Year behind the Veil as an English Wife in an Arab Country'.

Members of Wall WI continue to compete in competitions within the Northumberland federation and have a number of award winning knitters, crafters and cooks among our members. We are an active member of Chesters Group and enjoy joint meetings with Acomb, Wark, Humshaugh and Chollerton WIs.

Past Presidents of Wall W.I.
The First 90 Years. 1918 - 2008

Mrs. Waddilove	1918 - 1925
Mrs. Bell	1925 - 1939
Mrs. R. Wood	1939 - 1961
Mrs. G. D. Wood	1961 - 1970
Mrs. A. Hall	1970 - 1974
Mrs. A. W. Armstrong	1974 - 1975
Miss. E. R. Low	1975 - 1980
Mrs. E. M. Proud	1980 - 1984
Mrs. R. Spooner	1984 - 1986
Mrs. D. Charlton	1986 - 1989
Mrs. E. Mason	1989 - 1991
Mrs. E. M. Proud	1991 - 1997
Mrs. R. Berrill	1997 - 1998
Mrs. E. M. Proud	1998 - 2000
Mrs. E. Hill	2000 - 2002
Mrs. J. Hale	2002 - 2007
Mrs. J. Gaughan	2007 - 2008

WALL LADIES CHOIR - Elva Mason

The Wall Ladies Choir began life in July 1964 as Wall WI Choir under the leadership of Mrs Elsie Petch. For a while she acted as both conductor and accompanist until Pat Stewart returned to live in Wall and took over the role of pianist. I first saw the choir performing a pantomime and concert in the village hall in 1967 and recall that to some in Wall the group as affectionately known as the 'Wall Warblers'.

In 1972 following the death of Mrs Petch the baton was taken up by Mrs Ella Westle. Under her guidance and encouragement the choir became well known in the Tyne valley and beyond. Her faith was so strong that the choir was entered into the Tynedale Music Festival where they took first place in their class in March 1978 and 1979 and were awarded the Allendale Cup twice. Originally made up of WI members the choir would combine with other WI choirs, such as Chesters, for musical evenings to raise money for worthy causes; an example being a musical evening in aid of the Leonard Cheshire Homes at Matfen Hall in 1971. The choir would also be involved in Northumberland County Federation of Women's Institutes events where combined choirs from all over the county would join together. In 1974, for example, the choir took part in a festival of Christmas carols and music at St Nicholas Cathedral in Newcastle upon Tyne.

Although some founder members continued to sing in the choir for many years, Isabel Everatt, Gwynneth Wood, Connie Davidson, Shirley Mitchell and Doris Herdman to name but a few, only one remained until the choir folded and that was Dorothy Charlton. Dorothy was a real stalwart and not only served as treasurer but also became our 'bard'. Being very talented in writing verse, she augmented songs with beautiful tunes and not enough verses, and always ended concerts with a poem dedicated to the conductor, pianist and members.

By the mid 1970s the original membership, made up of WI members, was dwindling and so some non-members, mainly from the Hexham area, were welcomed into the choir. Concerts continued to be performed around the area and the choir travelled as far afield as Harbottle, Blanchland and Kielder. Whether at a WI meeting, Methodist Chapel

Anniversary or Harvest Festival the choir was always well received. No more so than in the village of Wall itself where the choir performed at an annual concert usually in late spring or summer and a carol concert near to Christmas; at both events it was the aim of the choir to raise money for local charities.

As the years passed by, the repertoire of the choir expanded but some numbers became, and remained, firm favourites with the choir members and audiences. In the early years a guest soloist would augment the programme but as more 'home grown' talent was drafted in the solo elements could be fulfilled by choir members. Programmes became more varied with the inclusion of Ella's famous 'Geordie' monologues, piano duets from Pat and Gwynneth, trios from the Charlton boys, tunes on the Northumbrian pipes and folk songs with guitar accompaniment. Then there was the 'Sketch'! These dramatic interludes, which were designed to add humour to the proceedings, began life as short plays read from hand held scripts. This method of performance, however, seemed to be lost on one member of the audience who, after one concert, was heard to say "It'll be alright when they get the words off!"

One concert worth particular mention was the 'Old Time Music Hall' in 1988. Dressed in period costume the programme included many old favourites and a take off of Hinge & Brackett (Binge & Hackett): a demure singing lesson, arpeggios and all, turned into a comic rendition of, 'Nobody loves a fairy when she's forty'. Another concert in May 1995 marked the 50th anniversary of VE Day: wartime songs such as 'White cliffs of Dover', 'We'll meet again' and 'Yours' were featured on the programme alongside, much to everyone's surprise, three tap dancing land girls!

Sadly in 1997, after leading the choir for 25 years, Ella Westle died suddenly and the choir was bereft of a conductor, a mentor and a dear friend. The choir paid their last respects to her by singing a two part arrangement of 'The Lord's my shepherd', a particular favourite of hers, at her funeral service.

At first it was thought that that would mean the end of the choir, but fortunately Lucy Davison, a retired music teacher from Humshaugh, came to the rescue and agreed to take over. For three more years Wall ladies continued to entertain throughout the district. Our final concert was on Friday 20 December 2002. A Christmas concert in Wall village hall, the programme included, appropriately, an arrangement of Silent Night from the WI carol book and ended with 'We wish you a merry Christmas'.

After Lucy's retirement it fell to me to keep the choir going for one more year. We met as usual on Monday evenings and continued warbling to our heart's content but our singing was for our enjoyment alone: we did not perform again. To conclude there is one person to whom Elsie, Ella, Lucy, myself and members of the choir will always be eternally grateful. She must be given special mention: our accompanist Pat, who gave her time and talent so willingly for all those years.

In writing this I am honoured to record for posterity some of the history of Wall Ladies Choir. I dedicate it to all those who put their hands together and applauded us over the years.

WALL FARMERS' SHOOT - Mike Douglas

Local farmers have traditionally enjoyed shooting game on their land, both for the enjoyment of being out in the countryside and also with the reward of the odd pheasant or rabbit for the pot. Back in the 1960s Kit Heslop of Low Brunton Farm and John Davidson of North Farm shot informally over their land at Wall on Saturday afternoons. After the closure of the railway in the North Tyne valley they also rented the railway land from Chollerton station to Wall station for the sum of £6 per annum.

In the 1970s the tradition was continued by Kit's son, Dick, and John's son in law, Freddie Henderson with their friend Hunter Adair and a couple of spaniels to flush the game. Shooting was very informal with everyone meeting in Freddie's kitchen at North Farm and ending the day there with a cup of tea provided by Freddie's wife, Connie.

Later in the 1970s John Lamb of Town Farm joined the team as did Ronnie Herdman and John McLelland of Wall and the shoot slowly expanded with more land to shoot over. Ronnie's engineering business in Wall assisted greatly in manufacturing hoppers used to feed wheat to pheasants throughout the winter months, as well as helping to build a couple of small release pens located on the railway and the fellside.

In the early 1990s Mike Douglas joined the shoot, and the Crag House land at Fallowfield was included. The shoot slowly expanded as new members joined but it always maintained its informal, friendly atmosphere, with all the work being shared amongst the members.

In 2004 the Fallowfield farm land owned by Nick Straker and farmed by Kit and Paul Dinning was added onto the shoot and in 2008 George Johnson joined the shoot and included the Half Way Farm at Acomb.

The shoot now includes access to approximately 1500 acres farmed by John Lamb, Peter Heslop, Eddie Ripley, Paul Dinning, Nicholas Robinson, George Johnson and Mike Douglas and we are indebted to these landowners.

The steep, well wooded terrain provides excellent habitat for game birds and allows us to show extremely challenging and sporting birds. In the past, generations of village children helped with the beating on shoot days. The majority of shoot members and helpers live in and around Wall and all the work, both administrative and keepering, is shared among the members.

We shoot approximately ten days per year with a typical day starting at 9.30am. As an introduction, the shoot captain for the day welcomes all guests and describes the format for the day and the sequence of drives. Great emphasis is always placed on safety and high standards are expected. After each of the drives all birds are picked, checked and hung in the game cart. There are generally four drives before lunch, which is taken out on the fell if the weather is good or inside John Lamb's barn if poor. Everyone lunches together and the morning's sport is discussed, usually with much leg pulling. After lunch there are usually two or three more drives, following which we reconvene in John's barn to layout and record the bag. Following this the game is distributed to guests, shoot members, helpers and beaters for eating at home. Following this everyone retires to the Hadrian Hotel for steak pie and chips and the odd beer as we reflect on the day.

The shoot has come a long way since Kit and John started their Saturday afternoon walkabouts and continues to develop as new enthusiastic members join. It will hopefully continue to be an integral part of Wall life for many years to come.

TYNE WATERSMEET FISHERY

Tyne Watersmeet Fishery is an angling syndicate which covers areas of both the North and the South Tyne above the watersmeet (the place where North and South Tynes join to form the River Tyne). The riparian landlords are the Strakers of High Warden. In our parish this includes the riverbank of Wall Mill Farm, which is between the river and the old Wall railway station. On the site of the old railway line, near the mill stands a fishing hut for members to the record days fished and their catches. At the sandy planting and the folly pool there are rest shelters. Members hail from a variety of places.

The fish sought by the fishermen, are brown trout and salmon. Over the last few years, as the waters of the industrial lower reaches of the Tyne, have been cleaned up, salmon catches have improved.

CHAPTER EIGHT
OUR RANDOM MEMORIES

Watching the otter hunt down by the river with the huntsmen in blue and the dogs barking, one well-spoken huntsman was 'throwing his weight and voice about'. He was on the flat shelves of rock which go out into the river. Needless to say, the inevitable happened as he marched over the edge and into the deep river, much to the glee of the on-looking crowd from the village, especially the young lads.

****

Many of the cottages had earth closets. One memory from childhood is when John Huddleston came with his horse and cart to remove the contents, which were taken along the Brunton Quarry lane and shovelled onto the old tip.

****

During the war years the young boys used to ask the troops for badges.

****

Mr and Mrs Ridley had a three piece band and played for dances in the village hall.

****

It is said that when the announcement was made that war had broken out, village women began locking their doors.

****

John Davidson always seemed to carry a hen.

****

Children would be given a jug to go and get fresh milk at milking time. One memory is of drinking half of it, still warm, and then having to go back for a 'top up'.

****

Ella Hill remembers that when she was a child at Planetrees farm, she was sent to fetch drinking water from the White Well in the Old Lane with a wooden yoke on her shoulders and two buckets hanging.

****

At Christmas time a group of enterprising Wall boys went carol singing. On visiting a house where two elderly spinster ladies lived, their choral attempts with seasonal greetings were received in a very chilly fashion. Buckets of cold water were thrown over them.

****

Many of the boys went to school each day with either a penknife or a sheath knife to cut wood to make pea-shooters or catapults.

****

I remember playing tennis with John, Raymond, John Elliott and Margaret Wood at Brunton House, every Friday night.

****

Pat Stewart (née Smith) remembers the poem 'Bonnie Tyneside' (refer Chapter 6) and this is what she has to say.

"This is the song I remember from a show put on in the village hall for two nights running, but I don't remember exactly when. Most of the young people and quite a few older ones were involved. It was organised by Mrs Crozier and her son Robin, who lived in 'Birds Cottage', and by Rev Alan Porteous, the vicar at that time.

Mr Porteous was supposed to be a hiker walking from the source to the mouth of the Tyne and at each village or town that he came to there was an item of entertainment. He introduced each item and where he was at the time.

I remember there was sword dancing by the younger boys and men, with music on his Northumbrian pipes by Harry Armstrong from Old Bridge End Farm, Acomb.

Various other songs and plays etc but I am afraid all I can remember is my own item which was the song 'The Cullercoats Fisher Lass'. I threw a real fish from a real creel into the audience at the end of the song! There was also a play entitled 'The Way to Where' about someone asking for directions and the last line was 'If I was you I wouldn't start from here'.

We had proper stage make-up and there was a report in the Hexham Courant. The village hall was packed on both nights and it was very exciting for us young ones".

****

The building beside the garage was a hidey-hole when playing hide and seek round the village.

****

In the days of Dr Monica Bell, there was a district nurse who lived in Ruahine Cottage which in the 1930s was two cottages. She rode to her patients on a motor bike!

****

Ivor Gray remembers the night, Sunday 5 August 1951, when with his friends, Doug Robson, Fred Thompson and Robin Crozier, they rushed to Brunton Crossroads to see the police road blocks which had been set up in an attempt to catch the man who had committed a murder in Bellingham that afternoon. When Ivor, in later years, spoke of this incident nobody seemed to remember. He was delighted to find the article describing what had happened in the archives in the Hexham Courant offices.

'Cars and buses carrying hundreds of holiday makers to towns and villages on both sides of the border were trapped in a cordon of some fifty policemen which was thrown around the Hexham and North Tyne Districts on Sunday night.' (Hexham Courant Friday 10 August 1951).

****

Margaret Seaby in Wall.

I was born in Wall. My mother had arranged for a mid-wife to come but she could not get to my home because of a snowstorm, the doctor being absent for some reason. The only people my father could reach were the vicar and his wife. Neither had attended a birth before but they helped me into the world. The only snag was they could not get me to breathe! After some anxious moments the vicar asked Dad if there was any whisky in the house. Poor Dad did not know what it was for and did not know whether he should admit that he had. When pressed again he said he had and produced a small glass. The vicar put his little finger in it and put his finger in my mouth whereupon I drew in a big gasp of air and everyone was happy.

Growing up in Wall was idyllic. There were three farms in the village to play in and about a dozen children to play with. My mother had the village shop (sweets even in the war years). We had an orchard behind the house that we could raid, there were hills to climb, hazel trees to gather nuts from, fields to pick mushrooms and a river to walk beside to pick bluebells and primroses and even go paddling in, in hot weather. Our school was a Church of England school. We had scripture every morning and once a month we had childrens' Eucharist. At eleven I realised that I was different from the other children because I did the unheard of thing and passed the grading exam which made me eligible to go to the grammar school in Hexham. My parents decided that I should have the chance. Both of them had passed but their parents had been unable to afford it. I was the first girl from the village ever to go to the grammar school. I went on to St Hild's College at Durham University and went to teach first in Leeds and then in Newcastle and then in Canada.

****

During the Glasgow Holiday fortnight buses full of holiday makers crawled up Brunton Bank heading for Whitley Bay. No A69 in those days!

****

In summertime the back green was the popular venue for Tyneside and coastal living folk to come in their cars. They played games, sat and read newspapers and enjoyed a picnic out in the country.

****

One hot sunny afternoon in July 1987 Joan Proudlock answered the door to a bus driver whose double decker bus with over fifty 7-9 year olds from a Scotswood school had broken down just close to her gate! Whilst the driver telephoned for a relief bus from Newcastle, Joan and friend Julie helped the teachers get all the children off the bus, took them onto the lawn and managed to rustle up drinks and biscuits for everyone. Trying to cope with toilets was another problem entirely! They all eventually got on the second bus and left at 4.30pm after singing and stories on the lawn. An exciting end to their trip to Housesteads! This is just one of the many stories of life on Brunton Bank.

****

Ray Craig remembers The Croziers who were interested in drama and had a drama club in the village. Another memory of Ray's is being part of the church choir and going to choir practice under the watchful eye of Mr Robinson, the Headmaster. It seems there were one or two 'mishaps' a particular occasion involving one of the choir stalls being overturned! He also remembers learning to sword dance along with other boys in the village.

****

In the late 1950s Mr Robinson started a young farmers' club. This lasted for a short while before becoming part of the Hexham club.

****

One unforgettable memory is of a Wall Ladies Choir Concert in the village hall. Elva Mason and her sister-in-law, Alison Porteous did a 'Take off' of Hinge and Bracket. Whilst Alison accompanied, a fairy, dressed in a pink tutu and with her wand, singing 'Nobody loves a Fairy when she's Forty' danced across the stage. There wasn't a dry eye in the hall and Elva's wonderfully funny performance nearly 'brought the house down!'

****

This story came from 'The Pub.' We are not sure which one, but are sure that sometimes fact is stranger than fiction! Many years ago two young men from Wall put a pig into the back of their van to go to the mart. Unfortunately either the pig was too heavy or the van floor was not strong, and all four trotters ended up on the road. There was only one solution to the problem, put the pig in the front seat and take it to the mart with one young man sitting across the holes in the back! Got the picture?!

****

Eva Reay remembers the day a coach took fire. It was in the early 1970s when holiday or day trip coaches still used the Military Road as a scenic route. They toiled up Brunton bank in danger of over-heating their engines. This one did! A lady on the coach spotted flames coming up from the floor. She alerted the driver, who drove past St. Oswald's farmhouse before getting everyone off the bus. He ran with his passengers back to the farmhouse where Eva showed him the phone for the fire brigade. Eva and Ridley then looked after everyone with cups of tea and comfort facilities until a relief coach came. The coach was burnt out but due to the quick thinking of the driver he got his passengers to safety and also the coach away from the farm as there could have been the possibility of an explosion.

****

"When did turnips give way to pumpkins for Hallowe'en?"

****

Most of us have, at some time, questioned whether our memories are playing tricks on us.

Ivor Gray, a resident in Wall in 1954, had a vague recollection recently and combed through the back issues of the Hexham Courant to see if his memory was correct. Sure enough, there was the story. A competitor in the Miss World Competition had been staying at a farm in Wall. Ella Hill (née Wardle) continues, "The story goes back to 1948 when most of the farms in the area still had German prisoners of war working on them, although many would go back home before the year was out. Times were hard in this country but in Germany they were even harder particularly for those who had moved from the east of the country. Letters from home told them how difficult it was and the mother of the prisoner who worked at Planetrees was worried about her 12 year old daughter who was lacking a healthy diet. Mr and Mrs Wardle who farmed Planetrees, decided that it would be a good idea if this girl was sent for a few months to Planetrees to help her recover her strength. She fitted well into life on the farm, stayed for five months and went home much fitter. That girl, Frauke, became Miss Germany six years later and came back to visit Planetrees while she was in this country. She did not become Miss World, but she came fifth in the competition, the winner being Miss Egypt."

****

In 1979 with snow 6 feet high and drifting over the roadside walls, Mrs Doreen Keen, living at Wall Fell farm was at the end of her pregnancy and awaiting the imminent arrival of her baby. Dr McCollum was most anxious to admit her into maternity before the snow got any deeper, as already the track into the farm was blocked. Snow kept blowing in so quickly and there were white-outs. Dr McCollum was dealing with another patient in Stonehaugh in the same weather conditions at the west end of his practice and realising the worsening weather situation contacted John Proudlock, who he knew had a vehicle with snow tyres, in the hope he could help. John managed to get as far as St Oswald's farm and Ridley Reay. Together they drove on the hard-packed snow to the farm lane end. Ahead of them on the road was a high wall of snow which had not been cleared. Having turned the car they left it in the middle of the road. They then walked through a near white-out, following where they could, the line of a field wall eventually reaching the farm where Doreen was waiting with her packed suitcase. The white-out lifted and Doreen with John and Ridley was able to trudge in their footsteps, in the deep snow for the half mile walk to the road. Driving in another snowstorm, there was just enough road left to be seen for John to get Ridley home and to drive down to his house with Doreen. Lunch was had and then John and Joan took Doreen to maternity where Dr McCollum was able to moniter her progress more easily and a few days later her son Richard was born.

****

From Heather Tailford (née Ballantyne) comes this memory,

"I remember when I was a teenager John Huddleston would come on his horse very early on some Sunday mornings, bang on the door with his riding crop shouting it was time to get up and go riding.

John Huddleston - Riding Lucky

Mam would get me out of bed, I'd throw on my clothes and off we would go riding way up the North Tyne valley to Birtley where we'd stop to see a friend of John's and then we'd ride around until it was time to go home, sometimes visiting other people he knew. I learnt so much about riding from John, he knew all about horses".

****

In September 2004 one of the stone flower troughs which welcome us into the village featured in the National Magazine Private Eye. The photograph was headed I-SPY Northumberland, and showed the tub taken from a low angle so that it looked like a small wall bearing the word WALL

****

CHAPTER NINE
ISABELLE EVERATT'S WARTIME MEMORIES

INTRODUCTION TO ISABELLE'S STORY - Mary Herdman and Joan Proudlock

During wartime the school played an important part in the daily life of, not only the children of the village and out-bye, but also evacuees who were sent from Newcastle to live with the good folk of Wall.

Miss Isabelle Robertson was a young teacher at Wall school from 1939 to 1948 and from her arrival soon became a key figure in the life of wartime Wall. Miss Robertson stayed for nine years and left in 1948 to marry Charles Everatt. She loved Wall, but Charles worked in Newcastle. The couple were happy to return to the parish in 1968. They moved into the school house at Bingfield when she was appointed head teacher at Bingfield C of E School. Charles died on 15 June 1973 at the age of 58. Isabelle stayed in the house for the rest of her life and died on 10 March 1994, at the age of 75. She is greatly missed by all who knew and loved her.

JOAN PROUDLOCK

When Isabelle's house was being cleared by family and two of her dearest friends a 'Miracle' occurred. As the friends were leaving one of them went to make sure the rubbish bin was secure and spotted an old notebook. Curious, she pulled it out and saw it seemed to have notes, handwritten by Isabelle. As they were leaving she popped it into her bag to read at home. Several years later, as she was going through some things in the house she found it again, realised that it was Isabelle's notes and records for the talk she used to give on Wartime in Wall, in other words her memoirs of those wartime days living in the village. Fortunately Maureen and David McCracken knew me, and one morning I received a small parcel with a note inside saying, "This might be of interest to you." It was a wonderful moment of discovery! I used the notebook, as it was written, to form a talk for the Village Society, ten years after her death entitled, 'An Evening of Isabelle's Memories'. Isabelle had a great interest in local history and Northumbrian life, she loved people, so when the Wall Local History Society (now the Village Society) was formed in 1989, she became the first secretary. In October 1992, she gave the talk herself to the society entitled 'Wall School in the War Years'. She gave us so much interesting and valuable information that it is right we print it in full on these pages, as it is the best record we have of those years in Wall.

Footnote. Margaret Gillespy's account of her time as a nurse at Brunton House was at the same time Isabelle was living in Wall. They did not know each other then but later in their lives, when Margaret retired to Humshaugh, they got to know each other through mutual interests.

The following pages are an accurate transcription of the notes she wrote for her talk. Her memoirs tell of activities in the village during the Second World War.

WAR TIME IN WALL - Isabelle Everatt

Well, how did I get to Wall in the first place? The catalyst – the person who made it all happen, I saw only once and for only about ten minutes. Because of this person I went to Wall. Because I'd been to Wall, I returned to Bingfield and because I returned to Bingfield, I'm back in Wall – here tonight – full circle.

At the beginning of the Autumn term in 1939 (which started in late August in those days) I was sent as supply Headmistress to Carrshield School, in West Allen, a one teacher, all standard school (5 – 14years), and all of nine on the roll.

Then came 3 September. I heard Neville Chamberlain at 11 am in the Post Office kitchen in Carrshield. They were the only people in the village with a wireless – so it's that long ago!

The post of headmistress had already been advertised. Eventually an appointment was made and I discovered that it was the assistant teacher at Wall, Miss Barnfather. She came to Carrshield and I was sent to Wall. It was as simple as that.

I came on the Sunday evening 1 October. I can't remember who made the arrangements. All I knew was that I had to catch Moffit's bus at Hexham, that left at 7.30 pm for Bellingham and I had to get off at Wall Post Office. I would be met off the bus. I can't say I first 'caught sight of Wall' because I couldn't see a thing. It was the 'blackout'. Every window had to be blacked-out with heavy curtains in case of bombing raids. I got off Moffit's bus at the Post Office. I knew I was being met there and taken to stay at North Farm. My memory is shaky at this point, but it can only have been Mr John Davidson, Connie and Hilda's dad, who met me. The Davidsons told me that the schoolmaster was nice and there were two evacuee teachers and some evacuee children as well as the village children.

I went to bed totally unprepared for the next day. I didn't know who I was going to teach, what age or how many. So next morning it was daylight. Mr Davidson pointed me in the direction of the school, and that was it – the first day of nine happy years at Wall School.

I'll talk about the school first. It was a stone building, built 1850-60 and would probably have been one large room. By 1939 there was a partition of wood to about 4/5 feet and then glass. It was fairly soundproof. So now there was the big room and also the little room, plus the master and the teachers – and 'please Sir' and 'please Miss'. We were never named personally.

At the start of term there were 80 children. 42 were local children, 22 were Walker evacuees and 16 private evacuees. The official evacuees arrived on Friday 1 September, before war was declared, but several returned home after a few days.

The first day I was there, two little lads were climbing up a tree in the plantation in front of the school. So I shouted to them "get down you silly boys – you'll fall and hurt yourselves". A voice behind me said "God made trees for little boys to climb!". I knew from that moment I was going to like Mr Parker.

The evacuees and their teacher were from East Walker Infants School. Children from this big school were housed in Wall, Chollerton, Colwell and Corbridge. At that time there were schools in each village. Wall and Chollerton schools were C of E; the school at Colwell was a Catholic School. Colwell was an estate village. The squire (and owner) was the Catholic Squire Riddell.

The Headmistress of East Walker, Miss Robson, was billeted with Mr and Mrs Wardle at Bibury, Ella's and John's grandfather, and the assistant teacher stayed at North Farm with me. She was called Miss Bowmaker, and it was nice to have someone of my own age.

When I think of the conditions under which we worked, it was a wonder the children survived educationally. No teacher would nowadays tolerate the conditions, nor would their unions!!! Incidentally, on my first day, during the dinner hour, part of the ceiling fell down in the big room and a plasterer had to be sent for. So that was a dramatic start.

I think there were about 60 in the school when I went: 42 local and 18 evacuees. The two evacuee teachers taught the infants in the little room. Mr Parker and I shared the big room. He had the seniors (10-14); I had the juniors (7-10). It really was a trial – two teachers in the same room. The children were inclined to listen to the other person.

I remember Eric Robson was in that first class. He was born to be a detective, which he later became. He knew everything about everybody. I remember being curious about the two eccentric old ladies who used to wander round the village, rather weirdly dressed. I found out that they were sisters, the Miss Squires who lived in the bungalow below Halton Grange.

Mr Parker was a lovely and loveable man, but he had a short temper. When he 'lost his rag' my lot switched off from me, to watch the drama at the other side of the room. Later we found the perfect expedient. Whenever the temper arose, he said "put your pens down – we'll have some music, Miss Robertson": all in the middle of whatever I was doing!! He was full of music himself and a devotee of Gilbert and Sullivan, so I often found myself, in the middle of geography lesson, playing 'Who are the yeomen, the yeomen of England'. Then it was back to the atlases. One of the older boys, Barney Mitchell, had the most beautiful voice. I remember him singing 'Linden Lea' – wonderful!!

I'm sure there was a timetable somewhere in school, but it wasn't used. I attended to the 3Rs and kept records of their work, but when the present stock of writing books was finished –we didn't know when it would be replaced.

That first term ended with a concert in the Church Hall: the usual nativity play and carols, with only 12 of the 38 evacuees still here. Evacuees throughout the war came in waves, whenever the fortunes of war took a turn for the worse we'd get a few more coming to the village: times like heavy bombing raids and the scare of invasion.

Mr Parker was small in stature. Some of his seniors, boys and girls, were head and shoulders taller than he was. He used to look up at them to tell them off. Stanley, Edward, Emma and Kitty Bowman were all tall. I remember one incident involving Stanley Bowman. He sat in the back row near the door. I don't know what it was all about, but I heard Stanley say, with his double negatives "Please Sir, I wasn't doing nothing" while Mr. Parker was prodding him in the chest. He said "Well this will let you know what you'll get if you wasn't doing SOMETHING"!!!

As I mentioned, Wall was a C of E school. One thing I hadn't encountered before was 'the Creed'. Being a Presbyterian, I knew nothing about the Book of Common Prayer. Mr Parker took morning prayers. We said the Creed and the Lord's Prayer and I played for the hymns. There was a lovely new piano at Wall school, about the only new piece of equipment there. When the vicar came to school the children all stood up and said "Good morning vicar", then repeated this when he went out. When Mr Robinson came the first custom he discarded was standing up when the vicar came in.

BARRING OUT DAY

The most interesting experience of my life at Wall with Mr Parker was something which happened a few days before Christmas 1939. I was reminded of it just a few months ago, when there was a special exhibition of paintings, in the Laing Art Gallery, Newcastle, by Ralph Hedley – a northern renowned painter and wood carver. He did all the carving in Newcastle Cathedral. All the angels he carved had the same face because he used his daughter as a model.

I was there at a special showing, organised by the Association of Local History Societies. Mary Herdman went later to see the exhibition. Before the conducted tour of the paintings, we had lunch then went into a small hall, where a projector was erected. The curator said he had chosen 20 paintings and had put them on slides to show us and explain a little of the background of each painting. He showed us a few of the slides, then he came to one which portrayed a number of children with their hands against a door, trying to keep it shut, and a figure of a man behind the door trying to get in. The curator said that this was called the Barring Out Day: barring out the schoolmaster. He said it was a local custom that died out at the turn of the century. (I think he got this information from a book by Rev Hastings Neville, onetime Rector of Ford, and written in 1909. It was inaccurate information. The book is called A Corner of the North – well worth reading, but the author said, wrongly, that this custom died out at the turn of the century.) So out of the darkness, I said "Oh no it didn't!" So he switched off the projector, switched on the lights and said "Tell us more!" So I told them, and after I'd finished he asked if I would write it down, exactly as I'd told them, for his records. And this is what happened, at Wall in December 1939 – long after the turn of the century. As far as I know the custom had existed for years and years, maybe as long as the school had existed.

The day started like any ordinary day: a dull, December morning, a few days before the end of term, Christmas only a few days away. I went 'home' to the farm for my lunch and went back to the school as usual for 1 o'clock. It was raining so I didn't expect to see children outside. I didn't expect to see the children inside either – certainly not where they were on the inside. You know how high those windows were: built deliberately high so that children couldn't look out and be distracted. All the children were on the window sills or on desks so that they could see out. Little ones must have been hoisted up by the bigger ones. How else could they have got up? They were laughing and waving their arms about. I wasn't worried about their falling off so much as what the master would say when he saw them. I shouted to them "get down before the master sees you". They took no notice. I went to the front porch door and found it was locked. All I could do then was to go to the gate at the other side of the school, and through the back door – hoping I'd dodge Mr Parker. What should I see as I opened the gate? Mr Parker was dressed with a poke over his head and shoulders, as workmen used to do when working in the rain. He had a broom in his hand. He ignored me and went to the windows. Then he banged the broom onto the windows: squeals of delight from inside! I thought I was having a bad dream. I really was frightened! I could hear myself saying "What's happening Mr Parker?" He knocked again and then the door was unlocked. In he went. I followed, bewildered.

There was more to come. All the children were now standing on the floor, along the sides of the room. Someone opened the door into the back porch and in flew a live duck, which naturally flew around the room, depositing feathers and other things with Mr Parker chasing it. I realised later that he had protracted the chasing for the pleasure of the little ones who were now stamping their feet in excitement. Eventually the duck was caught. Mr Parker took off the ribbon from the duck's neck – and there was a little parcel (tobacco in it) for the master's Christmas present. Someone – one of the big lads took the duck away; presumably back to wherever it came from, because that was the master's Christmas dinner!

All this chaos, mayhem and noise – and then, and I shall never forget it, he just flicked his eyes towards the clock. It was nearly 1 o'clock. Without a word from him they went back to their seats, stood while he said "Good afternoon children". They answered "Good afternoon, Sir", and sat down. Normality in no time! Such was his confidence in his own control that he could afford to allow this to happen.

Incidentally, after he left, his successor Mr Robinson said, near the end of autumn term, there was to be "no more of this nonsense" of locking doors at the end of term. So in one sentence he ended a custom that had continued for maybe 100 years. So there was no lock-out and he got no duck!!

During this first term a 'play centre' was organised in the church hall, which was leased by the Local Education Authority. It was on each week night from 5.45 to 7.45 – as much to give their foster mothers a break as for the children's own enjoyment. An entry in the log book said that the teachers gave of their own time 'ungrudgingly', but it was a bind after a whole day with the children, having to give up every evening for them. Mr Parker also organised Country Dancing for the older children. He took that himself. He gave up his evenings too.

After 7 years at Wall, Mr Parker left in 1941 to be head at Ponteland Coates Endowed School. He said he didn't want to go. It was said that Mrs Parker was ambitious for him! They had two daughters, Audrey and Maureen, and had a baby son, John, while they were living at Wall. John became a teacher and then a priest.

I met up with Mr Parker years later when I was living at Killingworth and was a member of the Townswomen's Guild. I noticed he was on a list of speakers. He was now retired and talked about his life as a magistrate. So I invited him to come and speak to us. The meeting was in my house and the lady who gave the vote of thanks said they'd enjoyed his talk and maybe next time he'd talk about 'Life as a Magistrate'. He'd talked about nothing else but Wall!! I attended his funeral a couple of years ago. The priest who gave the address said that in his last few months, Mr Parker spoke of little else but his days at Wall. He loved Wall and Wall loved him.

Mr Jim Robinson succeeded him. He had been Head at Bingfield for 3 years, and had lived in what is now my home. Wall was a great change for him and Mrs Robinson because there was, and still is, no public transport at Bingfield. Wall had Moffitts buses!

It was interesting to see the differences in the approach to teaching of the two headmasters. Both were dedicated teachers and good administrators, but completely different.

Jim Robinson was a slave to the clock. When Mr Parker was involved with anything, time didn't matter. With Mr Robinson one kept rigidly to the timetable. Mr Parker never talked about the theory of music, just the joy of singing. With Mr Robinson you learned that there could be 3 beats in a bar or 4 beats in a bar, and the difference between crotchets and quavers. With Mr Robinson everybody had to learn the words of a song before they sang a note of the music. I was very sorry about that.

He was keen on games and they (the boys) really enjoyed their football and shinty on the green. He was an expert on Rural Science. He introduced rabbit-keeping and poultry and had a well stocked garden. The older children really loved it. Speaking of games, here are two little anecdotes: One lunch time Mr Robinson was blowing up a rugby football when Andrew Wood came into the room. The conversation went something like this:

"What are you doing?"
"I'm blowing up this football."
"It's not very round is it?"
"What shape should it be?"
"It should be round so that it can bounce"
"Do you think this ball can bounce?"
"No."
"Take it outside and try it."
Andrew came in and said, "It bounced"
We realized he'd never seen a rugby football!

Mr Robinson had time for children, even though he was often sharp with them. He was very hard on Edward, his own son. I told him so one day, and I was told to mind my own b..... business!

By this time, most of the evacuees had returned home even though the war was still raging. I was now back into the little room by myself, and enjoying having a place of my own.

School meals began in 1945, and our cook must have been the best in the county: Mrs Matt Robson. She'd been a cook at the Hadrian before coming to school. In the paddock, where now stand the Mithras Court houses, there were two wooden bungalows. One, near the garage, was where Barney Mitchell and his parents lived. Near what is now the entrance to Mithras Court was the other. Here lived Mrs Matt as she was called (there were so many other Robsons). Living with her was her daughter and her little boy, Neil Scholes. His dad was in the army. He often toddled up to see his granny at the school kitchen and always appeared when I was taking a games or PE lesson outside. On one occasion we'd just got a consignment of PE ropes, bean bags and lovely coloured balls. Everything else was still in short supply – books, paper etc. All the children shared reading books and writing paper was so inferior.

But back to the lesson. Neil eyed these balls, so after we had finished the lesson I said "Would you like to play with our nice new balls, Neil?" His eyes lit up and he got one out of the box. Later his granny looked out of the window, saw him with it and asked "Where did you get that ball from?" He said "I got it from that big girl who plays with the bairns".

And there was I thinking I was a professional person!!

The school holidays were moveable feasts. They could be two weeks in June, four weeks in October. Teachers staggered their holidays in the early days and the school was open all the time. Mr Robinson and I had to be on standby. Fortunately Mr Robinson seldom left Wall, but often I had to stay the weekend, just to be there in case of emergencies. Times of starting and finishing school varied throughout the year. One year summer time was extended. One year after we had Double Summertime. In November children were allowed to go potato picking, but only in the afternoons, at Fallowfield, Planetrees and North Farm.

I doubt if people in the village today realise the distance children had to walk to school – from Fallowfield (Frank Charlton) and from Brunton Bank (Muriel Young, Ella and Isobel Wardle). Leslie Sisterson came down to school on his pony and tethered it on the village green. On wet days their clothes were dried on the big fireguard round an open coal fire. The room smelled like wet sheep.

We had a string of HMIs all throughout the war: Mr Paget, Mr Raymont, Miss Armstrong and Mrs Iceton the PT county organiser, came relentlessly every term. This was an important item on the agenda.

I remember an evening visit to Wall school by Professor Brian Stanley, Professor of Education at Newcastle University. I think such visits were in the nature of pep talks.

I remember his saying that if he wanted someone to have good journalistic training, he should join the Hexham Courant, which (I quote) "must be the best paper of its kind in the country". He was so eloquent and so interesting, but I overheard one elderly lady say to another "It took a long time to say very little!" So there is no pleasing everybody.

The church hall, (it was the church hall in those days), was put to good use. There was great enthusiasm for country dancing and, later, the village had expert advice from Bill Scott, a Newcastle headmaster evacuated to Hexham, and an authority on country dancing. Both adults and young people found it great fun. It bored us to tears. We seemed to be gathering peascods every night in the week! There were weekly dances, sometimes more than one a week, whist drives and concerts. Some concerts were given by local people in the Red Cross who gave recitals and songs. There was plenty going on socially in Wall. Being a church hall, there was a rule that at dances on Saturdays the last waltz was 11.45. The hall had to be vacated by midnight and Sunday had begun. The vicar was very strict.

THE ARMY

The military appeared very soon after the beginning of the war. This was a marvellous area for the distribution of ammunition dumps which were hidden in the many woods and plantations in the area. They were manned by military police and the manual work of moving these huge boxes was done by the Pioneer Corps.

There were six large Nissen Huts on the green below the school. The men of the Pioneer Corps were a mixed bag. Some were, to say the least, inadequate, and there were some misfits. I remember one who was very withdrawn. He was a brilliant violinist, supposed to have played with a London orchestra, and there he was playing 'Roll out the Barrel' at our village hops. There was a quick turnover of officers. I was told that they were men who had been at the front, actually on the battlefield, and had been sent here for a breather. There were several complaints from the school managers (the vicar and Mr Seaby) to the army for dumping ammunition so close to the school. One thing did aggravate me, and it was the contempt shown by the Military Police for the poor Pioneers. These MPs – to quote Shakespeare – "dressed in a little brief authority" were so rude and contemptuous. I could see the Nazi in some of them. I remember telling my father about it. He said "Put a man in uniform and it brings out the best in them – or the worst".

We observed all this because some of us worked in the Wall YMCA canteen. This was in the schoolroom of the Methodist Chapel. It was open every night from 7 to 10 except Saturdays and Sundays. Thursday was our busiest night because the men weren't paid till Friday. We dispensed gallons of tea; we made sandwiches and sold biscuits, note paper, razor blades, soap, cigarettes, sweets and chocolate (the few that we got, because they were on ration). Occasionally we got Royal Engineers who were stationed at Chollerford and The Chesters. A lot of them were cockneys, and I didn't understand their twang. Doris Herdman and I worked together, usually on a Friday night: their pay night. They spent the evening in the Hadrian, then they all landed in at 10 o'clock for a cup of tea, so we made a lot of money in a short time. Margaret Wardle was the secretary and did all the ordering of things to sell, the vicar was the treasurer. All during the war, and especially when the Second Front started, there was traffic going through Wall at all hours of the day and night. By this time I was living with Miss Herdman, Jean's great aunt, in Orchard House on Front Street where Jean and Lionel now live.

At night travelling was done with headlamps dimmed. I don't know how anyone found their way. At the beginning of the war, when there was fear of an invasion, every name on every road sign was obliterated. Even the local post offices had to have their names removed. One night a convoy got lost. A soldier was out on the road shouting "How the h... do we get to Bellingham?" I opened my bedroom window and said "You'll have to turn your wagons around first, you're heading south". There were about 40 wagons nose to tail. They were on for hours. All the directions I could give them were to turn left at the crossroads and follow the road to Bellingham, but I'm sure that it was Otterburn they'd want to get to eventually. Another night a huge military wagon broke down at the Temperance Hotel, and they were digging into the innards of this enormous vehicle. I heard several words with which I was not familiar!

I've mentioned the village hall and the canteen in the Chapel Schoolroom. There was also the Reading Room which was in constant use. It was a two roomed building. One room housed the County Library, a large table and chairs for meetings. The other had a billiard table. There wasn't a 'Men Only' sign, but I never saw any females in the billiard room. Both rooms were in constant use – what we would call a community centre nowadays.

The WEA met in the Reading Room as did the WI. During the war there were series of lectures given by the WEA, the Workers Educational Association. They always had (and still have) excellent lecturers. One lectured on International Affairs. He was so eloquent and had such a command of the English language. He used words I had to look up after getting home. G D Pearson did a psychology course with us. He was the best ever. He gave me a copy of his notes which I greatly treasure.

The chapel building hasn't altered since the war years. I never attended a service there, but I remember one occasion going to a sale of work or bazaar. This was opened by Gwynneth Wood shortly after she returned home from Canada. I can't remember the year, but I remember Andrew and Deborah Wood coming to school. It was the first time we had seen a T-shirt, which Andrew was wearing. English children were still wearing shirts and jerseys. One of the Arthurs remarked that Andrew just had his vest on.

The church has also remained unaltered. During the war it was filled every Sunday morning by the local soldiers, supposedly because they escaped doing drill if they attended church. Rev Westgarth was there all during the war. He droned on, poor fellow. I'm sure the content of his sermons was good, but his delivery wasn't. He was a wonderful calligrapher, and did beautiful lettering with pen and Indian ink long before the days of biros and felt tips.

The Post Office housed three unmarried sisters and an unmarried brother. Phyllis was the postmistress. Her sisters, Maggie and Kate, assisted her. Phyllis was a very dominant character, but very efficient. She dispensed pensions and papers, magazines and stationery, and, I believe, some food. When there were telegrams Maggie delivered them. There wasn't much going on in the village that Phyllis and her sisters weren't aware of. The brother, Nevison, was a wonderful tailor. He had his workroom above the Post Office. He actually sat crossed legged as tailors are supposed to do.

No village in England was without its Home Guard, formerly Local Defence Volunteers. Most of the local lads were in the Home Guard before being called up into the army. Charlie Watson of the Chare was Captain, Cecil Herdman was Lieutenant. There were a series of sergeants who were eventually called up. They worked closely with the military and had access to rifles and ammunition. I was one of the few female members of the Home Guard. I dearly wanted a uniform, but all I got was a round wooden badge with HG in the middle surrounded by laurel leaves. I kept the books showing records of ammunition spent at the weekly practices. They worked in close collaboration with the military, especially the officers Charlie Watson and Cecil Herdman. They met in the village hall once a week, and, of course, went on exercises, and occasionally on weekends. I was always very curious as to what they did, but they kept their own counsel.

Well, eventually the war was over. The YMCA canteen ceased to exist. The military left. The Nissen huts were pulled down (the cement foundations will still be there under the turf). The local lads came home. There was great sadness as well as relief over the homecoming of Norman Craig because of his war wounds. Blackouts were finished and village names reappeared. But there were still shortages. Some foods and all clothes were still to be rationed for some time. There were still grave shortages in equipment for schools and for years it was a case of make do and mend.

The people of Wall had a really excellent record for their work towards the war effort, and a lot of it was motivated from the school. Mr Robinson instigated the War Savings Scheme, and we were involved with all the schemes and special events, such as Wings for Victory Week, Warship Week and Welcome Home Week. The Regional Organiser for National Savings presented an Illuminated Certificate of Honour to the children in 1945. I wonder who has it now. As early as August 1941 the school was registered as a Working Party under Northumberland and Durham War Needs Fund, and the older girls did some wonderful work, knitting for the forces.

All villages have their characters and I'd like to end by recalling a few of them.

THE RAT CATCHER

He was full of knowledge about the local wildlife. He talked of stoats, weasels, badgers, foxes, the birds, which birds nested in which trees, the seasons and the weather changes. And he could forecast the weather. One day he came up to school and said that he had a dead badger. Would the children like to see it? I was a bit anxious about little ones seeing a dead animal. I took my children down first. It was lying exactly where the seat is now, outside the church. I'd never seen a badger before, nor had the children. It was as big as a pig. I had told the children that they were awake all night, hunting etc, and they slept most of the day. Mercifully they thought it was asleep. He carefully pulled its lip back to let them see its teeth, and said "There, I haven't wakened it up!" The rat catcher was an absolute mine of information.

COMMANDER HORNBY

The village eccentric: he was gentry and very well connected. His uncle was the greatly respected and loved Bishop Hornby, and he was related to Mrs Enderby of a landowning family at St John Lee. He liked to go about like a tramp: old mac, string round the waist, sandshoes and no socks; summer and winter. Like a tramp he walked miles and miles. They said that he walked to the Shire every day. He never conversed with anyone. He was a permanent resident at the Hadrian, every year he was 'turfed out' so that they could clean his room. One year he went up to Maxfield,(now Springfield), the bungalow next to the school (Mrs Walker and her daughter lived there). It was a very hot dry summer and Maxfield had a very erratic water supply. One day he complained; "What shall I do about my barth? I must have my barth!" So he made several trips to the pant with a pail, to get water – enough to fill his bath (a cold barth!), then put on his dirty old togs and went on his way.

JAMES HERDMAN

The village intellectual, he taught 40 years at the Royal Grammar School in Newcastle. He taught modern languages: French and German. He had a room full of books, all French and German. He was so proficient in the French language that he could recognize and speak many of the dialects of France. He could hold one entranced with descriptions of the various places he had visited all over the world, and the interesting people he met when he stayed with families (his friends) in France, Germany and Italy. Yet he loved the village folk here. He had endless stories of incidents that had amused him. He was a 'raconteur extraordinaire'. He had a beautiful speaking voice, and loved to use his local dialect when telling a funny story about incidents he'd witnessed in the locality, or conversations he overheard. One concerned Moffit's bus. The bus was very full, and waiting to leave Hexham bus station. There was silence all round, then a local in the back seat shouted along the bus to her friend in the front seat: "Here Meg, is your Margaret expecting?" Meg never turned her head, just shouted: "No, but wor Willie's wife is!"

MARY JANE DARE

My favourite, Mary Jane Dare, lived next door to John and Shirley Mitchell's old house (Fellfoot). I always seemed to see her at the pant when she was getting water. I am sure she would be poor (money wise), but what a contented person she was. I never saw her in anything else but black clothes: a long skirt and a shawl. She once told me she never got married because her mother neglected her when she was young. I was never able to figure that out. The last time I remember seeing her was at the pant on a cold winter's day. We both commented on the cold weather, and she said: "My feet are starving. I'll have these things off when I get in!" I looked down at her feet. Someone must have given her a pair of galoshes, but she hadn't put any shoes inside them.

By the time I left Wall in 1948, it was more or less just as I had seen it first, nine years earlier. Charles had been demobbed in 1946 after six years in the army; mainly in the desert and one hair-raising year in Palestine. We were married in 1948. If we could have got a house in Wall, and if my husband could have travelled to Newcastle each day (it was in the days before commuters) I'd never have left Wall. How eventually, I got back to the parish after 20 years, well that's another story.

If, on your way home, you say to your travelling companion (as the local lady said of Prof Stanley): "It took a long time to say very little". I shan't be in the least offended: because I've enjoyed remembering.

Thanks for listening!!

1939 – 1945.
Wall's Home Guard.
Back Row. Willie Mitchell, Fred Thompson, Fred Elliott, George Lamb, Billy Muse, Cecil Meikle, —, Tommy W Robson.
Second Row. Jack Moore, Ken Smith, Alex Mason, Isabelle Robertson, Ted Muse, Arthur Henderson, Tommy Tait, Jack Young.
Third Row. Sandy Nichol, Alf Young, Herbie Robson, Cecil Herdman, Eddie Watson, Willie Mason, Ernie Robson.
Front Row. Tom Scott, Arnold Elliott, Harry Robson, Eddie Ripley —, —.

CHAPTER TEN
OUR CELEBRATIONS

Memories are somewhat sparse regarding early celebrations, but to start we are fortunate in having a record of one early celebration day which took place in 1905. This report is taken from the pages of the Hexham Courant dated 10 June 1905 and is exactly as it was written up in that time, save for a very long list of heats which we have omitted. It was discovered by Ivor Gray, whilst he was trying to locate articles with reference to Wall happenings. In it we have a gem of a record of a celebration day for the folk of Wall, a day away from work.

THE READING ROOM PICNIC - Saturday 3 June 1905

'The annual picnic and sports in aid of Wall Reading Room were held on Saturday last. The committee had been fortunate in securing the same field as last year on Wall farm, Mr Davidson again kindly lending it for the occasion. The day was beautifully fine and there was a good attendance. There has been a great falling off in the number of country picnics held in the district to what was the case a dozen years ago, but there seems to be a renewal of interest in these pleasant little gatherings, and there are a good number arranged for this summer.

When held in such pleasant surroundings as the one under notice they provide an excellent method of enjoying a quiet afternoon's holiday. The wooded valley of the North Tyne, with its clustering villages and stately homes, stretches away to the far off hills that fringe the borderland, while on the other hand over Cocklaw quarries runs the pastoral landscape of the valley of the Erring burn. The light was exceeding good on Saturday and the range of country visible was most extensive. During the afternoon a capital programme of music was rendered by the Acomb band, under the leadership of Mr Henderson. A public tea was provided in a large marquee and was largely partaken of. The ladies who presided at the tables and others who assisted were, Mrs London, Mrs Telford, Mrs Gray, Mrs Wray, Mrs J Bell, Mrs Bell, Miss Woodman, Misses Laing, Misses Henderson, Miss Graham, Miss Davidson, Miss Fisher, Miss Johnson, Miss Hetherington, Miss Rowell, and the Misses Mews.

The lemonade was attended to by Messrs R Grey and W Bell. Messrs Sewell and J J Scott were doorkeepers and Messrs John Bell, Edward Herdman, W Forsyth and J J Scott, gatekeepers.

During the afternoon a capital programme of sports was brought off. The 120yds handicap again fell to the local 'ped.' R Mitchell who is still running well, and conceding start, all round he won his heat and the final smartly. The football kicking seemed immensely popular, as did the dribbling competition. The walking competition was smartly won by H Darlington, who walked fair but some of the other competitors 'lifted' in such a way they should have been disqualified. The judges were Messrs Little, starter M J Maddison and handicappers Messers Little and Maddison.

Omitting the heats, here are the final results.
Results; 120yds Handicap 1st. £2, 2nd 10/-, 3rd 5/-.
Mitchell 1. Ridley 2. Dodd 3. Batey 4. Capital race. Mitchell getting up to win by half a yard.
High Jump. T Welch Hexham 4ft. 7ins. 1. E Robson Wall 2. Football Kicking.
R Mitchell Wall 1. Air Gun Competition. W Younger Wall 1. Bowling at Wicket.
H Harding Acomb 1. Walking Competition. H Darlington Hexham 1. T Robson Wall 2. W Graham Wall 3. Darlington who walked well won easily. Dribbling Football Competition. T Welch Hexham 1. J Maddison Wall 2.
At the close of the sports the prizes were gracefully presented to the winners by Mrs W W London. A Ball was afterwards held in the marquee and was largely attended.
Capital music was supplied by the Acomb Band while the MCs were Messrs
Geo. Graham and J Bell. The lemonade stall was attended by Mr J Little. The arrangements were ably carried out by the general committee, Messrs J Reay, J Little, J J Scott, J Bell, W Sewell, E Herdman, W Lamb and Rev W W London with Mr M Telford as Secretary'.
It would seem a good time was had by all!

From 1905 we take a jump to 6 May 1935 when Wall celebrated the Silver Jubilee of King George V. The following was found by Ivor Gray in the 11 May 1935 copy of the Hexham Courant. 'Children's sports were held in the afternoon, followed by a children's and public tea. Sports for adults held later included a football match - Old v. Young, and a bonfire on Wall fell at night was lit by Mr J Wardle.'
Ella Hill remembers sports on the back green on 12 May 1937 for the Coronation of George VI.
The Second World War followed in 1939 and though there are memories of VE Day plusFifty, no-one has told us about celebrations in Wall for VE Day in 1945.

V.E. + 50

On 8 May 1995, Wall celebrated VE + 50. A barbecue was held in Town Farm Yard with seating in the barn. Through the generosity of George Lamb, this was always a place of refuge in times of doubtful and inclement weather (now lost to the housing development). The Wall Ladies Choir gave a concert during the evening. Later, a bonfire was lit on the back green. This was lit by Joan Ormston who had been a naval nurse during the war. Joan had received a British Empire Medal in 1942 after risking her life to save patients when the north east hospital in which she was working was bombed.
Maureen Proud remembers the Coronation day of Queen Elizabeth II, in June 1953.
"It was so wet that the children's fancy dress and the parade of decorated bikes took place round the billiard table in the Reading Room. In celebration of the event, the school's older pupils were given a book about Northumberland. The younger ones received a Coronation mug. In spite of the weather a fell race was held."
Later in 1977 came the Silver Jubilee. The day was much finer. The fancy dress and the decorated bikes could be shown out of doors. Lisa Proudlock aged four was

dressed as the Coronation Crown, her father having worked several nights at The Garage, welding rods together to make the frame, whilst her brother Mark was a two year old Yeoman of The Guard! There was also a competition for the best decorated house. Again, a fell race was held. The bonfire on the fell top was lit by Jack Seaby.

Another quarter of a century brought Her Majesty's Golden Jubilee. The village celebrated in style. 2 June 2002 fell on a Sunday. A joint service of the Anglicans and Methodists was held in St Oswald's Church at Heavenfield. This was followed by a picnic lunch. It was fine enough to hold this in the churchyard. Other celebrations took place on the following day. Again a fell race was organised with a course 2.5 - 3 miles long. Events, mainly on the back green, included a boules tournament, a tug of war, a rounders tournament and a scrimmage hunt. The beautifully decorated village hall housed a tea and Jubilee crafts for children of all ages.

A marquee was set up on the green for evening events. This was home to a bar and the serving of food. In the nearby hall there was dancing to Big Dave and his Elastic Band. To fit in with the national timetable the beacon on the fell top was lit at 9.45pm. The final beacon was lit by Her Majesty at midnight in London.

Ten years later, on Sunday 3 June 2012, we celebrated Her Majesty's Diamond Jubilee. Unlike our Queen in London, we enjoyed a sunny day. The day started off with a fell race, which was won by James Gillespie for the men and Sarah Dodd for the women. A children's tug of war proved great fun and once again there was a fancy dress parade, with The Queen on Horseback riding in with first prize. Phoebe Proudlock Cottiss carried on the tradition her mother started, when she wore a Coronation Crown in 1977!

Once more a marquee was set up on the green, with a hog roast and barbecue. With such a village setting as Wall enjoys, the safety of the green for picnics, space for a marquee and the village hall with its amenities close by, the feeling is that nothing much has really changed over all the years when it comes to the way Wall has of creating happy community gatherings. The day was enjoyed by a large number of villagers and was very successful and we are always grateful to the band of folk whose hard work makes these events happen.

MILLENNIUM EVENTS

During the Millennium Year, a number of major improvements were made to the interior of the village hall, to ensure that it was a worthy centrepiece for village life. Four years before that however in 1996, the Wall Millennium Committee was set up. This consisted of: Chris Allcock (Chairman), Jimmy Bell, Ella Hill, Clive Price, Maureen Proud, Joan Proudlock and Christine Proudlock (Secretary).

They sought suggestions for events, activities and projects to mark the year 2000, and called a public meeting in the village hall on 12 September to discuss them. The outcome resulted in a variety of programmes:

The Parish Map, The Events for New Year's Eve, The Summer Barbecue, The Millennium Walk, Bulb Planting and Wildflower Area, The Wall Hanging, The Photo Montage.

THE MILLENNIUM CROSS

In addition to our own activities we were one of the venues for the Millennium Cross. During 2000 a glass cross, made at Sunderland Glass Works, was handed on from parish to parish along the line of Hadrian's Wall from the Solway Firth to Wallsend, being transported in a stout carrying case. Its final home was Lanercost Priory.

Wall received it from Humshaugh parish on Palm Sunday 16 April, with a short service at the Roman Bridge Abutment by the side of the North Tyne. It rested in turn on the altars of the Methodist chapel, St George's and St Oswald's. It was used for the Easter Day service at St Oswald's before being handed on to Hexham Abbey on Low Sunday.

In August, the annual St Oswald's Day Pilgrimage from Hexham Abbey to Heavenfield included the carrying of the cross on the journey. For this occasion it was borrowed from a church in Benwell.

MILLENNIUM – NEW YEAR EVENTS

Wall celebrated the New Year in style. Mike Burch and a loyal band of helpers had organized a memorable 'bash'. They had raised funds, and a lot of interest from the people of Wall. A marquee was hired to supplement the village hall as so many were expected.

The first event of New Year's Eve was a very well attended treasure hunt. This was an event to encourage families to take part, and it certainly succeeded. There was much rushing about the village as everyone searched for answers to the clues which centred on 'Knowledge of Where You Live'. Afternoon activities in the hall were centred round the children. A large frieze of drawing and colouring was made by the children, who all wrote their names on it. Millennium mugs decorated with village scenes were given to them, and bought by adults.

Evening events started at 8pm with music and chat while food was cooked on four huge barbecues. An amazing selection of food organised by Elva Mason with her band of helpers (one of them being Jill Taylor's sister having travelled from New Zealand), was served in an outside marquee, the weather being reasonably kind. Entertainment continued in both the marquee and the hall with instrumental music and singing. Children charmed everyone with song and dance routines.

Three ladies rang the Church bell at midnight, signalling the start of the new Millennium. They were Angela Watson's mother, Evelyn Cramer, Jill Taylor's mother, Mona Ottley, and Molly Thompson, wife of the then Chairman of the Parish Council, Roy Thompson.

At midnight Chris Allcock lit the Millennium Beacon on the fell. This was one of nine in Northumberland some of which could be seen as the night was clear and frosty. With such a bright night sky there was a clear view looking up the North Tyne, enabling those on the fell to see the firework displays, bonfires and beacons.

Chris, with helpers, had dug the hole into which, just after midnight, Jenny Harrington having come down from the fell, and the only one sober enough, planted a copper beech, still to be seen on the back green today!

John Proudlock assisted by Mike Burch started a firework display in the garden behind Braeside the fireworks rising above the house with the fell woods as a backdrop. A wonderful show was produced by using two boxes of sequenced display fireworks and everyone safely watched from the green and the marquee.

Dancing went on in the hall until 4am then the first footing started.

1 January saw a United Church Service with the congregation enjoying half a service in St George's Church, then moving to the Chapel for the other half.

The Summer Barbecue

On Saturday 17 June we had good weather for another barbecue. This was held on the green outside the hall, starting at 5pm. At 6pm Charlie the Magician performed for the children in the marquee. Later we enjoyed hearing, and dancing to, the Queen Elizabeth High School Band.

The Millennium Walk

It was fine weather again for the walk on 9 July. Walkers met by the swings on the back green at 12.15pm, complete with picnics. They enjoyed a saunter along a circular route across Wall Fell, with a fascinating commentary about flora, fauna, history and anecdotes by Derek Proudlock who had produced leaflets for all those taking part showing the route.

THE WILDFLOWER AREA AND BULB PLANTING

A wildflower area was sown on the back green and many bulbs were planted throughout the village. Whilst some of the bulbs are still being enjoyed, the wildflower area subsequently became victim to the Council grass cutters.

THE PARISH MAP - Mary Herdman

The idea for a parish map was first put forward by Chris Allcock after he had seen an article concerning such maps in the Weekend Telegraph of 4 May 1996. He sent for information from Common Ground, a conservation charity which was promoting parish maps. He discussed it with the millennium committee and with me. It was approved. The Village Society became sponsors of the map.

Over the course of two and a half years I worked on the map, discussing and consulting with the committee at all stages: showing my ideas and layouts for their suggestions and approval. Through the Parish Newsletter I also asked what others wished to be included in it. As I was involved in an intensive study course with Open University at that time progress was slow for the first eighteen months.

In 1998 it proceeded much more quickly. Work so far was displayed at The Village Society AGM in January. In July the layout was nearer completion. It went on display in the Methodist Chapel schoolroom on the day of the Three Churches Fête. In September I took it to the Wall Village Wall Hanging working party for comments and suggestions. On all these occasions some useful ideas were put forward.

I consulted with John Proudlock concerning which fauna should not be omitted from the natural history border, and with Ella Hill regarding flora. A small committee consisting of Chris Allcock, Ella Hill and me decided which of my vignettes of human history should be used, along with the accompanying text.

At my request the final layout was examined by several people with regard to the accuracy of the map or any features that I might have missed.

From September onwards the business side was underway. I obtained a licence from Ordnance Survey. We sought estimates from printers. I ordered postal tubes. We decided who should do the framing.

On 7 October the map was finished. We had 300 copies printed. The original was framed. Copies were sent to Common Ground, and to Ordnance Survey who required one for royalties' assessment.

2 December 1998 saw the launch at the Village Lunch. The framed original had been hung in the village hall. It was covered by the Northumberland Flag. Chris Allcock made the presentation speech. It was unveiled and accepted on behalf of the village by the Parish Council Chairman, Roy Thompson. Sales of the copies were started. The price was £10 each. A Hexham Courant reporter attended the occasion.

Chris became publicity agent and chief salesperson. Good articles were published in the Hexham Courant and in the magazine The Northumbrian. Following this, Newcastle Central Library ordered a copy.

I had in the main financed the production. After my expenses were recuperated, I received a proportion of the profits; the rest was used to finance other Millennium projects. Copies have gone to many parts of the world. There are still some available.

THE MILLENNIUM PHOTO-MONTAGE - Joan Proudlock

As the Millennium was drawing near it was clear that with the planned celebrations for the

31 December 1999 into 1 January 2000 in the village hall, there would need to be decorations. I am not quite sure to this day as to how I came by the job of hall decorator, but there it was, work to be done.

I decided on a theme that was based on Wall Village as the centre looking out at the rest of Britain then the continents of Europe, North and South America, Africa and Asia. This would be depicted using large photo-montage pictures of our village, Britain and each continent.

The ceiling of the hall would be a representation of the universe with large, silver sprayed, spherical paper lampshade 'planets' hanging, with trails of small Christmas lights indicating stars. This was the future, as in time to come more discoveries would be made with space travel becoming a reality. On the stage would be large free standing figures of the nativity representing our Christian heritage that is so much part of St Oswald's and Heavenfield.

Wall Village was the centre panel on the long wall of the hall with three panels either side. Each panel featured faces of each continent and the countries that made up that continent. The faces were unknown, known, political leaders, royalty and celebrities but mainly the unknown. Sorrow, hunger, pain, joy and love were in the faces I had collected from magazines, National Geographics, books and newspapers.

The photo-montage of the people of Wall brought different problems, as though I had taken many photos over thirty years, I did not have the villagers of the late 18th century or the early years of the 20th century. This is when Raymond Craig and his wonderful collection of old photographs came to the rescue. He had gradually amassed a collection from the older residents of Wall, who dug them out of boxes, lent them to him to photograph before he returned them to their owners. John rephotographed them so I could cut them up to form a picture of faces and people. Still it wasn't complete as there were new residents in the village in several new houses, so cheekily I went knocking on doors, explaining what I was doing and was met, in every case, with pleasure at being included.

Then another problem arose, as I realised that there would be more people coming to live in the village on into the future in the 21st century. How would they be depicted? The answer was to cut out head shapes in silver paper and glue them at the bottom of the panel. They would represent those yet to come.

Following the Millennium celebrations the panels were removed from the long wall, but such was the interest in the village one, we had it mounted. It remains in the hall as a constant reminder that our village is, and always has been, a living people place, a community in which so many have lived and played their part and still continue to do.

WALL VILLAGE WALL HANGING - Joan Proudlock

One of the ideas put forward in 1997, when discussions were taking place in the village relating to the millennium, was to produce a community piece of craft work. This eventually emerged as a very ambitious community project: a fabric wall hanging of three collage pictures. Each picture was to reflect images of a particular area of Wall and its environs, the East, Central and West views. The aim was that it should hang in the village hall, on the wall behind the stage.

In 1997 we were fortunate in having local artist Kathleen Sisterson working in North Tyne Studios in Herdman's workshop. Kathleen, with another artist colleague, had put forward the original community project idea, for a quilt, but since that time it had metamorphosed into something huge. Kathleen took on the role of designer. Following a large gathering of Wall residents offering suggestions of items for inclusion in each picture during a village coffee morning, she began the task of painting the three pictures from which stitchers, knitters and embroiderers would work.

It was obvious that with such an ambitious project, funding would be needed. Those of us who were committed turned ourselves into the Wall Village Wall Hanging Association and moved forward on the administrative side. A community bank account was opened at Barclays Bank and Mary Mason took on the role of Treasurer. As a community we began to hold events to raise money. The Village Hall Committee and the Parish Council were the first to support the work. Rural Action, Barclays Bank Community Support Grants and Millennium Awards for All, along with individual contributors and proceeds from events gave us all we needed financially to complete not only the triptych wall hanging but the accompanying Art Book.

As an exhibiting artist and part of the Art Tour, Kathleen had met Marjorie Graham, a fabric artist living in Hexham, who had experience of working on and nurturing along community needlework projects throughout the country. She agreed to come on board.

On Friday 13 March 1998, all superstition set aside, we began to work. Gifts of material had come rolling in. We had selected and bought the large amounts of new material needed for the backing and large areas of colour, the tables were set up in the hall, Kathleen's three pictures were on show and the decision was made to start with the west view.

During the two years it took to complete the transition from painted picture to fabric wall hanging new friendships, births, marriages and deaths, grief, problems, happy events, companionship and love were all part of the weekly sew-ins, as we sat for the afternoon cup of tea and biscuit. This was prepared most often by Judy Yeoman, a new arrival in Wall who, along with Doreen Mitchell became two of the 'treasures' with the practical support they gave. We all looked forward to our meetings each week as for a while we shared our lives working on the Wall Hanging.

Thursday afternoon 27 April 2000 saw David and Jill Brookman and John and Joan Proudlock in the village hall, mounting all three hangings which was not an easy task and required 'fine tuning' to centre the middle picture, then match exactly the two either side. Job complete, all was ready for the following day, Press Friday.

On Saturday 29 April 2000, two years, one month and sixteen days from the start, probably the largest number of people in the history of the hall squashed in, with standing room only, to celebrate the unveiling of the Wall Hanging.

Before that could happen there was another task to perform. It was the right moment to remember and celebrate all that Rachel Lowther had done in securing the hall for the village, not only that but her involvement in so many community activities. Unable to take an active role any longer, it was Rachel who had wholeheartedly supported the idea of this community project. Chris Allcock spoke of Rachel, and Maurice Lowther unveiled the plaque, which will for ever associate Rachel with Wall Village Hall.

On the stage, Georgina and Nicole Lamb aged six, the twin daughters of John and Susan Lamb of Town Farm, then slowly raised the protective blind to reveal the fabric pictures. It was a morning of speeches, but that moment of utter silence as the blind was raised followed by a communal gasp and resounding applause, gave those dedicated folk, the Wall Hangers, all the appreciation they so richly deserved. They had risen to every challenge, and week by week there were many, to produce a magnificent work of art.

An open afternoon followed the more formal morning. In the evening, with the Millennium Wall Hanging as a backdrop, David Oliver and his Ceilidh Band, The Hedgehog's Skin, played the composition he had created especially for our Celebration Day, 'The Wall Hangers Waltz'. We have included a copy of this, but the copyright belongs to David Oliver and any playing of it either in Wall Village or elsewhere should have reference to him as the composer, and the reason for the composition. He has graciously given permission for The Wall Hangers Waltz to be published here.

A cake was baked and iced by Ann Burch. It showed a bee in one corner celebrating all Rachel Lowther had done for the village, and the Wall Hangers Logo, of needle, cotton reel and scissors in the other. Jimmy Bell, a long-time Wall resident, with much involvement in village life, and whose birthday it was, shared the cutting of the cake with Joan.

The Wall Hangers Waltz

A tune to commemorate the inauguration of the
Wall Village Millennium Wall Hanging
29 April 2000

David Oliver

Thirteen years have elapsed since the unveiling. It was borrowed for an exhibition in Hexham Abbey and is now nationally recognized as part of the Stitch 2000 project. The hanging has a place in the NNR (National Needlework Record) for all time: a fitting tribute to the work of a dedicated group of ladies in Wall Village.

THE WALL HANGING ART BOOK

This is a 'spin off' from the wall hanging. It was realised as we were working, that when complete, though each picture would show an area of the village and its environs, there was no way of knowing who had contributed, or the story of individual items and the unveiling celebrations.

To overcome this Joan began to write about the work, and realised that it had a focus on only adult involvement. She liaised with Irene Tomkinson, then Head of our school in Humshaugh and together they worked out a programme, which brought the children for six Friday afternoon learning sessions, into the hall. David Brookman, with his people carrier, and accompanying teachers with cars, provided transport. The children took walks around the village in order that they could produce writing and pictures, and finally, with the generous permission of Maurice Lowther, they visited Wall's Old School, now his home. Mrs Reed, who taught at the school, was there to tell the children all about it. All of their work is collected in the book, and those children are now fourteen years older. The ladies of the wall hanging group created stitched vignettes of the children's drawings, which were mounted on the front and back covers, the latter stitched by Valerie Lowther, whose advice at that time was so valuable. John Proudlock made a protective wooden case which is attached to the wall under the hanging and it is there in the hall for anyone to look at.

The following is the poem that the late Dorothy Charlton composed to commemorate the completion of the Wall Hanging. In it everyone who played a part is mentioned. To bring it up to date you will find at the end a small addition.

THE MILLENNIUM WALL HANGING - Dorothy Charlton 2000

Every Friday afternoon 2pm 'till four
Some dedicated ladies entered the village hall door.
Ladies, who for many years
Had knitted lots of blanket squares
These were stitched into blankets gay,
And then, we gave them all away
To underprivileged people
Beset by disasters and wars.
Our knitters deserve a mention –
Supporting each worthwhile cause
Then Kathleen painted three pictures
Scenes of our village you know.
Joan said, "Could we make a collage?"
We said, "Yes we'll have a go!"
The collage for the Millennium,
May be better than the dome
We even took work home.
Then, like a jigsaw, every bit
Was embroidered, painted, snipped to fit.
So we stitchers and knitters gave of our valuable time
Dorothy Charlton said, "I'll name them all,
Just hope the names will rhyme!"
So would you believe, three Marys,
Two Dorothys and our Joan,
Jill, Doreen, Ella, Margaret and Eva,
Hasn't our work force grown!
Mustn't forget Marjorie who put the collages together,

And Judy, who plied us with coffee and tea
Each meeting, whatever the weather.
At stitching blanket squares, Audrey headed the list.
Knitted by Pat, Margaret, Doreen and Mona,
'Till she fell and broke her wrist.
Mary Doyle and Dorothy Iveson stitched
Wall Station and Wall Mill.
Dorothy C did a leap of salmon,
Fields machined by Ella Hill.
Marjorie appliqued the seagulls
Swooping over the North Tyne
Jill did a lovely mill wheel,
Tish's water-splash looks fine.
Then Dorothy C. did a riverside tree,
With Ann Burch's apple blossom, lovely to see.
When we were finished our first collage
We were all as pleased as punch.
It was admired by WI members, and
Friends at the Village Lunch.
So we started the second collage,
Ella had finished the fell.
Dorothy Iveson's done the school house
With Rachel's bee skeps as well.
Jill embroidered the painter, sketching
The white horse on the green,
While up in the corner St Oswald's
And the Heavenfield Cross are seen.
We think Eva's mini-tractor
Looks as if it ploughs,
Ann Slack had lots of fun,
Making her mini cows!
Audrey stitched the village pant
Where horses drank long ago,
Maggie silk painted a line of trees
Eva did the foreground below.
Dorothy C did her second tree, and
For the last collage brought her total to three.
Mary Mason stitched the hall,
Joan's people go in at the door.
Mary Herdman's goats are great
With fences around, what's more!
Joan and Ann Burch cut linen stones
Which mustn't all look the same
Then we embroidered the stones,
With village dwellers names.

There's just not room for every house,
"We've been missed out" someone's sure to grouse
As all of Front Street couldn't be done,
We put the little blue bus on its daily run.
We made cross stitch pictures
From drawings the school children did,
Valerie's stitching them together
To cover the journal, and box lid.
Angela's swings on the old back green,
Where children laugh and play
Elva's gorgeous pheasant
The little chapel, grey.

We're on to collage number three,
Hooray we're getting there!
Dorothy Iveson stitched St George's Church
With time to spare!
Janet and Joan appliqued gay stalls
At the three churches fair,
While Dr McCollum's spectators
And little Sam, all stare.
We couldn't put the three farms
Around the village green,
But Herdman's engineering works
And Coronation tree are seen.
We couldn't put Eddie, Fred or John
Taking cows to milk each day
For now the only milk cows
Are at High Barns, sad to say.
Farm buildings are now dwellings
Things have changed a lot,
But we hope we've shown in our collage —
(and now, Book)
WALL IS A MUCH LOVED SPOT.

The Best Kept Village Sign

AND FINALLY…

JOAN PROUDLOCK

As the co-ordinator of this project I have been allowed to have the last words!

The idea for this book came to me in 1999 when working on the Art Book which describes all the items in the Wall Village Wall Hanging. It seemed that there were many more stories of the lives and people of our village that needed to be told before they were lost. What became apparent then, and has come through so clearly whilst working on this writing, is the love that so many people have for this small village. The chosen title of this book is Wall - Our Northumbrian Village, and that expresses just how we feel about the place where some of us grew up, and where some of us have chosen to live. Is it the buildings we love, is it the formation of the village around the green with the countryside around, could it be that commuting is easy or is it perhaps that in this village people care about each other? It is probably all of these things, and more, which make us able to take possession of Wall as Our Village and have brought this book into being.

We needed to fund this project and the response from our community was, as always, wonderful, but we also needed more finance in order to print our book. Here my thanks go first to the **Community Foundation with Vivienne Rodgers and Gill Lowing** who made it all so easy, and then **I'Anson Family Fund** who so generously gave us the money we requested.

I have so many people to thank for turning a dream into reality. When I threw out the idea to **Mary Herdman** she quickly took it up, and with her wonderful archive collection was able to supply much of the factual writings. Initially there were just the two of us but it soon became necessary to have a working group and this came from the members of the Village Society Committee. To **Jenny Harrington, Mary Mason, Jill and David Brookman, Tony Cattermole** and **Mary Herdman** who have cheerfully steered me through, sometimes troubled waters with patience and humour, my gratitude is unending. Each in their own way have brought part of themselves and their feelings about the village they love to this work, but with her skills and knowledge of art and design my special thanks goes to **Jill Brookman**. Her guidance regarding the cover design and her commitment to supporting and educating me in the detail required in producing a book of quality has been so appreciated. Both she, and her husband David, not only have supported me, but given me their time for on-screen proof reading, the latter being a test of real friendship! This book is a testament to the many hours **all my team have spent reading and discussing and finally deciding upon the contents. Thank You.**

Sharon Slater took on the job of treasurer and certainly deserves my thanks for keeping the finances in order. I knew we were in safe hands with her banking experience as she set up an account for the book, with its own small logo, a smiling book on legs ensuring the account would grow.

The most onerous job of all, and she volunteered to do it, was taken on by **Valerie Lowther**. With absolute precision she read every word, considered every punctuation mark and corrected all the mistakes she found – and there were many! Her experience in proof reading has been an invaluable help to me and I am so grateful for it. She made doing the corrections a pleasure!

Then along came **Tina Wiffen,** who happily gave me her time and patience as she untangled some of my computer muddles so easily, and made sure everything I did was copied on to a disc. Yet another person to whom I owe thanks for being part of our book.

So many people have come my way as information has been gathered and I have had such pleasure from meeting folk and hearing their stories. To **All of You** out there who have given of your memories, who have taken time to write them or have patiently answered my telephone calls requesting information, thank you for you have given us much of what has been written here.

Particular thanks to **Ivor Gray** for foraging through the Hexham Courant archives to find snippets about the village he loved, and also to **Ray Craig** for the use of his collection of photographs. Not only for Ray's collection, his amazing knowledge of natural history, but also his memories of growing up in Wall, which brought many laughs as he recounted stories in our kitchen, not all of which could be written in this book!

At a moment's notice when suddenly needed, **Marjorie Baillie** came to our rescue, and graciously set the Book Group around the village pant for the photograph you will have seen at the front of our book.

When it came to many of the photographs help was required to restore the old ones and both **Alan Mason** and **John Cooper** at **Pattinson Photography** took on the laborious work. I am most grateful for their generosity, time and experience as Alan transformed them.

Many of the photographs came from Ray Craig's and Mary Herdman's collections and the source of some of the original photographers is unknown. We acknowledge and credit the **Hexham Courant** with several of the photographs and articles. My thanks go to the **Editor** who responded so positively, making what might have been a difficult issue, very easy. The same is said for the staff at the **Newcastle Chronicle and Journal** who gave permission for the use of the photograph of the Northumberland Rural Community Council 'Newcastle Journal' Trophy for the Best Kept Village, designed by Leonard Evetts and won by Wall.

One of our aims was to use local skills as much as possible in producing our book and it has been a pleasure working with **Neil McKie** and **John Vinton** at **Robson Print Ltd** in Hexham. They have patiently guided the book through to publication and through them I have learnt about the processes involved in printing. Neil has been ready at all times with advice and help, and has proved that 'keeping it local' is good.

Whilst it has been time consuming work I have always had my husband **John**, bringing common sense to bear when I have lost the plot, and meals, when I have forgotten we actually do need to eat! It was through John that I came to Wall and little did I know then that the people I found here, and so many of those I have known through 42 years, would be the inspiration for this book. It has been such a privilege to be able to bring the story of Wall and its people to these pages. The community life of Wall has been a constant and yet changing thing and hopefully will continue on into the future, giving roots in an ever changing world. Wall is a small village with a big heart; it is my home and indeed a 'much loved spot'.

And finally… **Thank you for reading.**

OUR CONTRIBUTORS

Chris Allcock, Elizabeth Archer, Ernie Bainbridge, Margaret Bainbridge, Marjorie Baillie, Daphne Bannister, Harriet Benson, George Benson, Lorraine Bewley, Billy Bilner, John Blacklock, Jill Brookman, David Brookman, Mike Bruce, Christine Bull, Sandra Burgon, Peter Burgon, Tony Cattermole, *Dorothy Charlton, Ted Charlton,* Raymond Craig, *Mona Craig*,* Steve Cram MBE, Richard Dodds, Melanie Douglas, Mike Douglas, Barbara and Ralph Duggan, Tish Easby, David Easby, John Elliot, *Isabelle Everatt,* June Gallagher, Jacqueline Gaughan, Margaret Gillespy, Patricia Gillespie, James Gillespie, Ivor Gray, Julia Grint, Alan Grint, Kathleen Handyside, Jenny Harrington, Alison Henson, Mary Herdman, Ron Herdman, Ella Hill, Ken Huddleston, Gordon Johnson, Ruth Hicken Jones, Chris Jones, Douglas Jordan, (Field Operations Leader, Arqiver, Stagshaw Mast), John Lamb, Jackie Lewis, David Lindsay, Valerie Lowther, Maurice Lowther, *Frances Mason*, David Mason, Elva Mason, Mary Mason, Maureen McCracken, David McCracken, Doreen Mitchell, Shirley Mitchell, David Oliver, Maureen Proud, Joan Proudlock, John Proudlock, Stuart Proudlock, Eva Reay, Jean Reed, *W B Ripley*, *Jasper Rootham*, Alison Say, Rob Say, Margaret Seaby, Ged Short (Bellingham Heritage Centre – Railways), Kathleen Sisterson, Ann Slack, Stan, (our postman), Pat Stewart, Jill Stewart, Eunice Storey, Frank Stubbs, Susie Swan, Heather Tailford, Fred Thompson, Joan Turnbull, Angela Watson, David Watson, Mrs Weir (Tyne Valley Coaches Acomb), David Westle, Jemima Westle, Tina Wiffen, Althea Williamson, Margaret Wood, Ann Woodcock, Judy Yeoman.

* Those whose names are in italics are no longer with us but we have been able to use their work.

Acknowledgements are made here to those unknown people who originally contributed photographs to Raymond Craig for use in his album, and whose photographs we have chosen to appear in this book.

We have tried to record everyone who has made a contribution but it is inevitable that we will have missed out some names and our apologies go to whoever they may be.

BIBLIOGRAPHY

Breeze D J & Dobson B, Hadrian's Wall
Bruce J C 1978 Handbook to the Roman Wall
Bulmer T F (Editor) 1886 History, Topography and Directory of Northumberland (Hexham Division)
Burton A National Trail Guides – Hadrian's Wall Path
Davies H A Walk along The Wall
Eagles J 1992 Landscape and Community: A World Heritage Site in Rural Northumberland
Evetts Leonard Master Designer p182. Privately Printed 2001
Grint A I The Faith and Fire Within: In Memory of the men of Hexham who fell in The Great War
Grint A I & J In Silent Fortitude: In Memory of the men of the North Tyne who fell in The Great War
Grint J A Bastle Village
Hall M 2005 The Artists of Northumbria (Art Dictionaries Ltd)
Kinghorn R Lost Railways of Northumberland (Countryside Books)
Mary Lascelles Village Life, Publisher unknown
Marsden J 1989 The Illustrated Bede (Floris Books)
Millard J 1990 Ralph Hedley, Tyneside Painter (Tyne and Wear Museums)
Parson W & White W 1828 History, Directory and Gazetteer of the Counties of Durham and Northumberland
Potter B 1902 The Tale of Peter Rabbit (Frederick Warne and Frederick Warne & Co)
Robertson A 2004 The Walton Family, A Lead Mining Dynasty of the Northern Penines (Hundy Publications)
Rootham J 1978 Reflections from a crag (Unit Offset Ltd)
Sewell G W M The North British Railway in Northumberland (Merlin Books Ltd)
Tynedale Council 2008 Wall Conservation Area Character Appraisal
Young R 2004 Wall and the Chesters Estate of John Clayton (Compiled for the Oxford University Advanced Diploma in Local History)
Census Records for 1881 & 1901
English Heritage Guide to Chesters Roman Fort
Newcastle Chronicle and Journal Ltd - Copyright
Hexham Courant - Copyright
HMSO British Regional Geology 1971
Northumberland Archives, Woodhorn Colliery, Ashington, NE63 9YF.
Sales Catalogue of the Chesters Estate
The Northumbrian Magazine
Wall Village Archives
Wall Village Wall Hanging Art Book and Records
Ray Craig's Photograph Collection and all those who have in the past contributed to it.
www.keystothepast.co.uk

OUR HISTORY

Circa 1890. The old thatched building that stood in front of the site on which St George's Church was later built.

Circa 1890. Front Street Wall, looking south.

1914-1918. Wall's Working Party under the direction of Mrs Waddilove.
Back Row. Winnie Clark, Phyllis Laing, Molly Mitchell, Polly Mitchell, Frances Stobbs, Mrs Wilson, Mrs Ridley, Mary Curry, Becca Smith, Edith Johnson.
Second Row. Bella Bell, Frances Urwin, Lizzie Herdman, Elsie Muse, Miss Fisher, Ethel Walton, Hilda Muse, Lizzie Herdman, Mrs Ridley, Cissy Wardle.
Third Row. Mrs Davidson, Mrs C Watson, June Scott, Mrs London, Mrs Waddilove, Mrs Waring, Mrs Robson, Mrs T Davidson, Mrs Telford.
Front Row. Maggie Robson, Gladys Watson, Albert Laing, Willie Mitchell, Jimmy Bell.

1906. Waiting for the first car to come through the village.

OUR ENVIRONMENT

1920s. The A6079 at the top of the village with Crook Hill and the School, before the Garage was erected in 1929.

1964. The making of the concrete cricket wicket on the back green with Lewis Mason, David Mason, Barney Mitchell and John Elliott.

1970s. Wall Reading Room.

2000. Wall Village Hall. Commemorating and remembering Rachel Lowther's work as Maurice Lowther unveiled the Plaque.

OUR COMMUNITY

1890-1910. Wall School is out.

Early 1940s. Wall Sands.

2000. Some of Our Community

2000. Some more of Our Community

OUR INDUSTRIES TRADES SHOPS AND SERVICES

Early 1900s. Black Pasture Quarry workings.

Some of the workers of Black Pasture Quarry.

Steam train near Wall Station.

Foster's bus returning from Newcastle on B6318 and stuck in a snowdrift and blizzard at St Oswald's Farm

Late 1940s Farming. Eddie Ripley, Willie Ripley and Isaac Maddison taking a tea break.

1973 – 1988. Wall's Postmistress and shopkeeper, Mrs Ella Westle.

1950s. Fred Henderson with Alex Mason and Dick Heslop going to the fields.

OUR CHURCH CHAPEL AND SCHOOL

Early 1900s. Wall Church Bible Class. Back Row. William Graham Quarryman, Ernest Robson, Jack Scott Joiner, Nevison Laing Tailor, Ephraim Jewitt Railwayman, George Graham Chauffeur,—, Robert Little Signalman, Robert Maddison Quarryman, William Urwin Signalman —. Front Row. —, Thomas W Robson Quarryman, —, —, Matthew Telford Schoolmaster, Rev John Southwell Curate, William Bell Quarryman, —, —, —, —.

1927. The Dedication of the cross at St Oswald's.

1957. School playtime.

1965. Methodist Music and Arts Trophy Winners.
Back Row. Margaret Lamb, Joan Huddleston, Jennifer Robson, Margaret Marran, Hazel Armstrong. Second Row. Anne Fairhurst, Anne Potts, Lorraine Henderson, John Marran, Billy Mitchell. Third Row. Christine Ripley, James Bowman, John Kitchen.
Front Row. Lesley Mitchell, Evelyn Mitchell, Andrew Ormston.

1968. The Chapel Sunday School Centenary.
Back Row. Graeme Wood, Andrew Ormston, Peter Heslop, Lesley Mitchell, Christine Ripley, Evelyn Mitchell. Second Row. Tim Ormston, George Charlton, Tim Charlton, Trevor McLean, Sandra Heslop, Mandy Bilner, Chris Bilner, Susan Ripley. Third Row. Trevor Holliday, Stephen Stubbs, Tommy Mitchell, Sandra Wood, Ian Storey, Gillian Mitchell, Jackie Proud, Graham Storey. Fourth Row. Alison Reay, Althea Reay, Yvonne Holliday, Roger Mitchell, Elizabeth Reay, Alison Foster.

1971. The last school Christmas Party with Mrs Reed and Mr Bobby Wood.

OUR CLUBS AND SOCIETIES

1964. Wall School Football Team.
Back Row. John Kitchen, Derek Thompson, Bobby Bowman, Gerald Huddleston, Bobby Wood, Michael Robson, Billy Mitchell. Front Row. John White, John Rutherford, James Bowman, Graeme Wood, Peter Heslop.

2. 1988. 70th birthday party for Wall WI.
Back Row. Gwynneth Wood, Marjorie Holliday, Betty Bell, Nancy Potts, Sheila Cook, Ella Hill, Mona Craig, Kathleen Spooner, Pat Stewart, Maureen Proud. Second Row. Doreen Mitchell, Joan Ormston, Mary Huddleston, Evelyn Carr, Doris Herdman. Third Row. Elva Mason, Phyllis Smith, Mona Harrison, Nancy Dodds, Dorothy Charlton, Nancy Armstrong, Ella Westle. Front Row. Eva Bowman, Ella Bowman, Peggy Seaby, Madge Johnston, Edna McMillin.

1989. Carpet Bowls Presentation Night.
Back Row. Adrian Proud, Eddie Herdman, David Woodcock, Tommy Potts, Len Woodcock, David Armstrong, Norman Doyle, Tony Ormston, Billy Armstrong. Second Row. Ella Hill, Daniel Price, Ella Westle, Mary Doyle, Doreen Mitchell, Herby Robson, Maureen Proud. Third Row. Phyllis Smith, Ada Armstrong, Evelyn Carr, Doris Herdman, Mona Craig, Lucy Robson. Front Row. Jimmy Carr, Rachel Lowther, Nancy Armstrong.

2013. Some of the Village Society members and guests photographed by Marjorie Baillie, who gave the evening's presentation.
Back Row. Dennis Harrington, Valerie Lowther, Joan Proudlock, John Proudlock. Second Row. Martin Kitchen, David Brookman, Maurice Lowther, Jonathan Carter, Gill Carter. Third Row. Renée Baillie, Mary Herdman, Ann Woodcock, Eva Reay. Front Row. Shirley Mitchell, Mary Mason, Jenny Harrington, Doreen Mitchell, Jill Brookman.

OUR RANDOM MEMORIES

1952. Alnmouth Camp.
Back Row. Olga Purvis. Second Row. Jimmy Robinson, Doug Robson — Peggy Robinson, Robin Crozier. Third Row. Eddie Robinson, Ann Hutchinson, —. Front Row. Bobby Arthur, Margaret Leadbeater, George Leadbeater, Maureen Armstrong, John Proudlock, Jean Austin.

1954. The Drama Group.
Back Row. Jimmy Robinson, Eddie Robinson, Elsie Bowman, Fred Thompson, Mrs Crozier, Doug Robson, Robin Crozier. Second Row. Maureen Armstrong, Daphne Huddleston, Jean Austin, Pat Smith, Nancy Bowman, Irene Bowman. Front Row. Bill Marran, John Elliott, Ray Craig.

1964. Tennis at Brunton House. John Proudlock, John Elliott, Pat Smith.

"Nobody loves a Fairy when she's Forty."
Elva Mason on stage, this time in Wall Village Hall.

ISABELLE'S STORY

Young Miss Robertson

Mrs Isabelle Everatt

OUR CELEBRATIONS

1911. Handing out the Coronation Mugs.

1972. Wall Village, winners of the Best Kept Village Competition.
Addie Hall, Mona Craig, Phyllis Smith, Nancy Armstrong, Maureen Proud, Nancy Maddison, Willie Ripley, Reg Dodd, George Milburn, Jack Seaby and Alison Proud.

1982, 26 May. The Queen and HRH The Duke of Edinburgh drive through Wall following the official opening of Kielder Water and Dam.

1987. The official opening of the village hall extension.

1987. Wall School Reunion Celebrations

1998. The unveiling of the Parish Map at the Village Lunch in December. Chris Allcock, Chairman of the Village Hall Committee, Mary Herdman, Artist, Roy Thompson, Chairman of the Parish Council.

2000, 29 April. The Wall Hanging Group with Nicole and Georgina Lamb. Back Row. Ann Burch, Eva Reay, Dorothy Iveson, Jill Brookman, Dorothy Charlton, Doreen Mitchell, Veronica Robson, Ella Hill. Front Row. Mary Herdman, Maggie Birch, Mona Harrison, Kathleen Sisterson, Joan Proudlock, Mary Mason, Valerie Lowther, Margaret White

2012. Diamond Jubilee Celebrations in Wall.

2013. Nicole Lamb, part of the Rowing Team GB in the Youth Olympics in Australia. She won Gold, Silver and Bronze Medals.

NOTES